*WITHIN THE SOUND
OF THESE WAVES*

"In her lustrous black hair she wore a white hibiscus."

WITHIN THE SOUND OF THESE WAVES

The Story of the Kings of Hawaii Island, Containing a Full Account of the Death of Captain Cook, together with the Hawaiian Adventures of George Vancouver and Sundry Other Mariners

BY WILLIAM H. CHICKERING

ILLUSTRATIONS BY JOHN KELLY

GREENWOOD PRESS, PUBLISHERS
WESTPORT, CONNECTICUT

To

Ronald Kamehameha von Holt

ACKNOWLEDGMENT

The first section of this book is a combination of early legends from which I chose what seemed to me the most logical sequence and detail of events. For the second and third sections I used Hawaiian sources also, but for the most part relied on the written evidence of the various mariners and missionaries who visited the islands.

The account of Cook's death is, I believe, the first comprehensive description of this event. Many of Cook's men were ardent diarists and on the return of the ships to England most of their diaries were confiscated by the British Admiralty lest an account be published unfavorable to Cook; only in very recent years have these journals been made available at the British Museum and (in photostatic copies) at the Archives of Hawaii.

Thanks are due to the Archives of Hawaii and to the Hawaiian Historical Society for giving every possible assistance in the compilation of this work.

W. H. C.

CONTENTS

CONTENTS

ILLUSTRATIONS

INTRODUCTION

How can I justify bringing to your attention the story of a Polynesian Island, a record of such unimportance in the wide scope of man's historical interests that there will be but three or four names in it you might recognize? Why, I cannot!—unless, by chance, you share my delight in discovering tales of pure romance existing as factual history, and unless you have the faculty for discerning in such tales parallels to the complex dramas of more civilized nations. If your mind is thus lenient with your tastes, you will probably also enjoy the scenes where the two ways of life are juxtaposed against each other; and because civilization is apparently far from being the ideal state, you will perhaps sigh regretfully that the Hawaiian mode of living has vanished—but it hasn't vanished really, for as much of your mind as you are willing to give to Hawaii that serene island can give back to you of its half-forgotten charm.

I am deeply fond of the Hawaiians, but I cannot suppose that you will share that sentiment merely from reading about them. You will see, though, that they have a joy of living, a rare humor, and an intuitive sense of man's proud heritage, things which set them apart from other primitive races and make them worthy of your acquaintance, even though they built few lasting monuments.

I like the Hawaiian language, too, and in that I have even less hope of sympathy from you, for at first sight it looks fantastic. But it was never a written language till the missionaries took it over and reduced it to a strict phonetic code; it is that system of phonetics that startles you, and if you will tackle it bravely, pronouncing each word to yourself, you will find it—different, yes—but strikingly harmonious and rhythmical. It is a language of vowels and each vowel is given full value.

One thing more: the first few pages are in the nature of an ethnological study. It is necessary to understand something of the *mores* of the people to understand fully their history. These matters might have been relegated to footnotes at appropriate points, but too many footnotes detract from the narrative, and it is as narrative that this history should be presented. And as a narrative I hope you will read it.

WILLIAM H. CHICKERING

Honolulu

WITHIN THE SOUND
OF THESE WAVES

PROLOGUE

ONE BRILLIANT MORNING HUNDREDS OF YEARS AGO, as the silver rays of the Kona sun were beginning to touch life and color into the night-drenched slopes of the volcanoes, a man was sitting cross-legged on a smooth tumulus of lava not far from Kailua Bay. In one strong brown fist he gripped a flinty chisel, in the other a stone with which he pounded the chisel, hard, rhythmically, biting gradually into the lava face and making there a curious symbol.

The sound of chipping stone was harsh on the still air and reached the ears of a woman who, seated in the shadow of a near-by pandanus-thatched hut, held a baby to her breast. The mother smiled down on her drowsy infant and once, as though to tell him what she thought of his father's loud activity, she raised her brows, rolling her warm dark eyes upward with a sweetly absurd expressiveness.

If you stand on this tumulus today and contemplate this symbol and the others there with it, feeling on your skin the same hot sun that burnt into the skin of that ancient, and, lifting your eyes, if you give yourself wholly to this same view—twisted masses of lava, broad sloping plain, and magnificent sweep of volcano ascending through farm land and hoary forest to the fleecy regions of the sky—it is almost possible in that moment to hear the scrape of stone against stone, the labored breathing of the artisan even, the croon of a mother to a child who grew old and weary and died long, long ago, under this same sun, within the sound of these waves.

PART I

IDYLL OF SIX CENTURIES

THE ISLAND

SOUTHERNMOST—AND LARGEST—OF THE HAWAIIAN IS-
lands is the island from which the group takes its
name . . . Hawaii. Born out of dark turbulence in
the depths of the sea and emerging as a mass of fiery
cones, Hawaii has been the familiar of chaos. Even today
at least one of her great volcanoes, which sprawl like
three sleeping colossi over the central and southern por-
tions of the island, has not forgotten how, in moments of
awakening, to stretch out fingers of red-hot lava and
crush the land in paralyzing grip; but these moments are
rare, and have become spectacles rather than catastrophes.
Man has probed the volcano's secrets, anticipates its erup-
tions, and has moved out of the paths of its flows. As for
the rest of the island, its soil has been made fertile by the
volcanic ash. Each new tide of settlers has brought its
own particular knowledge of the uses to which rich earth
may be put and today there are forests of great trees,
vast green fields of produce, and grassy slopes and plains
where herds of cattle graze.

7

The landscape is a study in paradox, from the blazing tropic shores to the lofty, frequently snow-clad summits of its massive mountains. Because of its remarkable climate variety, Hawaii has always been a pleasant place for man to live, and until the deep-drawing ships of the western world showed preference for the harbor of Honolulu on the island of Oahu, Hawaii supported the bulk of the islands' population.

The Polynesians who settled on Hawaii lived mostly by the sea to be near their first source of food. Wherever the ragged lava shores were indented sufficiently to form tiny bays, or jutting arms of rock made breakwaters behind which a sandy beach could form, there they built their homes. Even when, as in some parts of Puna, steep cliffs made landing a canoe difficult, they built their thatch houses at the cliff's edge and hoisted up their canoes by means of simple davits. Along the leeward shores fresh water was scarce, but that caused little inconvenience. There was always the sea for the many daily baths and usually brackish pools in which to rinse off afterward. Food was baked in earth ovens or eaten raw, no water was needed;—and the Hawaiian had the minimum of laundry. For drinking water, he knew places along the shore where springs of fresh, cold water gushed from coral ledges below the surface, and by diving down with a carefully stoppered calabash he could bring up all he needed. Too, when he went to the wet uplands to exchange his fish for the other staple, taro, he could bring back gourds of water slung in nets over his spear or carrying pole. And there were everywhere plenty of coconuts, with their cool reserves of nourishing liquid.

The easiest mode of travel from village to village was by outrigger canoe, but there was also a well-defined trail which completely encircled the island. A narrow line of smooth stepping stones across the lava wastes, it became, on approaching a village, a wide, dusty path patterned with the imprint of many bare feet. After the remorseless heat of the open country the shade of village trees was welcome to the wayfarer. There were many trees—a grove of palms,[1] stencil-leafed breadfruit, the huge, shaggy, blue-green whorls of pandanus, tousled bananas, shimmering *milo*,[2] *kou*,[3] and occasionally clumps of bamboo. In this plenteous shade high-peaked, yellow-thatched houses were grouped behind neat stone walls; each family had its special houses for cooking, sleeping, eating, prayer— and women ate and prayed separately from the men. Most domestic chores were performed outside in the clean-swept yards. One might see men squatting on their haunches pounding cooked taro with stone pounders,

[1] The Hawaiians planted a palm over the afterbirth of each child that it might carry his spirit upward.
[2] *Milo*—Thespesia Populorea.
[3] *Kou*—Cordia Subcordata.

making the glutinous, gray staff-of-life, *poi;* the women pounded too, but with wooden beaters on wooden anvils, turning sodden bark into the thick, sturdy cloth called tapa. Sows with trundling companies of shoats nosed for scraps in the lanes; chickens strutted and squawked; and a pen of dogs, being fattened on vegetables for a feast day, protested the sedentary life.

In the palm grove, which was the village meeting place, games were usually in progress; men bowled with round stones, wrestled, fenced with crude staves, shot with small bow-and-arrow at mice in a pit, or perhaps played more quietly at *konane* (a form of checkers) or at guessing games. If the surf allowed, many would spend the day in the water riding the waves on their light, slender surfboards; in the shallows children frolicked, shouting and making a brave display of small brown buttocks. There was always a generous welcome for the wayfarer in these villages, whether he chose to linger for an hour or for a month. The people were invariably friendly; they seldom quarreled even among themselves, for how could one quarrel when life was so full of laughter!

THE PEOPLE AND THEIR GODS

FOR MANY CENTURIES NOTHING HAD BROKEN THE line of the glittering southern horizon. And then, suddenly, as a pencil makes its first mark on an empty sheet of paper, a dot appeared. Moving closer it became a sort of raft: two large dugout canoes joined together by a platform jammed and cluttered with men, women, chickens, dogs, pigs, vegetables. In the eyes of the infinite this barge was little better than a bobbing coconut shell, yet it had conquered three thousand empty miles of sea, and now the thirsty, famished men and women claimed their trophy—the superb volcanic islands of Hawaii.

They were not the first. In some forgotten age other Polynesians had mastered the secrets of the Pacific and claimed its islands as their empire; proof of this conquest is hewn in living stone on many a far-flung atoll and barren island. But the first "vikings of the sunrise" had now, in the Twelfth Century, A.D., exhausted their destiny, and, except for a few weak remnants of their people still living in Hawaii, had vanished, as footsteps in the sand are obliterated by the rising tide. Yet such was the nature of the Polynesians that a second group of conquerors had challenged the wind and the sea and in their sturdy double canoes had brought their gods and their new civilization to Hawaii.

These new conquerors came directly from Tahiti . . . unusually tall men with handsome, swarthy, clean-cut features, red-brown skin and muscles as hard as steel. The Tahitians died . . . Hawaiians were born. But the Polynesian gods lived on.

To understand that which a man calls God, one must first understand its function in spiritual temples. The wood and stone temples are built merely to satisfy the senses, man's eternal desire to make his soul something he can see and feel. But the gods are the inner flame. The stone temple of the Hawaiian village bristled with grimacing wooden images; it was easy, if one had eye only for the obvious, to decry these as symbols of idolatry, mumbo-jumbo, barbarism. To the naïf Polynesian they were simply decoration—something to inspire awe, to remind the pedestrian man that his spirit has strange wings. Can one understand Christianity by studying the gargoyles of Notre Dame? The Polynesian had other images within his temple, but neither were these worshiped for themselves; they were but symbols, equivalents of which can be found in any church the world over. For the Polynesians were not idolaters. They worshiped nature's mystic force, and to give definition to their worship they personified aspects of nature and thus created their gods.

When the westerner came to Polynesia he sought to persuade the natives that there was but one god, defined and palpable. Yet at about the same time that the first missionaries were arriving a western poet, musing near a Christian abbey, wrote of his religion as follows:

". . . a sense sublime
Of something far more deeply interfused,
Whose dwelling is the light of setting suns,
And the round ocean and the living air,
And the blue sky and in the mind of man:
A motion and a spirit that impels
All thinking things, all objects of all thought,
And rolls through all things."

Religion was a living, a dynamic, thing. This same thought was the very heart of the barbarous religion which the missionaries came to Polynesia to decry.

"Mana" was the Polynesian word for the "motion and . . . spirit that impels all thinking things, all objects of all thought." Out of the concept of mana the gods evolved. The gods served as something from which man might derive energy, but also—and this is the important idea—man charged the gods with this energy by religious ceremony and worldly accomplishment. The purpose of the temple, the sacrifice, the prayer, was to increase the mana of the gods, to generate for the satisfaction of man's senses (the first psychological factor in a simple person's religion) a sort of spiritual electricity from which man drew his physical and moral strength. Mana was a positive force. The negative of this spiritual electricity is found in the concept of tabu,[1] but the words are not autonomous —breaking a tabu meant a negation, or at least a canceling out, of mana.

The idea of human sacrifice, an idea which has been revived among the new politico-religions of the world, was scarcely so barbaric as its modern equivalent. The Polynesian who was sacrificed to his war god, for instance, was—once his fate was sealed—quite honestly an altruist. He believed that in giving his life he gave mana to the god—a tremendous fund of energy from which the tribal warriors could draw strength to defeat the enemy. It was one life for many. Doubt the ritual if you choose, but there can be no doubt that such a sacrifice, given in that spirit, provided others with—if nothing else —the "will to conquer." When the chief of a conquered province was sacrificed to the war god, he was not wholly amenable, perhaps, but at least it was something he ac-

[1] The Hawaiian form of this Polynesian word is *kapu*, or *tapu*, but as the other spelling is more familiar I shall use it throughout.

cepted as part of the code; if he were to be tortured, however, it would be a barbarous breach of the code. The purpose of this type of sacrifice was to liberate the conquered chief's mana to be absorbed by the conqueror's war god and this mana was as much a part of the conquest as the lands themselves.

The degree to which a Polynesian could share mana with his gods depended on two things—his position in society and his achievement. The preference of the gods was about equally divided between these two considerations and a man could have a fairly accurate idea where he stood in the divine lists: weigh blood, weigh achievement, and take the mean. From this double system arose a unique form of sovereignty and one which had its undoubted advantages. If a prince of the dynastic line—an *alii kapu*—proved to be a weak king, he was frequently overthrown by a strong warrior chief who set himself up as *alii aimoku* (chief possessing the land); but such a kingship was temporary—at the death of an *alii aimoku* the rule reverted to an heir of the dynastic line, unless some other strong chief took the throne first. But an *alii aimoku* could secure the succession of his own heir if he married a woman of the dynastic line and hence incorporated the sacred blood with his own.

Caste was determined through the social standing of both father and mother, but in the old society it was sometimes difficult to be sure of a child's paternity, and hence the mother's blood was considered more significant than that of the supposed father. Sons were heirs by primogeniture. Priests were in a special category paralleling that of the chiefs.

The first Tahitian chief to be lord over the island of Hawaii was Hika-po-loa ('Hika of the long night') who settled in the Kohala Province. Hika's canoes brought from Tahiti the idea and symbols of the four major Polynesian gods. These gods were: Kane, god of nature; Ku, god of war; Lono, god of husbandry and peace; and Kanaloa, god of the sea. In the process of Hawaiianization Kane and Ku came into ascendancy and were made first gods of the pantheon; Kanaloa became a servant to Kane; Lono returned to Tahiti to appear again in Hawaii after many years . . . in the uniform of a Captain of the British Navy under the pseudonym of James Cook.

The next Tahitian of importance to arrive in Hawaii was Pa-ao, the high priest. Pa-ao had been high priest of the greatest of the Tahitian temples, a sort of Vatican of central Polynesia. He left Tahiti stricken by the loss of a son, whose stomach he had caused to be cut open to refute the charge that the boy was a food thief. He introduced to Hawaii the walled temple, the red tapa as a symbol of royalty or divinity, and the ceremony of human sacrifice.

As the religious ideas developed in Hawaii, taking on their own distinctive characteristics, a large pantheon of minor gods was evolved. Special attributes of the four major gods were taken and, as though they had been so much spiritual clay, lesser deities were fashioned from them. There were gods for thieves, for women, even a god whose sole business it was to right upset canoes. Symbols of these gods were fashioned from homely materials or found in the form of birds, fish, animals.

But these various developments did not take place at once; they were the larger product of the fertile Hawaiian imagination. Religion was all art to the Hawaiian, and because Hawaiians have a great and constant welling up within them of artistic feeling, their religion grew rich and colorful in its trappings, dramatic in its ceremony, intense in its meaning.

LILOA

SOME SAY THAT LILOA WAS THE FIRST ABSOLUTE SOV-
ereign, the first *alii aimoku,* of the whole island of
Hawaii. That was five hundred years ago.

(Remember?—the king of England lost two sons to
the murderous treachery of his brother; the king of
France, in cloth cap, stalked the dirty corridors of his
palace mumbling and chuckling while outside in the
streets of Paris starvation trod the same gaunt measure;
the emperor of China was wrapped in ultimate ceremony
and the delicate exquisiteness of Ming.)

E inoa o Liloa! [1] Lord of giant mold, copper-skinned,
lithe and strong. His nose is straight with flaring nostrils;
his dark eyes squinting, slightly bloodshot; his stance
proud, straight as the spear of dark, polished wood he
holds in his hand, and from his shoulders flows a long
cape of soft yellow feathers. This is the king—a living
god even—ruler of the massive blue mountains and the
wet green valleys, lord of the tall brown men of Hawaii.

[1] "Glory to the name of Liloa!"

18

Liloa was a chief of the sacred tabu. The pale blue of heaven alone possessed spirits of greater divinity. Walking with long stride through the spacious palm groves of Waipio, he was heralded by the cry of *"Tapu O! Tapu O!"* [2] and a noisy village was hushed. The people bent down making an aisle of naked, glossy brown backs for the majesty of Liloa. Woe to him who was slow in bending:—behind the king in the procession of chiefs holding aloft sacred feather standards marched a somber warrior, the royal executioner, alert to seize upon the offender and mark him for death. But Liloa was not unnecessarily cruel; he had the reputation of being an affable, generous man. It was usually his pleasure to stay the hand of doom . . . to put instead a large, gentle hand on the trembling shoulder and say, "E! Just a worthless crab! Let him live!" *E inoa o Liloa!*—he was the first, perhaps, in that line beloved by Hawaiians . . . the politician.

The king lived in Waipio, a wide green valley cut into the sea-bound cliffs of Hamakua on the windward shore. Deep in mountain jungles of the Kohala range huge, white waterfalls had beaten downward seeking passage to the sea, and the concentration of their perennial force had cut away the soft earth, and a powerful stream poured down through the valley. The Hawaiians had diverted

[2] Proclaiming his tabu.

this stream far up and made from it tame rivulets which leaked down through level after level of walled meadow wherein grew the finest taro on the island. Every foot of the valley floor was so cultivated except at its wide mouth by the edge of the sea where huge white rollers ran in to break on a beach of gray sand. Behind the beach were dunes, and atop these dunes stretching back perhaps half a mile along the river's edge were the royal grounds, a place of sanctuary, a gracious estate wherein grew many palms, bananas, breadfruit and other trees and flower-bearing shrubs. Across the stream and set back against the mountain walls was Waipio village, and farther up were other small hamlets.

Waipio had first become a royal residence in the middle of the Thirteenth Century and was sacred to the line of Pili from whom Liloa was descended. The *alii* (chiefs) of this line had had their moments of greatness, moments historically obscured by the feuds of these early times, but now the line was indisputably established under Liloa; completing the conquests of his warrior father, Liloa had made himself suzerain of the whole island, *alii aimoku* (chief who eats—i.e. possesses—the lands). From his father, Kiha, he had inherited a fabulous nautilus shell, brought in some obscure period from Tahiti, and which Kiha had studded with the teeth of the chiefs he had slain; when blown by the rightful king, this horn would emit a tremendous, earth-shaking sound, in which could be heard the battle-cries and death-screams of the chiefs whose teeth were its decoration.

But although his royal palace was at Waipio—and it was a place one would seldom care to leave—Liloa liked to be close to the people of his kingdom, and was wont to make frequent tours of the island. He talked well—a kingly virtue, carefully cultivated—and he talked to all kinds of people; not only his chiefs, but the simple farmers and fishermen and craftsmen who constituted the majority of his subjects. He knew he could not be the one strong man in a race of warriors, and so he had to be the shrewdest.

The island lands were marked off into many divisions, great and small, each with its governor, supervisor, or petty chief. The government was feudal: each landowner was responsible for his tenants to an overlord. And, as in the case of all such systems, each landowner was inclined to have individual ideas concerning the limit of his powers. It was the king's task to define these limits and enforce his definitions, a task which could be performed either through the services of a large, standing army or a lively internal diplomacy. Liloa preferred the latter.

Communication, of course, was difficult. It took eight or nine days for a runner to make the circuit of the island;

and a runner was unhampered—an army on the march might take three times as long. Further, the trails were rough and the sun fiercely hot; an army that was forced to march overland was at a great disadvantage. Nor was an attack by sea any quicker; and even though it conserved the warriors' strength, such an attack was easier to fight off. Under these circumstances it was reasonably simple for a powerful warrior chief to make of his own district or province something akin to a small kingdom and successfully repel the disciplinary action of his nominal sovereign. Frequently, high chiefs would possess more lands than the nominal sovereign and hence more warriors; such chiefs felt free to govern according to their own whims. The fact of professing allegiance to a superior was wont to give them a feeling of irresponsibility toward their own tenants and, safe in their provinces, they would exercise an arrogance against which the common people had little recourse. In the province of Kona—which was particularly productive of this type of governor—the common people had built themselves a fort tactfully removed about half a mile from the palace of the provincial high chief at Kailua, and set at the entrance of a cave euphemistically called Laniakea ('Boundless heaven'), an extensive lava tube which had an exit three miles farther up on the slope of the volcano; when the high chief was in an antagonistic mood, his tenants took refuge here.

Martial government on the part of the king might lead to his own overthrow—or at best avail him little. Shrewd diplomacy were better. And the home diplomat has seldom wielded a better weapon than taxation.

Liloa kept a fond and wary eye on Kona. He was well aware of the temptations offered the governors of this province. Being enthusiastic about Kona himself, the king welcomed the political necessity of paying the province frequent visits; something in the silvery quality of the sun, something in the brave dash and color of the Kailua surf, something in the very air—a feeling of challenge, perhaps—seemed ever to renew his youth and bring out the best of his humor. The days moved leisurely in Kailua, as befitted the days of a king; and the nights!— he could stay awake until dawn by the flickering yellow light of kukui-nut torches watching the supple pantomime of hulas, or, lying on mats by the sea listening to storytellers whose wondrous tales were underlined by the soft swish of the inner surf.

But if Liloa liked Kona, it seems improbable that the governor of that province liked Liloa. The king's ways were devastating. The sight of eight or nine large double canoes, thronged with courtiers, coming round the rocky point headed for Kailua Bay, sent quivering darts of gloom into the spirits of governor and local gentry. The Kailua court was a notoriously large and commodious establishment, but it was neither large enough nor commodious enough to accommodate expansive royal parties. Neighboring personages of rank were turned out of their homes, forced to live with their tenants, and, as if that were not enough, asked to provide food, clothing, and wives (for the king's party, in the spirit of holiday, preferred to leave their own wives at home in Waipio).

This provision of food and clothing for the king was called *hookupu* (gift-giving); the provision of wives was but normal hospitality—and not too annoying, for every man of rank had wives in reserve. But the *hookupu* could be annoying, the way Liloa exacted it. Each landlord had to raise the taxes of his tenants, and these taxes continued to be raised and raised as long as the king stayed on. The consequence was that a severe economic depression ensued throughout the province; in some districts the people had to abandon their lands and remove to another province until their production recovered. Liloa was not unaware of these consequences; indeed, they were part of his system of "diplomacy." He knew that even if the mood were right there would be little danger of insurrection or private rule after his departure; the men would all be needed to fish and till the fields. And the common people did not resent Liloa; it was their immediate overlords they resented, those who forced them to work. The king was sacred, one to be revered;—but more than that, he talked with the common people and was their friend. Such a strange power may the magnetic leader wield.

Toward the end of the year 1460 Liloa made a journey for the purpose of enlarging and restoring the famous temple, Manini. After a particularly exhausting ceremony, he was weak and dispirited and his one desire was to rest his spirit in solitude. He decided, therefore, to return to Waipio on foot, unguarded and in the guise of a poor, landless chief. He enjoyed going among his people incognito; like many another ruler he found such excursions helpful in the formulating of governmental policies.

Early one morning when the sun was still but a promise over the rim of the eastern sea, he set out along the dusty trail, carrying only a war-club and clad in a *malo* (loin-cloth) such as any fisherman might wear; the only thing that set him apart from the lowest class was the chiefly pendant of carved ivory, which he wore about his neck. The way led him up over barren headlands high above the sea, wound down, down, into deep-cleft valleys and tediously up again. As the morning wore on, it grew hot; the sun seemed to hang motionless, a plate of fired steel in a cloudless, chalk-blue sky. About mid-day Liloa found himself in a shady ravine and his dusty bare feet were tempted by the cold waters of a mountain-born stream which tumbled down from above. He left the trail then, and began wading up the stream, pushing aside the tangled green overgrowth, ducking and scrambling, climbing over huge boulders. In time he reached a pool, wide and deep, with a small cataract racing down over smooth rocks above. The heat glistened on his brown chest; drops of perspiration clung to his eyelids making his eyes smart with the salt. It took but a moment to strip off his *malo* and dive into the icy depths. Then the clinging heat vanished from him; his skin grew firm and elastic again; all kingly care fell away. He floated on his back luxuriating. The sun, glinting down through a network of yellow-green kukui leaves twinkled in silver flecks over his dark body and sparkled in his glossy hair. Taking a mouthful of water he spurted a crystal jet upward toward the fretted dome of leaves.

While he lay thus, kicking his feet now and again to keep afloat, a white hibiscus flower, drifting by in a gentle eddy, softly touched his cheek. He started; the flat of his hands smacked the water. From behind a cluster of ti-leaves on the bank came a tinkle of laughter.

"E! Who's there? Who spies on me?"

The long, shiny, toppling leaves were parted and a young girl stepped forth. In her lustrous, black hair she wore a white hibiscus and this was her only adornment. She needed no other, so exquisite was her youthful, golden body. There was no shame in her nakedness; her race regarded the human body with honesty. But there was modesty—a laughing shyness which made the girl lower her long black lashes as Liloa, with a few swift strokes, reached the bank and pulled himself out to stand dripping, tall, questioning before her.

"*Owai tou inoa?* (what is thy name?)" he asks softly. "Who art thou?" A goddess? A child of Pele who watches over mountain streams? No—he need have no awe of her; she is but the daughter of an impoverished chief who lives near by. But who is this lordly one she has surprised in his dreaming solitude?

Liloa speaks his name.

The girl's brown eyes cloud over with fear. She falls, weakly, terrified to her knees, prostrates herself before him. The throbbing of her heart is pain. She has looked upon the king. She has stood in his presence. Perhaps even her shadow has fallen upon him. There is no greater blasphemy. And she has done these things, unknowing; there has even been laughter in her heart. This is fear beyond weeping, fear that turns the body to ash. Death, the inevitable punishment for such a violation of the tabus, is to be welcomed;—to live this blasphemy were worse.

But Liloa speaks again, and his words are tender.

The cool grass is at her cheek, the cool earth. It no longer sinks away from her. It is strong and life-giving. She feels it cool against the length of her and she is calm.

She dares look up. She dares raise herself and kneel before the king and look into the king's eyes.

At this time Liloa had six wives and was well on in his fifties, but no Polynesian is ever so old as his age—and romance is with him till he dies. When, some days later, he returned to Waipio there was an unwonted buoyancy in his step and his lips were smiling. But it was not these facts that created the sensation in his court; like an up-country boor he wore a *malo* of ti-leaves, and about his neck the chiefly pendant no longer hung! *Auwé!* The courtiers nudged one another. Some smiled. Others whispered, Was the king mad?—had he gone native, wreathing himself in vines and leaves? Liloa gave them no answer.

Considering his position and the easy custom of the era Liloa might have dallied with the girl as long as he wished, and then left her with no further thought about the matter. But something in her ethereal beauty had stirred him deeply. When he left her, he left with her his war-club, his *malo* and his ivory necklet. By so doing he made her his wife—adding one more queen to the seraglio. But this gentle country queen knew intuitively that her rule would be the stronger for reigning in memory rather than in the thatched palaces of Waipio. She chose to live on with her father and when that old chieftain died, she married a prosperous farmer.

One morning some fifteen years later, Liloa, having

finished a hearty breakfast of fish, *poi* and roasted dog, was taking his ease on a pile of finely woven mats in the large thatched chamber which served him as a council hall. In a few minutes he would meet with his spies and other confidential agents to learn what events of importance had taken place since the day before. Now, however, he lay back and rested his tired old frame. With him were only his *kahili* (feather standard) bearers who languidly waved away the gnats, and his spittoon-chancellor, a nobleman whose duty it was to see that none of the royal spittle came within sorcering distance of evil priests. Suddenly, there was a loud commotion outside— shouts and the sound of running feet. A moment later there burst through the king's private doorway a young boy, tousled and breathless.

Liloa sat up. It was tradition that "nothing ever startled a sovereign of the line of Pili," but Liloa had been startled at least once before in his lifetime. And he was startled now.

"Insolent child! How dare you!" he cried.

Laughing, the boy pranced up and sat himself down on the shaky knees of the old monarch. One of the *kahili* bearers stepped forward grimly, but Liloa had recovered himself: spreading his legs, he sent the boy sprawling to the pebbled floor. Thus did he refuse parental recognition which had been sought according to custom. The boy stood up, brushed himself off, and, looking into the king's fierce, bloodshot eyes, laughed again.

"Does my liege see nothing familiar in this countenance?" he said. "Then perhaps he will recognize this *malo*, this *palaoa*,[3] and this war-club!"

"*Tahuhu!*" cried one of the *kahili* bearers. He recognized these things the boy held out for the king's inspection.

The wrinkles of Liloa's big, old face creased into a smile. "It is true," he said. "I do indeed recognize these gifts, gifts of honor bestowed on the loveliest girl in Hawaii. *Auwé!* And your name—your name, boy, is . . . ?"

"Umi."

"The very name I gave her for you."

Liloa then summoned his counselors and the *alii* (chiefs) of his court, amongst them the heir apparent to the throne, Prince Hakau. To this august assemblage he presented Umi as his son, a prince of the royal blood. He made the boy a gift of lands, and appointed a staff of warriors and attendants suitable to his station. Runners were dispatched to make a circuit of the island, announcing the news and summoning to a conclave all the provincial governors and their retainers. A fortnight later twelve hundred alii were assembled in Waipio Valley to witness the ceremonial

[3] Ivory pendant.

investiture of Umi, a ritual wherein was symbolically indicated the cutting of the child's navel cord. Thus he became a prince of Hawaii.

Umi was taken in hand by priests and warriors, to be trained in the traditional chants and ceremonies as well as in the intricate arts of warfare. He proved remarkably versatile, learning quickly, and in his twenties became all a Hawaiian prince should be: one of the first athletes in the kingdom as well as one of the most skilled in dialectical exercises. The king made no secret of the fact that he preferred Umi to his elder son, Hakau, who was both arrogant and vicious. Likewise, Umi became a favorite with the people of Waipio. He had that remarkable magnetic charm one sometimes finds in Hawaiians, a charm that attracts all whom they meet. Undoubtedly, the people recognized great mana in this quality.

Not unnaturally this favor was a source of envy and hatred to Hakau. The heir to the throne was a vain man; he had been known to have men killed whose looks were considered handsomer than his, or even whose tattoo marks had been compared to his. Praise of Umi grated harshly in his ears, but he was powerless to affect his half-brother so long as the old king remained alive. In his bitter heart, therefore, he kept his dreams for an ultimate revenge, for Hakau was indisputably the heir—both by primogeniture and by blood, his mother being no country chiefess but a lady of the highest rank in the land.

It was customary for the king to make formal appointment of his heir when he felt the end drawing near. Old Liloa, his hair grizzled and white, his face seamed, his great gentle hands trembling and gnarled, had heard his doom whispered in the wind, had seen it in the fading skies of sunset, yet for a long time he hesitated to make known his choice. He loved Umi so well, seeing in him the finest traditions upheld, while in his father's heart he found not the slightest glow of affection for Hakau. And so he waited. And finally he conceived a scheme.

At a meeting of the high chiefs in the temple at Waipio, Liloa pronounced his decision.

"My son, the tabu chief Hakau, will succeed me as *alii aimoku* over the chiefs and peoples of Hawaii. His lips will blow the great horn of Kiha to summon his men to war."

He paused. A murmur ran through the assemblage; it expressed neither astonishment nor pleasure, but there was in it for Hakau—had he heard it as he stood there in pride and scorn—an ominous note.

"In the charge of my son Umi," the old king went on, silencing the audience, "I place the terrible war-god Ku-kaili-moku ('Ku-the-land-grabber') . . . and further,

32

Prince Umi shall be custodian of all the gods and all the temples in the land."

Now the murmur was one of astonishment indeed. Never before had the executive and religious powers of the king been so divided. All eyes were upon Hakau, who, after a first start of surprise and anger, curled his bearded lips back in a disdainful smile.

A few days later Liloa was dead.

HAKAU

THE HEAVY STILLNESS WHICH PERVADED THE MOUN-
tain forests of Hawaii was broken by the monoto-
nous *chuc-chuc* of stone adzes and the occasional
shattering rips and crashes as great trees toppled to earth.
Ohia trees, *koa* trees, these furnished the hard wood out
of which were fashioned the materials of war—canoes,
spears, daggers, war-clubs. In the villages games of *pahee*
(sliding a sugar-cane javelin) and *ulumaika* (bowling with
rounded stones) gave way to sports of a martial nature,
exercises in spear throwing and spear dodging, the practice of slings. The powerful chiefs were preparing for an
insurrection.

King Hakau was contemptuous. His representatives
were sent regularly among the provinces to exact tribute
from the landlords, tribute in the form of the very weapons they were making, and in the form of foodstuffs and
tapas which were destined to rot away from disuse in
the royal storehouses of Waipio. Spies brought him information as to the state of his kingdom, news from the

courts of the dissident chiefs;—when such news particularly angered him, Hakau made predatory raids on the neighboring districts in order to work off his wrath. As for the rest, let them arm! He could afford to be contemptuous, for were not the chiefs so lacking in confidence in each other that none dared strike for fear of leaving his own flank exposed to his opportunist neighbor? Perhaps they might one day settle their difference . . . but when that day came they would find themselves so impoverished that all of them together could not conquer the king.

Umi had remained in Waipio. Simple and honest, he conceived it his duty to serve his half-brother; it did not occur to him that Hakau might be jealous. This naïf faith was admirably suited to Hakau's plans. He did all in his power to discredit Umi: attendants were bribed to be disrespectful, to call attention to Umi's inferior birth; the young prince's retainers were arrested on charges of violating minor tabus, and executed with over-elaborate ceremony to impress upon the public mind his unworthiness as a leader. But for all Hakau's scheming, Umi still remained an idol to the people. It was not until the king began to tax Umi's tenants—his mother, even—beyond their ability to pay that he realized how unwelcome he was to Hakau. Two venerable priests, Nunu and Kakohe, who had been friends and counselors to Liloa, urged Umi

to leave Waipio lest Hakau be tempted to commit the ultimate crime and bring down the wrath of the gods on the
whole kingdom. Sadly, Umi admitted the wisdom of their
counsel.

One moonless night when the sky was sprinkled
thickly with stars, the prince, accompanied by two loyal
friends, set out up the steep, shadowy trail that led out
of Waipio. As they reached the summit, and paused for
a moment to look back, it was as though Umi then abandoned all claim to rank and privilege, for he had determined to leave the field to Hakau.

Traveling leisurely through Hamakua, affecting to be
landless chiefs on a tour of the island, the three young
men came to the district of Lau-pahoehoe ('Leaf of
smooth lava'). The village at the mouth of the green valley attracted them. Umi said, "Why do we go farther?
No one knows us here, and Hakau is well satisfied with
Waipio; he will never seek us out. Let us stay, then, and
find ourselves a living."

Now, the Hawaiians loved to gamble; many a wealthy
chief had squandered his lands away on the roll of a
bowling stone—Umi's maternal grandfather had thus exchanged goodly properties for a taro patch and a life of
obscurity. A man with luck—! And why should not the
custodian of the kingdom's gods have luck? Mana?
Among the chiefs of Lau-pahoehoe, Umi represented

himself as a skillful surf-rider and inquired whom they considered their champion. The chiefs admired his self-confidence; his tall, muscular build seemed to justify it. One of the prominent young men raised his eyebrows and smiled hopefully at the others. They told Umi that a man named Paiea was not only the champion of the village but of the whole region. Umi, followed by a small, delighted crowd, promptly sought him out.

"E! Paiea. They tell me you are the finest surf-rider in all Hamakua." He paused for effect. "A bandy-legged little fellow like you? And what puny arms! How do you get out to where the big waves break?—hitch on to a sea turtle?"

Paiea, a petty chief, was a thickset man with a morose, scowling face. At these words his big lips twitched angrily and his wide nostrils flared.

"You talk—a skinny slave with not enough wind in the calabash to blow a nose flute! When have you ever seen big waves? The children's surf would tumble you like a shell. But you challenge me?"

"We'll have a wager on it," suggested Umi.

"What have you to offer? Ha!—a clumsily-carved chief's necklet? Not worth one of my spears. Still, I may as well have it, and to show you how much you frighten me, I'll match a canoe against it."

One of the chiefs in the crowd cried out that if the

stranger had nothing more to offer, he personally would back him and match everything Paiea could offer. A roar of pleasure went up. This would be an event indeed. The corners of Paiea's mouth turned down like a fish; his eyes blazed beneath lowered lids.

"I have but one thing more to offer," said Umi, "—but if Lau-pahoehoe has no better surfer than this sickly dog-face, I gladly wager that . . . my bones!"

Paiea smiled sourly. "Your brittle twigs then—and let your foolish friend match my four canoes, my houses, my mats, my weapons, and my tapas!"

The Lau-pahoehoe surf is treacherous. Turgid lava oozed out from the mountain long ago, leaf upon whorled leaf, to set the sea a-boil and then grow cold under its persistent onslaught; shelves of lava stretch out and have been broken off, leaving sea caves and jagged edges, against which huge waves crash and eddy in ceaseless turmoil. Surfers catch the waves far out and are hurled in toward the snag-toothed ledges. Just as catastrophe yawns they dive back into the wave and with powerful strokes fight their way to safety. Umi surveyed this prospect from the shore on the day of the contest, and turning to his friendly patron he smiled cheerfully. He had not bothered to give the surf a preliminary try.

Paiea was ready. The two men ran down the stony beach, hurled their long flat boards into the foaming water and leaped upon them to paddle with long steady strokes out to the bigger surf. Reaching a point well out where the waves first raised their choppy crests, they rode in the trough for a time, awaiting one on which they might agree. Finally it came, a high formidable ridge of water growing momentarily larger and larger, moving as though driven by some power intent upon crushing the very shore in tidal fury. A few deft strokes and both men had risen with the wave and were flashing along just ahead of the crest. They knelt and then stood upright, delicately and gracefully poised while the huge curl of water, gaining greater impetus, flung them toward the lava crusts. The boards were but a few feet apart. As they approached the rocks, Umi shifted his weight slightly to the right, turning his board as though to cross in front of Paiea. The Lau-pahoehoe champion was incredulous: could the stranger be intending to avoid the lava and by some superhuman deftness surf on into the beach? He didn't believe it possible, but he would take no chances. The instant was at hand when he must dive. With a quick shift of his weight he turned his board against Umi's—and dove under. When he emerged from the violent compulsion of the surf, he looked quickly to discover Umi's fate. His rival was coasting in to the very edge of the beach.

The impact of Paiea's board had deflected Umi and cannoned him against the perilous lava, a projecting tusk of which had ripped the flesh from his shoulder, but by some incredible skill he had managed to keep his footing on the board and turn it away, catching the wave again as it curled down the ledge. Thus by his virtuosity did Umi acquire property, wealth, and a host of new friends.

Lau-pahoehoe made much over its new champion and his two comrades. There were *luaus* (feasts), boxing matches, games of every sort. Bards commemorated the occasion in singing verse, and hulas were performed to pantomime the valor and good looks of the three stranger chiefs. Young girls brought them flowers and leis of fragrant leaves. The gaiety and good nature of these people of Lau-pahoehoe appealed to the exiles. What a contrast it was to the gloom and fear of Waipio! *Auwé!*—one sighed at the thought. Flung out upon the ground in the cool shade of the murmuring palms, the sweet scent of flowers in one's nostrils, how delightful it was to watch the naked and laughing villagers disporting themselves in the surf with all the ardor and high spirits of children; and how pleasant to have the attention of these comely, bright-eyed girls! The two handsome daughters of one of the chiefs were particularly enamored of Umi. And he was not unresisting, even though he delighted to pretend he was asleep when they came shyly up. Through his lowered lashes he would watch them whispering to each other and growing bolder. In time he capitulated wholly and visited the girls in their sleeping quarters; as he did not leave before the morning sun warmed the thatch, they became, in the eyes of the community, his wives. In a like fashion did his two comrades marry. Two of the fathers-in-law had no complaint to make with their new sons; the young men proved able farmers and assisted willingly in the chores of home-life. But the chief who had lost his daughters to Umi was slightly disgruntled. He admitted that Umi was the noblest of the three strangers—yes, but he was utterly worthless when it came to doing any work. It wasn't lack of skill either—he had proved himself perfectly capable on one or two occasions, but he was always too preoccupied to pound the household *poi* or even to cook his own food; he allowed his father-in-law to do it for him. Yes, there had never been a finer or more daring surfer in the memory of man, but still Umi's father-in-law grumbled, *"Na-wali-wali!"* (useless) into his beard.

In a small but fertile valley near Lau-pahoehoe lived a priest named Kaoleioku, a tall, thin, middle-aged man with a flowing beard, a fine thin nose and penetrating eyes. Although nominally the high priest at the temple, Manini, he had inherited lands from his chiefess mother and preferred life as a country gentleman to the exigencies of priesthood. As a man of high caste both in priestly and chiefly rank he was widely influential and many persons came to him seeking advice. His mind was a rich storehouse of tradition and he was never at a loss for words of wisdom bearing on any subject from the curing of a child's cough to the thwarting of a sorcerer's evil prayers. Acquainted with the young chief who had made himself the hero of Lau-pahoehoe, the thoughtful priest often wondered as to his antecedents; he guessed even that he might be Umi, for Kaoleioku was kept abreast of the kingdom's affairs by a small group of loyal spies, and was familiar with the story of Umi's disappearance. He kept his speculations to himself, however; he had no reason, at first, to wish to penetrate the chief's disguise. But after Umi had been several years in Lau-pahoehoe, news reached Kaoleioku that a group of rebellious chiefs had finally come to an agreement among themselves, and that the revolution, smoldering so long, was being fanned into a flame—a flame that, in the priest's opinion, threatened to consume the whole kingdom in anarchy. Meditating on this serious turn of events, he was visited one night by a prophetic dream and was prompted thereby to seek out the hero of Lau-pahoehoe.

Approaching the young chief one morning while he was busy oiling his surfboard, Kaoleioku invited him to dine. Umi accepted eagerly; it had been long since he had enjoyed the stimulating conversation of a priest. When he presented himself at Kaoleioku's house, he was cordially received. But before many words had passed between the two men, a small black pig, a pet of the priest's which had been snuffling about in the compound, was seized by a strange compulsion; approaching Umi in a dazed, unsteady fashion it lay down at the young man's feet. Before a word of astonishment could escape him, Umi saw the priest follow the pig's example and prostrate himself on the pebbled floor.

Umi pretended surprise . . . protested . . . took the priest by the arm and sought to raise him, asking him what made him act so strangely. But his protestations were in vain. A black pig would always recognize Hawaiian royalty, and, as though to confirm the omen, a double rainbow was seen at that moment against the slope of Mauna Kea. Umi sighed and acknowledged the priest's chant of subservience and devotion.

"Heaven-born prince," said Kaoleioku when he had risen to his feet at last, "dark clouds are gathering over your kingdom; you alone can pierce them with your divine radiance. A vision sent me by Kane shows me that you must conquer your brother Hakau and set yourself up as the *alii aimoku* of Hawaii."

"I have no right," said Umi.

"The gods give you the right."

"I have no warriors."

"I will give you the warriors, and the spirit of the ancient priest Pa-ao will give you mana. When my glorious forefather came from Tahiti, he brought with him a war-god, a war-god whose mana has never been revealed to the peoples of Hawaii. This god was secreted in the temple of Manini, and Pa-ao admonished the priests that it was never to be removed unless the peace of the whole island was imperiled, or Hawaii invaded by a foreign foe. As high priest of the *heiau* [1] of Manini I declare that the peace is imperiled and that the god of Pa-ao must be invoked."

Kaoleioku then summoned his protégé, the warrior, Mauka-leoleo ('Towering-to-the-peaks'). He was a man of prodigious size. Seven feet was not an unusual height for a Hawaiian warrior, but Mauka was nearer nine. Because the Hawaiians, like children, were inclined to cruelty toward deformity (and madness), Mauka had lived the early years of his life far up in the mountains to escape taunts and also to avoid frightening people. Kaoleioku had found him and brought him to this quiet valley where he had trained the young giant in the arts of warfare, as he had trained a select group of other young men for just such an eventuality as this. He dispatched Mauka now to summon the others, and to bring from its hiding place Ke-akua-paao ('The god of Pa-ao').

Eight large thatched huts were built in the little valley, each housing twenty warriors. When the god-symbol had

[1] Temple.

44

been set up at a small shrine, a ceremony was performed to arouse its mystic powers. According to the divine direction, trees were sought out in the mountain forests and cut down, to be brought to the camp and hewn into arms. Umi's two loyal comrades were put in charge of the regiments that formed the right and left wing of the little army; Umi himself commanded the center. Through various methods, Kaoleioku sought to achieve communication with the god-spirits and one night was visited by another vision. Its import was at first obscure: it told him that Umi would never conquer until Hakau's spears were out of Waipio Valley and only the king remained there alone. Such an opportunity was scarcely to be hoped for even from the heedless Hakau. For several days Umi and Kaoleioku pondered over this vision.

Back in Waipio Umi's old friends, Nunu and Kakohe, had fallen upon hard times. Hakau had no use for priests, possibly because he had no authority over them. On an occasion when the two old men had been feeling ill, they had taken an herb cathartic, a powerful remedy which cured them but left them weak and ravenously hungry. They sent to the king for their usual allowance of food and *awa*—a semi-intoxicating herb drink used constantly by the higher class Hawaiians. Apprised of the plight of the old men, Hakau sent back word that there was no more food or *awa* for them in the royal storehouses;

thenceforth they were to consider themselves independent of the royal bounty. For the first time in their lives they had to work for their living, but they were too weak to do much more than gather herbs and set nets for small fish. The villagers took sympathy on them, and those who could afford it secretly provided the old men with taro. But their leathery skins grew shriveled and hung about their puny frames, and the weight of their long white beards seemed almost too great for them.

In time, Hakau was informed of his dangerous position and became thoroughly frightened. He had the walls of the palace compound made higher and thicker, and a sturdy gate put across the entrance. In his adversity he began to bethink himself of his ancestral gods, as all men who fail themselves turn to a superhuman power for comfort. He regretted that he had treated Nunu and Kakohe harshly and decided to try to conciliate them to him once more. He found the old men solemn and surprisingly willing to listen to his woes. Relief flooded over him. They fetched chickens and swine and cutting them open examined the entrails for omens. Hakau said he had heard the cry of the *alae* (a type of mudhen) every night recently, a sign of evil foreboding. The old priests shook their shaggy heads and admitted the situation was most grave. "Cannot we invoke the power of the mighty war-god, Kukailimoku?" asked Hakau, knowing that the feathered symbol had been left by Umi in the care of the priests. The old men said that they must consult the oracle. Hakau was led to the triangular, tapa-covered scaffolding which stood at the head of the *heiau*.

Kakohe prayed, and after a time they heard words of prophecy emerging faintly from the concealed sanctum (Nunu, who crouched within, could no longer speak above a hoarse whisper). This oracle said that in order to placate the potent Ku, who had been placed in Umi's charge, Hakau must send his warriors to the mountains for feathers . . . red and yellow feathers . . . to be sewed onto the symbolic god mask. Thus only could Hakau hope to obtain Ku's mana for himself. "It shall be done!" cried Hakau. "At dawn tomorrow my warriors will be sent to the mountains."

That evening Nunu and Kakohe hobbled slowly and painfully up the steep trail to the cliff summit above Waipio. At a point which was cupped from the view of the valley below they lit a fire. Far down the Hamakua coast, Mauka, who was standing sentry, saw the faint flicker and hastened to bear the news to Umi and Kaoleioku. Their warriors were then summoned, and the god of Pa-ao brought from the shrine. Then Kaoleioku chanted a soft wailing prayer; it might have been the sound of wind soughing through the mountain forests . . . there was something in the sound that was ageless, unearthly. A moment later there was a murmur of voices, and then silence; the tall shadowy figures began to file out of the valley, down the trail that led to Waipio.

Since the warriors had gone off to the mountains, Hakau had found it comforting to have the frail old priests with him. They looked somehow invincible, as they sat cross-legged on the ground, leaning their frail, withered brown bodies, their over-burdening manes of shaggy white, against the dusty thatch of the royal council chamber. On this morning the king was stretched out in the shade of banana trees; he talked volubly, nervously. Suddenly he cried out. With trembling hand he pointed to the steep trail descending the headlands above. Gray figures could be seen against the cliffs, marching down the trail.

"Those are but your warriors returned from the mountains," said Nunu calmly. "The hunting has been good and they have brought many feathers."

"But how silent they are!" said Hakau. "No shouting, no songs; they might be spirits of the dead."

The priests said nothing, but their eyes were bright and the bones of their hands stood out as they gripped their thin brown arms.

The eyes of the king were bright, too—feverishly bright —as he watched fascinated for the first men to appear at the foot of the trail across the stream.

Now they appeared. First a tall, powerful man of proud bearing, and close on his heels a giant, and others and others, pouring forth, eagerness in their step, no baskets in their hands, but spears! Umi!—Hakau could never forget the splendid virility of that figure. He cried out, and his voice sounded strange to him. "Bar the gate. Make firm the walls. We are attacked!" The few attendants left to him started up and ran frantically to do the king's bidding. Hakau himself was trembling. He ran into his sleeping house with no thought for the two ancients, who continued to sit in the sunlight unmoved. Within the darkness of his house, he seized a huge calabash and began fumbling through the clutter of things it held until he found what he wanted: the horn, the horn of Kiha! Putting the big shell to his lips, he blew with all his wind. But only the ordinary hoarse note of a fisherman's horn came forth.

Outside there was fierce shouting; he heard the impact of weapons, screams of the wounded, moaning, and then a rending crash as Mauka's great shoulders battered down the gate. Sucking in his breath in a mighty gasp, he put the horn to his lips and blew again; the eyes fairly starting from his head. Still only a dull honk emerged.

He choked; the blood sang in his ears; his heart hammered frantically. Catching his breath, he tried to listen. There was now no sound from without, only the faintest whimper from someone down by the gate. His heart seemed to stop beating.

And then he heard it—the soft pad of bare feet moving on all sides of his house. From his lips issued a scream of fear.

At that moment, Umi entered, followed closely by Kaoleioku. Gone now were the mild manners, the gentle air, of the Umi of old; his long, lean, duskily red face was contorted, hideous as a temple image. In his hand he held a poised spear and would have run his brother through but for sudden intervention of the eager priest.

"Hold!" cried Kaoleioku. "The eel must be sacrificed to the god of Paao!" With a length of sharpened *koa* wood, he dug viciously at the king, ripping him open from chest to groin. Umi, standing motionless, watched his brother crumple and lie twitching in an ugly pool of blood and dirt. After a moment he bent over and took from Hakau's hand the ancient nautilus shell. Setting it to his lips, he blew. A tremendous sound rose and clamored against the cliffs;—set free, it flowed over mountainside and plain in a terrible burst of thunder and wild shouts and moans. Hakau's warriors marching slowly homeward with full baskets of feathers heard the sound and quickened their pace. But when they emerged from the trail into the valley they were met by the mana of the god of Paao.

U M I

A MAN OF SIMPLE BIRTH, AN ACUTE MAN WHO HAS shared in the unassuming life of the common people, tilling the soil, catching the fish—a man who has not been exposed to the complicated, and often fettered, processes of government, religion, or even higher education, until he is already accustomed to think for himself—such a man frequently has sharpened perceptions, an eclectic ability, a sense of balance, which give him an advantage over others who have been the unthinking children of a system. A man of the fields may solve with simplicity and dispatch a problem which has long challenged the specialists whose ways are tangled by the necessity of weighing precedents and judging potentialities. And yet it is likely that this man of the fields will set great store by these specialists whom he has momentarily outwitted—greater store than even they may set on their own abilities. Often it is he who, when elevated to a position of power, becomes the most devout worshiper at the door of tradition, the most loyal supporter of an aristocratic regime. Why? Because even though his clear wit may penetrate many faults and inconsistencies in this regime, he knows the importance of respect. Hence, he wields the weapons of the autocrat, but with a difference —there is discrimination on whose shoulders they fall. He forces respect where none was before, but where respect is innate he is mild and even benevolent.

Such a man was Umi. He was wise, yet crude; mild, yet tough and sometimes savagely cruel. But he was a good king.

His first action on taking over the royal valley of Waipio was to invite the aged priests Nunu and Kakohe to go on a short expedition with him. Reaching a certain place, he turned sternly on Nunu: "Now run, old man, run as far as you can and don't trip over your beard. Be off with you." The poor old man had no choice in the matter; horrified at Umi's sudden metamorphosis from friend to enemy, he started off at a lumbering pace, breathing in short gasps, and with large tears rolling down his withered cheeks. When he could go no further, he fell and lay almost dead with the exertion. He heard Umi's hearty laugh at his plight, and felt the king's hand on his shoulder. "Thus, old friend, have you defined your property; your land extends from here to the sea, and is just as wide as the distance you have run." It was Kakohe's turn next; the weak old man saw what the game was, and striving with every ounce of energy in him, managed to run a few paces farther than had his friend. He likewise was rewarded with the land.

Although of humble birth himself, and now in a position to dictate, Umi determined that his heir would be a chief of the highest tabu. He knew that though he might force the outward respect of the provincial chiefs—a petty lot who had been all too willing to forget their grievances against the *alii aimoku* and to genuflect before a strong man so long as they were no longer forced to trust their fellow chiefs—he knew also that he could not control their secret scorn of a king of lowly birth. Therefore, that his sons might be indisputably royal, he married his half-sister, a daughter of Liloa by a chiefess of the highest pedigree. And, as a further precaution—as well as a diplomatic gesture—Umi wooed by proxy for the hand of the princess royal of Maui, a tabu chiefess called Pii-kea ('White ascent').

Maui was willing. Word of Umi's defeat of Hakau and the iron-handed rule he had established on Hawaii convinced the Maui king that the line of Umi would be perpetuated. The girl came. As she stepped to the shore, the *alii* claimed a rainbow appeared, arching itself from prow to stern of the canoe. A tall warrior approached Piikea, picked her up like a child and set her upon his shoulders, and thus she was carried to Umi's court. In the green shade of pandanus, with their fretted circles of root, their smooth, ringed trunks, their dense tufts of long, bluish, sharp-edged leaves, she first beheld her husband. He stood there smiling, with tall warriors on either side; but he was the tallest, seven feet tall, and he had a splendid black curly beard, a feathered casque on his head, and a yellow cape hanging negligently over one shoulder. She saw these, but it was at his smiling face that she looked, feeling a queer contraction of her throat. It was a broad, strong face; the nose was rather small; the lips wide and sensitive, but the eyes were the man, wide-set, large, almost black, yet as clear as a mountain pool, honest eyes. After a moment of appraisal, he laughed aloud and the warriors laughed, too, and she was set down upon her feet and the king of Hawaii approached her to touch his nose to her cheek and whisper something very bold in her ear. In this first meeting Pii-kea was tacitly acknowledged as the queen above all queens of Hawaii.

For his first royal tour Umi wished to start by traveling overland to Kawaihae ('The wild waters'), a place which he had never seen. But Kaoleioku, now the royal high priest, said that a king should not circle the island from this direction; he must go even as the moon's orbit around the sun. The tour therefore was commenced through the province of Hamakua, and not unnaturally one of the first and one of the longest stops was at the village of

Lau-pahoehoe where Umi had spent his exiled years—
and where he was greeted by his two former wives, now
married to others. The old chief who had been his father-
in-law was dead and with him his muttered comment of
"Nawaliwali" which he had been wont to direct at Umi;
—and perhaps it was just as well, for the king had not
forgotten old injuries. Paiea, who had fouled him in the
surfing contest, was brought forth from his impoverished
obscurity and offered up on the altars to Umi's gods.

When the king finally returned to Waipio, after a tour
of nearly two years' duration, it was not to stay; he had
decided that the lovely valley was too far removed from
the other centers of island life and, though assuredly the
most comfortable and delightful place to live, not sufficiently strategic for a king who wanted absolute rule.
He had found a place high up on a plateau between
Mauna Loa and Hualalai from which he could descend
on any of the provinces with almost equal facility and
ease. To this place he moved his court. From it the most
inaccessible provinces were Kau and Puna and to remedy
the situation he had a paved road built over the shoulder
of Mauna Loa. On the plateau itself he had the *alii* con-
struct a *heiau* of hewn stone, an innovation in Hawaiian
engineering, and about this temple the capital village grew
up. To check on his subjects, Umi ordered representatives to come from each province and on the side of the

temple nearest their province make a pile of stones, one stone for each inhabitant; this was the first Hawaiian census and enabled the king to gauge with fair accuracy the amount of resistance each province might offer to his arms;—it also enabled him to regiment the taxes with greater uniformity.

But unfortunately this strategic capital was far from ideal as a place to live. It offered fine, unencumbered fields for the practice of war games, but this very lack of encumbrance allowed the wind to sweep down on the lightly constructed houses of grass and ti-leaves; it was cold, and one felt restless and almost too energetic—without much outlet for one's energy. All the men of Umi's court loved to fish, but the sea was far below, the calm sea of Kona, the finest fishing ground in the islands. More and more the king visited Kona, taking the people of his court with him. The capital became little more than a camp, a stopping place on his journeys, and other than the people of the court, none settled there; only the feather-gatherers used it regularly, for the mountain forests were close at hand.

A favorite resort of the kings was a village in the Kona district called Holua-loa ('Long sliding course') from the undulant stone pavement which ran from the hills to the sea and on which the *alii* displayed their prowess at sledding. It was a dangerous sport, one which was practiced only in the *makahiki* season, the four-month festival of the New Year. In this season the people of Holualoa brought leaves and grass from the mountains and with these they covered the course to make the surface slick. The sleds used were shaped somewhat like the modern ski, but several inches wider and built up slightly on two runners with a sturdy tapa stretched across for the rider to stand or kneel upon. The rider would take a running start, throw himself on the sled, and careen down hill; were he accomplished at the art, he would rise to his feet, and standing with one foot ahead of the other, poise himself with arms outstretched on either side for balance. The under surface of paving was rough, and was further complicated by occasional hillocks over which the sled leaped precariously, and it required an amazing sense of balance to negotiate the whole length of the course. The penalty of non-success was concussive. Despite his size and bulk, Umi was as adept at this sport as he was at surfing and loved it. But there was scarcely a sport that he did not enjoy; he had the athlete's intuition, the sense of timing, the fine, responsive co-ordination of mind to muscle. In later years, when he had grown stout and no longer played at the more vigorous pastimes, he devoted himself to fishing; the fisherfolk along his shores knew him affectionately as *"Poupou"* ('chubby').

To his court in this village came two old ladies. They

were from the island of Oahu. Their skins were burnt nearly black by the sun, and shriveled; thin, gray hair straggled down to their shoulders; their eyes were red-rimmed and deep-sunken into sharp, bony faces. But they were ladies of rank, and they did not bow down as they presented themselves before Umi who sat in his council chamber with the queen Piikea.

The moment Piikea saw them she gripped Umi's arm in fear and whispered to him that these women were her grandmothers, and that they had the reputation of possessing powerful mana.

"Ka-lani ('Heavenly one')," spoke one of the old women in a quavering voice, "we come from the island of Oahu. The royal line of Oahu is sick. A young prince of the highest blood is needed to give it strength again. We have come to take a son of yours . . . a son by our granddaughter, the tabu chiefess of Maui. Protest not. It is our privilege!"

It was a custom among Hawaiian chiefs to give children to their closest friends and to receive children similarly given to them; the gift was always treated with the honor implied, and these adopted youngsters brought up as if by their own parents. But Umi—perhaps because he had lived among poor people unaccustomed to this fashion—had never been able to bring himself to make such a gesture. He was fiercely proud of his sons and his daughters—and he had many (indeed, they used to say in after years that there was not a Hawaiian on the island who could not trace his ancestry to Umi). A suggestion such as this from strangers, people of a distant island, filled him with rage; his lips quivered.

"No son of mine has ever been given to another—nor ever shall be. No son of mine shall ever go to Oahu."

"*Auwé*—so be it!" sighed the old woman, raising an eyebrow cunningly to the other. Together they hobbled stiffly out of the thatched council chamber.

Shortly thereafter, a plague descended on Kailua. Without apparent cause, many of the *alii* began to sicken and die. It was obvious to all that a *kahuna anaana* (sorcerer) was at work. Piikea appealed to the king; she knew this evil influence was traceable to her grandmothers.

"We have other children to console us. Even now I carry a son next to my heart. Let us give them one of our little boys and lift this disastrous spell."

But Umi was not to be intimidated by the sorcery of two feeble old women. He went himself to the place where he had heard they were to be found. Peering into the gloom of a tumble-down hut, he discerned them crouching in a corner staring up at him; their pinched, ugly faces showed no expression whatever.

"Your methods are those of the eel—vicious and contemptible," said Umi. "And like the eel you shall be treated, cut into pieces and flung to the sharks. Not you yourselves, wretched creatures with your bones rattling around within you like stones in a gourd, but the gods on whom you call. Chant the message to them, drum on your calabashes, tell them Umi will meet them on the field of battle and give them a taste of the might of Kukailimoku."

The old women seemed not to have heard him; they continued to stare, but their muddy eyes began to suffuse with a strange glow. Umi, stooping, uncertain in the doorway, felt a slight uneasiness. He had seen many old crones who were said to be sorcerers, and many old men as well; he had found them to be crotchety but simple-hearted old people who were ready enough to be agreeable to *him*. But these ancients were from the island of Oahu; perhaps they were unacquainted with the reputation of Umi. Well, they should be acquainted soon enough. He withdrew from the doorway and was walking toward his canoe on the shore, when he heard a faint, hoarse voice calling after him, "Go, thou with the mind of darkness, and tomorrow the gods will try your mettle on the shore of Kailua Bay." Umi threw back his big head in the sunshine and laughed, a gusty and confident laugh.

He spent the afternoon picking among his many spears, clubs, and daggers, testing the weight, feeling the sharpness of the points, and giving orders to his attendants to oil and polish this one and that one. Feeling pleased with himself and in a humorous mood, he played at fencing with a few of his chiefs, calling them the evil gods and making his most ferocious faces at which, they, falling in with the game, would affect to die miserably. In the evening when the sun was sinking into its gaudy bed on the western sea, the king lay on a pile of soft mats by the shore while his masseurs kneaded the folds of his flesh and gave ease to his spirit.

At dawn on the following day, the villagers began to gather on the sandy beach near the *heiau* of Ahuena ('Flame-color'). By sun-up, people from other villages had arrived by canoe, and the tiny bay was packed with a hushed throng rising and falling on the gentle swell. As the morning advanced, a shimmering mist of heat lay heavily over land and sea. There was no breeze. All Kona seemed holding its breath. Then, from the royal stockade across the bay from the temple, came the booming cry, "*Tapu O! Tapu O!*" Low-voiced and in monotone, the chanting of priests commenced in the temple. The herald emerged with his tabu sticks proclaiming the king's approach. A murmur of excitement ran through the crowd. Umi appeared, huge, haughty, straight-of-back, stern-of-face; on his head a scarlet and yellow helmet, around his neck his polished necklet of ivory, the chief symbol, and falling carelessly from his shoulders a brilliant cape of feathers. He was followed by his courtiers, bearing tall, multicolored feather standards. But the people had no eyes for these. They crouched face down before the king. As he approached the arena through this aisle of backs, those few who dared to observe his face saw his eyes dilate and his nostrils flare.

On the edge of the sandy field just off the small crescent of white beach, the king paused to discard his cloak and helmet and take from an attendant a long, sleek, dark brown spear. The chanting in the *heiau* had ceased. Umi stepped forward, and throwing his head back addressed himself to the palm tops and the sky of faded chalk-blue.

"*E*, you niggardly gods, you inhabitants of the mudhen's droppings, you gods who dwell in rotting trees and stagnation, leave the bowls and the poisonous potions and show your pale spirits to the honest sun. It is Umi the king of Hawaii who challenges you!"

A sharp rustle and a clack of palm fronds. Frightened brown eyes squint upward—there has been no breeze. Pale shimmering heat; the receding sky; motionless day. The king is alone, thick brown legs, broad bare feet, astride the sandy field of battle—waiting.

And then the encircling throng, as by a common pang, sucked in its breath . . . gasped. Umi's face contorted

with a dark ferocity. Slowly he began to move, describing small circles as though performing a cumbrous, antic
dance. He brandished his spear with his arm held high
and wide, his other hand poised as in a hula gesture. He
thrust forward, and jumped deftly aside, and recommenced his slow circling movement. The muscles in his
broad, oiled back stood out in sinewy relief. Suddenly he
howled ferociously and flung his spear with all the force
of his body; it shot out to plunge deep into the sand and
quiver there on the far side of the arena. The multitude
on shore and on the bay groaned. Seizing a thick club
from an attendant warrior, Umi changed his tactics and
plunged forward flailing wildly; he leaped and ran off to
the side, like a black marlin with a hook in its mouth.
But his body could not keep this up; the folds of indolent
flesh quivered and shone with sweat. As though to defy
his flesh, he opened wide his mouth, and his nostrils
cupped upward against the small arch of his nose; the
breath came from him with the sound the sea makes ex-
piring through a fissure on the rocky shore. And now the
groan of the massed humanity turned to a sigh.

He was no longer invincible. He stood, his legs apart,
the club falling limply to the ground while he tottered,
and appeared to be able to see only dimly through a
cloud of perspiration on his frowning brow. A broken
sob escaped him, and among his sympathetic emotional

people the tears flowed freely. In a low tone, tremulous and melancholy, he began to chant. It was a king's chant of submission to a power admittedly greater than his own. When he had finished, he took his yellow cloak and putting it about his shoulders, held a portion of it across his face with a bent arm. In silence, he walked alone along the shore, through the prostrate throng, to the cluster of large straw-colored houses in the grounds of the royal estate.

The pebbles of the floor were cool under his feet as he entered the twilight atmosphere of the chamber where Piikea awaited him. For a moment he stood blinking his eyes before he became accustomed to the darkness. Then his heart pounded against his chest and seemed to stop beating. He saw his wife prostrate, motionless, on her low couch of mats. There was blood about her. Umi stumbled to the couch and fell heavily on his knees by her side. Was she dead? But no—her eyelids fluttered feebly.

"A man-child was born to us," she said almost with her breath alone.

It was not necessary to say more. Umi knew. The gods had defeated him in battle and the old women had taken the prize.

In the sunset of his days, Umi came to think often of what would become of his bones after death. He had enemies. A strong king makes enemies. And they would be eager to gain something of his mana when he was gone; this mana could be gained by securing his bones. A warrior was not afraid to turn ghoul and rifle a tomb when he could secure matter of such advantage. A chief of the highest tabu might be reasonably safe from depredation in his sepulcher, but Umi's tabu was only of the secondary class; his mana was the mana of achievement, and hence his bones had active rather than passive power. And so to thwart his enemies, he conceived a stratagem.

A boon companion and counselor from his earliest youth was a man named Koi. Now suddenly Umi quarreled with him, and in a fit of anger—which incited much gossip throughout the kingdom—banished him from the court. Koi chose to live out his exile on the island of Molokai where he became a chief of some importance. One day, four or five years later, he received word that Umi was dead and lying at the *heiau* of Ahuena at Kailua; he would lie half buried until the body had disintegrated sufficiently for the flesh to be removed and ceremonies performed over the bones. The moment he received this news, Koi set sail for Hawaii with his brother. Reaching a fishing village in Southern Kohala they put in for information. The heir to the kingdom, the Prince of Koloa (Keliiokaloa), had withdrawn from Kailua—as was the custom, lest his sacred person be profaned by the atmosphere of death—and was at Kawaihae with the other close relatives. The whole island was in mourning, a mourning which in the case of a king highly honored became a virtual bacchanalia of grief; the people ran riot, cutting their hair and beards in wild patterns, knocking out their teeth, tattooing their tongues, and indulging in a mad frenzy of licentiousness. Koi and his brother affected to fall in with this gruesome orgy, but kept their wits about them. At last they found what they wanted—a man of Umi's build and same general appearance. Taking advantage of the distraction that then prevailed, they lured this man away from the village and at a lonely spot set upon him and killed him. Stealthily they loaded the body into their canoe and made sail once more down the coast.

It was well on into the dark hours of the night when they arrived at Kailua. The townspeople, exhausted with their debaucheries, were dead to the world. Only at the *heiau* was faint light to be seen, a few flickering torches sending wild shadows flying up the palms and darting across the rocks of the shore. With sail lowered and cautious dips of their paddles, the two men entered the little harbor and drove the prow of their canoe into the sand with a gentle *sssh*. Lifting the corpse out they carried it between them to the *heiau*. Koi crept up the steps and peered into the walled enclosure. As he had hoped, the priests were nodding over their long, lime-caked beards. The brothers advanced stealthily with their burden toward the House of Mana, the small woven hut within which Umi's body was laid. At the entrance, two venerable priests were slumbering beside guttering lamps of hollowed stone. Once inside Koi set about quickly scooping away the sand and earth until the king's body, wrapped in banana leaves, was uncovered. Removing this shroud they wrapped it about the other body, substituting it in the king's place. Then with Umi's partially decayed corpse between them, the two brothers returned to their canoe.

Somewhere, in some remote mountain cave, or perhaps in one of the deep lava tunnels that form the hollow veins of these islands, Umi's bones still lie, where Koi and his brother hid them. Though there have been searches, the burial place has never been found. Hawaiians had a saying that "the bones of a bad chief will not stay hidden, but the bones of a good chief will remain hidden forever."

HAWAII'S GOLDEN AGE

SOMETIME BETWEEN THE YEARS 1528 AND 1531, A fleet of Spanish caravels under the command of Don Alvaro de Saavedra strayed in the south Pacific. A hurricane detached one of its vessels and carried it, sailless and rudderless, northward until it was wrecked on the shore of Hawaii near Kealakekua Bay. Only a man and a woman were saved. Because of their singular and beautiful hue, the Hawaiians considered them divine and absorbed them into the royal dynasty, thus providing Hawaii's blue blood with a Latin strain. These events occurred during the reign of Umi's son, the Prince of Kaloa, a mild, amiable, but inconsequential man.

On the death of Kaloa, the web of autocracy broke. The provincial governors were strong, the hereditary king weak. A period of internal wars and general domestic disorder ensued; a long period—fifteen years, perhaps. Seven men contested for sovereignty, each unwilling to give up his own effort to support another. But there was one who was stronger and shrewder than the rest:

Kaloa's younger brother, Keawe-nui-o-Umi ('Mighty Keawe, son of Umi'). Through these violent years Keawe's deadly spears cleared a path for him; one by one he slew his opponents until finally the bones of all six reposed in one huge calabash, a grisly trophy which he liked to carry about with him on his travels ever afterward.

Having bereft the provinces of their governors, Keawe, the *alii aimoku* appointed to these positions chiefs who had been loyal to him in the wars; although this was an act of necessity, it established a precedent—a "spoils system." Until this time, the lands had been hereditary; henceforth it became the custom for each new king to reapportion the lands, a custom which put a premium on loyalty and enabled a king to draw tight bands around his little kingdom. A court was established to look into the pedigree of applicants for lands and discuss the merits of their claims. A wise king saw to it that lesser chiefs were given the control of the provinces, while the great chiefs—the warriors, capable of organizing powerful opposition if they were given lands and tenants—were retained as members of the exclusive court circle. Despite this rule of reapportioning the lands, a king would occasionally confer small land titles in perpetuity to some particularly deserving *alii*; such grants were almost always honored by the succeeding kings.

Once Mighty Keawe was established as sovereign, peace came to Hawaii. The land was once more made to yield its vegetable wealth, and the people settled down to a period of great prosperity, uninterrupted by wars. Good minds which had been occupied solely with the finesse of spear-dodging and spear-throwing were turned now to other things and there was a general cultural awakening which brought about the establishment of many of Hawaii's most solid traditions.

The caste system became more sharply defined and the legal code—the tabus—made more rigid. The penalty of noncomformity was death; thus the mold quickly hardened. With such a simple people the establishment of a stern social code was an easy matter, for it was their nature to revere and their greatest pleasure to admire.

The king of Hawaii was a ruler one might envy. His subjects were amenable to his disposition. His life was never dull, for his tastes were not over-sophisticated. He could be—and almost always was—one of the best athletes in the kingdom, a warrior, a fisherman, a Lothario, without fear of indignity or reproach. He could play all the games, simple, bawdy or rough, with a child's delight in his eyes. He was king of a loving, laughing, lusty people, and was himself the gayest and most sporting of all—and no less a king, for all that.

The Hawaiian government, which was in itself a whole

system of society, not only provided amply for the physical needs of the people, it provided for their spiritual needs as well . . . by allowing them, or supplying them, occasional vent for the fighting impulses common to all men (without too much bloodshed, for the very nature of their weapons precluded the type of bloody slaughter common to the fields of Europe) and by giving them the pageantry and color that all simple people love; and, finally, by supplying the ultimate raison d'être—religion, a religion adapted perfectly to the needs of the Hawaiian heart.

The royal court was a cross-section of all the types and talent and ideas in the kingdom. The king surrounded himself with highest *alii*, the foremost warriors, the cleverest conversationalists, the most beautiful women, and the most skilled dancers, musicians, masseurs, wrestlers, boxers, prophets, priests, sportsmen, and cooks that the kingdom could provide. He also had more specialized attendants: back-scratchers, chancellor of the royal spittoon, orators, and discouragers of gnats. It was the saying that "an image is the only thing that does no work in a king's household"—but this was not strictly true in the society which grew up around Keawe. There was always one class which was unequivocally called the *hoopili-mea-ai* ('those who stick close to the food'—and don't do much else!).

The two most characteristic traits of the Hawaiian people were laughter and cleanliness. They were extraordinarily good-natured, seldom quarreling among themselves and much given to jokes and riddles; most of their humor derived from the simple foibles of human nature. They were scrupulously clean, swimming as many as eight or ten times a day—after each meal or any other action which might conceivably soil them. Where the nature of the place made it possible, the *alii* had small dipping pools of brackish water in which to wash off the salt after each swim.

Mighty Keawe was a liberal and cheerful monarch and was so well loved that upon his death a sepulcher was built for him at Honaunau, a sepulcher—called Hale o Keawe ('House of Keawe')—which was to become the established royal burying place in after years and a place of the deepest veneration. The terrace of stone upon which it was built is still to be seen within the "City of Refuge." It is probable that the latter was also constructed during Keawe's reign. There had always been places of refuge—caves and a few *heiaus* whither people might flee in times of war and where the criminal or suspected criminal might find sanctuary. But this new compound at Honaunau surpassed anything that the islands had yet known, and it is still standing. Built on hummocked, pahoehoe lava, it includes an area of perhaps three acres beside the small bay. A ten-foot wall of stones, six feet wide, surrounds it, and some of the blocks are so huge that it seems impossible that they could have been hauled there and put in place without any engineering equipment. The Hawaiians say that the big stones were put there by supernatural power, the priests intoning and the laborers concentrating trance-like to achieve the levitation. The wall reputedly had two entrances, one genuine and the other a blind; it was supposed that any person seeking refuge here would take the false entrance and be captured if he were really deserving of the wrath of the gods.

LONO

W HEN MIGHTY KEAWE HAD USURPED THE KING-
ship, the rightful heir had been a prince
named Ku-of-the-Sublime-Sea, eldest son of
the Prince of Kaloa. But this Ku had not been warrior
enough. His bones were among the first to rattle into the
darkness of Keawe's sinister calabash—with an uncle's
sigh of regret. Keawe held nothing against him: the lad
was merely in the way. To prove that this action had
been but a political necessity, Keawe set out to be kind
to Ku's relatives—in particular, the sister, whom he treated
as one of his own children. Her presence in his court was
slight drag on his conscience, for the girl, Ka-iki-lani
('The little heaven'), was a lovely child—and Keawe collected beautiful women. As for the girl's sentiments: presumably she did not hold it against her uncle for having
slain her brother; it was all in the family—some had to be
killed, and nearly all the contesting chiefs were related.
Still, Keawe himself was sufficiently concerned about the
affair to see that his charming niece was well cared for:

indeed, it was in the back of his mind that she would make an excellent wife for his own heir.

But the matter of his own heir was curious. The eldest son was an able and intelligent man named Kanaloa, born of a queen of the purest blood. Traditionally he should be the heir. However, there was a younger son, Lono (Lono-i-ka-makahiki, 'Lono of the new year'), who from his earliest childhood had proved himself a prodigy; his remarkable talents had marked him as a person endowed with mana to an extraordinary degree. When the lad was fifteen or sixteen, the aging king had a talk with him. He was asked if he would consent to become king on his father's death. Lono replied solemnly that on due consideration he felt himself as yet unfit for such a great task; he explained apologetically that while he had mastered the arts of argumentation and conversation and the lore of his people's religion, he was not sure of his left hook—in short, he felt that he had something to learn in boxing and wrestling and in the fine technicalities of warfare. His father laughed at this explanation, but at the same time was in sufficient awe of his astonishing child to respect his judgment. And therefore he called to him the girl Kaikilani. He told her that he proposed to do a remarkable thing—he would appoint her to rule upon his death; she was a chiefess of the high tabu and of the royal strain. It was the first time in Hawaiian history that a woman had ever been given such an honor. But before he drew the interview to a close he impressed upon her the advantage of having a warrior husband—such a man as his son Kanaloa.

Kaikilani, bred in the royal court, was not blind to the political advantages of such a marriage. She took Kanaloa as her husband—and as Prince Regent, for it was he who ruled the kingdom; . . . she could not be bothered by such cares. Kanaloa was intelligent and philosophical; he ruled ably, while the appointed queen set a new fashion for court life.

Lono meanwhile schooled himself under the kingdom's acknowledged masters in the arts of self-defense and warfare. After several years at this education, he set out on a circuit of the island, traveling incognito and at each village challenging the local champion to a contest. In this way, he gained practical experience; more and more frequently he emerged as victor in his public bouts of boxing, wrestling and spear-dodging. His naturally lithe, boyish physique filled out, and he became broad of shoulder and sleek of muscle. At twenty, he was the foremost athlete in the kingdom. His mastery proved, he returned to the court at Kailua and presenting himself to Kanaloa challenged him to battle, a challenge in which the regency was held forfeit.

Kanaloa had something of his younger brother's seriousness; he accepted the challenge unhesitantly. He had well known that this day would come; he was not a man defending his own—he was merely a *konane* (checkers) pebble in the hands of the gods. The time for each contest was set, and the place—the sandy arena on the Kailua shore already famous for Umi's battle with the gods.

Sunny, leisurely Kona was aroused; ah!—these were the events that made a man aware of his virility, that dispelled the sunny dream-cloud of daily living and made life something that man alone could enjoy to the utmost. On that first morning the tiny, green bay was once more swarming with canoes and alive with the throng of bareskinned people, laughing, whispering, gloriously excited. There was only one person in all Kona whose heart did not beat faster and whose lips did not curl into an uncontrollable grin of anticipation—Kaikilani, the queen; excess of flattery and pleasure had jaded her young spirits. She was bored. What if it did mean she might have a new husband to share her throne? The affair was political and meant little to her. She remembered Lono as a sober, ungainly boy, never willing to participate in the games of childhood, uninterested in the games of adolescence; she sighed a little at the thought. Indeed she would have preferred to stay in the royal enclosure during the first contest had she not found herself in danger of being unflatteringly alone. So she went. And for the first time in her life her slumbrous brown eyes opened wide.

The power of that hot, silver sunshine!—it seems to deaden the motion of morning. And yet the brown, easy-going Hawaiian has it in him to give the rhythm that nature has stilled. The heat seems not to affect him . . . the sun to give him slow but beautiful animation.

The first contest was a boxing match. A crowd of *alii* formed the circle, those in authority wielding sticks with which to belabor the ankles of any who carelessly destroyed its symmetry. Kanaloa, a somewhat portly man, entered first; his skin was oiled and glossy, a deep red-brown; his squinting eyes quite serious. And then Lono stood forth, as dark and glossy as his brother—but taller, more slender, in the physical perfection of athletic young manhood. Each struck a stiff pose, back straight, arms extended before and but slightly bent. They spoke to each other quite calmly. Kanaloa called his brother a feeble, spineless jellyfish. Lono compared Kanaloa unfavorably to a fat and sluggish lobster. Kanaloa made a face. Lono countered with one far more ferocious. They pranced ceremoniously. Kanaloa then spoke more heatedly and said that Lono could scarcely claim equality to a bird dropping. Lono replied that he felt far more warmly to the vomit of a dog than he did to Kanaloa. At that Kanaloa drew back his fist and jabbed at his brother; the blow was hard and true to Lono's jaw . . . he staggered. *"Hei-a!"* shouted the crowd in delight. One of the chiefs whacked Kanaloa's leg; he was too close to the edge of the ring. He moved out just in time to receive a swift blow on his temple. He scowled viciously. Thud! . . . his fist went home on Lono's cheek. Thud, thud, thud! The action became more lively. No blows were aimed below the head . . . that was unthinkable; nor did either contestant rely on more than the muscular spring action of his arms held before him. The red-brown skins glowed now with more than coconut oil. Kanaloa's breath came heavily. Too much *poi*, too much *poi! Auwé!* . . . how he regretted the half of a fat dog he had eaten for breakfast. He knitted his brows and leered in his most ominous fashion. Thud, thud! E-ah! . . . the boy was strong. They pounded at each other steadily with the rhythmic persistence of men chopping down a tree with stone adzes. Lono had cause to stagger under many of his brother's well-aimed blows, but the older prince was feeling the strength slowly ebb out of him. He wheezed now, and sweat blinded his eyes. And then with a hoarse shout he made his supreme effort—one, two, three blows, sure and hard, each one landing on Lono's battered face. The boy's knees seemed to buckle; he swayed. But suddenly he twisted like an eel, caught himself and heaved forward with his great broad chest. Kanaloa felt the terrible crunch of bone against bone; his jaw seemed crushed, and he dropped like a monument of stone. Shout after shout rolled up the blazing slope of Hualalai. Here was a warrior indeed, this proud young man who stood, legs apart to steady himself, gazing down triumphantly on the figure of his fallen brother.

Kaikiliani, viewing the spectacle from the shade of a pandanus tree, felt somewhat mixed emotions. At the first sight of her cousin Lono, her heart had given a great swelling beat and then fairly stopped; what a superb warrior! She had seen many, but none so handsome and graceful as he. And she cried out with the others when he had won—honestly and from the fullness of her heart. But now no one paid attention to her. Was she not queen! She took up a beautiful yellow cloak and rising quickly walked out into the ring. Before the delighted multitude she put the cloak around Lono's shoulders and then with a marvelous smile that changed her face to a thing of infinite beauty and desire she rubbed her nose softly against his cheek brushing his lips gently with her own.

That night was festival. A huge moon, plate of silver, floated above the palms in velvet sky, shone down the long slope of volcano and sent a wide sliver of light across the calm, dark sea. Kailua was a tiny spot of flickering yellow in the vastness. But the moon, the mountain, the sea, mighty as they were, could not shout and laugh and beat drums and dance as these happy brown men. There was a *luau*—a feast of staggering proportions; what warrior could not eat a whole pig after such a battle as they had witnessed today! *Lomi-lomi* [1] had eased the bruised and tired muscles of the contestants and they now sat side by side in the torchlight laughing, praising each other, and offering each other choice morsels of roasted pig and dog. Breadfruit and taro, bananas, yams and coconuts, sugar cane, fish—all these succulent things were heaped before them in profusion on a cloth of green leaves. While they feasted, there was dancing and chanting and two burly fellows acted out the day's battle for the amusement of Kanaloa and Lono. Later, the women came in—after the frugal meal which they were allowed by the tabus—and Kaikilani herself did a hula before Lono, her hands with feather-lightness describing the graceful motions that told of ancient glory, her supple slender body conveying a subtle music; and then she danced more tenderly, a dance that made a man's blood pound through his veins and his eyes glow with desire. When this dance was over she came to Lono and kneeling beside him placed around his shoulders a royal *mamo*, a yellow cloak of soft feathers. The *awa* bowl was passed and repassed, and one's body seemed a thing as light as a cloud. Kanaloa suggested a

[1] Massage.

game of *kilu*—which was something more than a game of quoits.

Two days later Lono met the champion wrestler of the court in the sandy arena. This man he vanquished easily, for he knew better than any the violent art of bone-breaking. Many times in his solitary wanderings he had met with robbers—those men whose bodies were greased and their hair cut short so that one could not catch well hold of them; with these men, bone-breaking was a profession—with Lono it was an art. And he taught them that art may be superior to trade.

The final trial, at the week's end, was in the handling of spears. Although it was customary to use spears with blunted ends, this contest was more than a mere game, and the warriors brought their sharpest, most nicely balanced weapons. Unarmed, naked except for a *malo*, Lono stood at the water's edge facing a line of warriors. His stance was easy; he held his arms slightly outstretched before him. Catching Kaikilani's eye—for he had learned to seek out the lovely queen—he grinned at her. It was Kanaloa's honor to hurl the first spear. Drawing back his long polished wooden shaft he flung it straight and true. Lono raised his arm, moved his body the slightest bit to the side, and the spear faintly grazed him—falling in the water and darting through the ripples. The enthusiastic crowd laughed happily at this bit of humor, and Lono laughed with them. Two men stepped out of the line and at a signal each hurled his spear at Lono's taut chest. He ducked. With a gesture so quick it could scarcely be seen his hand came up and caught one of the spears by the shaft; its impetus nearly pulled him over, but he recovered himself and before a man had caught his breath to cry out he hurled it back at the warriors who leapt aside with less grace, perhaps, but equal agility. The throng shouted with joy. Now four men gripped their polished shafts . . . hurled. Then eight. Then sixteen!—a veritable hail of spears converged on the spot where Lono might have been if his nimble feet and his finely co-ordinated body had not obeyed the flashing impulse of his mind. With ambidextrous skill he plucked from this deadly hail two spears; the arms of another man would have been cruelly jerked from their sockets, but Lono's practiced muscles stretched—and recoiled: the spears flew back almost before the others had touched the water. Crunch!— a luckless warrior lay writhing, pinned to the sand! Superb climax to the most amazing exhibition of skill these assembled Hawaiians had ever beheld. Who could now question that Lono was the finest warrior in Hawaii?

Kanaloa smiled proudly and a little wistfully. He sought out Kaikilani in the royal reception chamber whither she had retired.

He spoke gently: this, to him, was not easy news.

"Lovely one . . . you have seen! Of all the sons of Keawe none is more favored by the gods than Lono. If he has the god's favor, I pray that he have yours. The priests have read the omens; the *alii* have met with me in council during these days. It is agreed by all—myself included—that I must step aside to make room for the wiser and the stronger and the one blessed of heaven. We ask you to accept Lono as your husband and share with him the sovereignty . . . Will you?"

Kaikilani had listened to this speech with lowered eyes, but anyone less rapt than Kanaloa would have seen in the rise and fall of her young and golden breasts an intense, joyous excitement. Her breath was quick and she could scarcely speak in reply. At last she pressed her palms against the soft mat and threw back her proud head. "Since the gods favor him—well, then so must I!"

In this fashion did Prince Kanaloa become husband emeritus to the queen of Hawaii.

Educated to an active life, Lono had never been partial to the languid ways of the royal court. Nor could the persuasion of his beautiful new wife alter his spirit now. He was determined to be a vigorous and progressive ruler. Although well-known to the majority of his people since the days when he had roved the island trying his fledgling skill as a fighter, he went among them once more—as a hero-king now, as a man to whom they could come with their land problems and the more complicated problems of living; he found that a king who so wished might become in the eyes of his people a father, a priest, a magician, by merely smiling down upon them from the high pinnacle of sovereignty. By attending to their interests he became a palpable god.

But Kaikilani, herself an appointed sovereign, cared not for such dusty and tedious matters. The romantic love that had first swept her away proved a volatile thing. She soon came to think of her husband as a royal bore. How much better the carefree court of Kailua than the heat and discomfort of traveling around the island. *Auwé!*— such foolishness—all a ruler need do was to select his servants well. And Kaikilani began to select hers with a sly irony. She surrounded herself with the handsomest and wittiest men in the kingdom . . . and the most amorous. The part she played she was well suited for with her arrogant good looks, the trace of Castilian heritage in her bold and sparkling eyes, and her uninhibited sense of humor.

Lono, as all earnest men, was an idealist. No thought occurred to him that his wife might be unfaithful to him, but in time he did realize that his continued absences might make life somewhat dull for her. Therefore, when he felt the affairs of the kingdom had been put in good order, he decided to make up for his long abstraction by taking Kaikilani on a leisurely voyage through the islands. To surprise her, he ordered the construction of an enormous double canoe, having a raised platform seventy feet long and seven feet wide with a six-foot thatch around the sides. Within, many soft mats were piled up to form a continuous built-in couch and spread with tapas of gay colors and design; about the walls, festoons of flowers and fragrant leaves were hung; at the entrance were tall, multi-colored feather standards; and enshrined at the far end, a basket-work mask of Ku. The canoes themselves were painted with alternate black and yellow lines, and from the masthead a royal scarlet tapa pennon floated. This barge was Kaikilani's own; Lono traveled in his war canoe. The gay young queen was delighted by it, and she peopled it with attendants of her own choice—a goodly company of court *alii;* performers on the nose flute, *ukeke*[2] and drums; and hula dancers. She was tactful enough, however, not to invite the well-born chief with whom she had been having her most recent affair.

The first island visited was Lanai, not a very luxuriant island but an established way station for inter-island travel. At a small bay on the southern shore, the royal party made its encampment. Traveling was a leisurely diversion and Lono planned to spend several weeks there.

One evening while the king and queen were seated

[2] Gourd rattles.

near the shore playing an idle game, a sweetly plaintive chant arose on the heights above them and seemed to float on the still air. A lover's chant, soft, rhythmic, rich with longing. Lono tilted his head to listen and an appreciative smile formed on his lips, but the words he heard made the smile turn to anger. The song was addressed to his wife. She affected not to notice it, but her slender fingers trembled as she moved a black pebble on the heavy playing board of Hawaiian mahogany. The song came to an end and the soft echoes died against the cliff. There was a hush. With a stiff, deliberate gesture Lono's big brown hand swept the pebbles from the board. Then suddenly he gripped the heavy slab, raised it with a mighty effort and brought it down on the head of his queen. He staggered to his feet, and in the glance he gave her as she lay stretched out and motionless on the sand at his feet was a mixture of fury and pain. For one weak moment he felt impelled to kneel and take her hand, but he controlled himself and turned away . . . turned away to run as though pursued and sought out along the shore a small canoe. His two attendants, trusted friends, had followed him fearing that he might have gone out of his mind. Seeing them close by, he indicated that they were to help him launch the canoe through the pounding surf. They hastened to obey. When they were safely past the breakers, Lono dug his paddle savagely into the waters and in a few moments the canoe had disappeared in the gathering darkness.

This discovery of Kaikilani's infidelity left Lono quite wounded and bitter. He was determined never again to return to Hawaii, but to live out his days as a wanderer and one of those who seeks only sensual pleasure. He guided his canoe to the island of Oahu where, on the windward side, was another Kailua, well known throughout the archipelago as a place where all the restless spirits gathered in search of gaiety and forgetfulness.

And Kaikilani? Her attendants found her there, lying frighteningly still, her soft black hair and yellow feather coronet clotted with blood. But she breathed. The gaudy barge bore her back to Hawaii. Its flowers were wilted, the fragrance had left the *maile* leaves and the drums were stilled. The voluptuous tapas made a restless couch for the fretful girl's body. Home in Kailua all was changed. The shock had done more than physical hurt—it had shattered the touchstone of her spirit. Kanaloa heaped tinder on the fires of indignation that flared out against Lono; chivalry's call found ardent response in the Hawaiian breast. The illusion of the paternal monarch was destroyed . . . carefully, by *alii* who had been secretly jealous of Lono's prestige among the common people. And, as it should be, the leader of this revolution was perfectly sincere—Kanaloa, the former husband of Kaikilani, was convinced that his brother had lost his mind. Kanaloa's love was humble; once more he took Kaikilani to wife and assumed the position of Prince Regent.

Two years passed. Kaikilani grew stronger, and as her health returned she understood why she had been so crushed. She loved Lono. The romantic love which she had thought was all now appeared to her as nothing. She saw that true love was selfless. She was ashamed that she should have ever thought herself worthy of demanding so much. In search of absolution she became a mild and dutiful wife to Kanaloa; she bore him a child—the child, indeed, that was to continue the royal line. This obligation fulfilled, she felt herself justified in renouncing her home and setting out to search for Lono.

It was nearly three years since he had come to Oahu, and Lono was still at the court of pleasure. Without a kingdom to think about, the life suited him very well; he became at once the leader in all sports and festivity for none were so careless, so strong, as he. His name was unknown, but his nobility was patent.

As he sat one day beneath a spreading breadfruit tree in the chiefly enclosure playing a game with a few of the *alii*, his sport was arrested, as it had been once before, by a chant, a love chant. It came from beyond the wall of the sheltered garden; Lono's back was turned. He sat very still. The other chiefs listened, for this was the song of

Lono and Kaikilani whose romance was already legend throughout the islands. The soft voice of the singer welled with emotion and then, with a broken sob, ceased. Still Lono had not moved. And then, after a long moment, he took up the song. He turned around and Kaikilani saw the tears coursing down his cheeks. After lonely months of wandering throughout the islands, her search had ended.

A great celebration was arranged by the friendly Oahu chiefs whose sentimental hearts were moved by the reconciliation of the king and queen of Hawaii. The feasting and song were prolonged for several days. But after the first joyous hours together, Kaikilani told Lono that the kingdom was no longer his; he knew that he must return.

Adventurous Oahu warriors offered Lono their services; it was a generous offer, and without it he might have been helpless. Canoes were provided for him, and arms. Thus, when he landed once more on the shores of his kingdom he had a small but formidable army, sufficient to overthrow the petty chiefs of Kohala and win once more to his side a great body of the common people who had long dreamed of his return. Kanaloa met him on the sloping plain north of Kailua, and though the Hawaiian army was greater, its spirit was not wholly with the uninspiring Kanaloa, and Lono was victorious. With footholds in Kona and Kohala, it was easy for him to march into the other provinces and put down all further resistance; indeed, after the defeat of Kanaloa, the kingdom fell apart for his taking as easily as a pit-roasted pig. Instead of killing the rebellious chiefs whom he conquered, Lono contented himself with depriving them of their lands and keeping them in his court where he could have an eye on them. Kanaloa was forgiven and restored to his former status as friend and adviser to the king. Lono was aware of the chivalry that had prompted the revolution, and he was determined to be equally chivalrous in its quelling. Peace restored, he set out once more on a circuit of his kingdom to reconfirm his suzerainty.

At this time it pleased destiny that the king of Maui, one Kama-lala-walu ('Kama of the eight branches'), should look out across the blue channel that separated his kingdom from that of Hawaii, and muse upon the prospect. A fat parcel of lands to be added to someone's empire! The Maui king had been friendly to the great Keawe, but friendship ceased where envy begins!—and there were rumors afloat that Hawaii was divided against itself. Kama was old and fat, but his warrior's heart throbbed youthfully; the war heralds were sent out to scour Maui for troops.

Lono was in Hilo when word reached him that a huge fleet of Maui warriors had landed at Kawaihae. There was no question as to what this meant. The king set out at once marching overland around Mauna Kea. Meanwhile,

Kanaloa raised the best army he could on such short notice and set out for Wai-mea ('Cloudy water'), a village which commanded the tableland between Mauna Kea and the Kohala mountains. He suspected that the Maui armies would march up from Kawaihae and cross the great plain in order to sweep down upon Kona from above, and he hoped to forestall them; also, with his small army, he needed the advantage of surprise. When, as anticipated, the Maui force appeared over the rim of the hot, arid tableland, Kanaloa kept his men out of sight behind rocks and such shrubs as there were. Relentlessly the sun glared down on the sweating Maui warriors and when, about noonday, they approached Waimea, the hearts went out of them at the sight of three small but compact crescents of fresh Hawaii troops moving swiftly down. Kanaloa, as high chief, was at the head of the center crescent, and when the armies were within hailing distance, he stepped forth and contemptuously hailed Kama.

"E!—you fish-bellied slave, you atrophied gnat-snapper, you king of stones and dust . . . you wish to gain for yourself the rich lands of Hawaii? We laugh at you. We come, a mere handful of sportsmen, and in a moment we shall wipe out your whole wobbling army."

The Maui troops were fair marks for this description; exhausted from toiling up the slope in blistering heat, they were unfit for battle and panic-stricken by the sudden appearance of Kanaloa. But old Kama and his general had fought many a battle and were not to be dismayed by scornful words backed up by only half a regiment. The Maui king answered Kanaloa in the same vein, shouting boldly to inspirit his warriors; he himself flung the first spear at Kanaloa. This the Hawaii warrior caught and flung back with a will, and in a moment the armies met.

Under the serene blue vault of heaven, isolated on the vast yellow plain, what paltry ant battalions were these! The sound of their fierce cries and shrieks and groans were lost in the heavy hot stillness that shimmered and pressed against mountain and plain; the thick swirling dust found ceiling scarcely twenty feet above the fray. Two miles away a wanderer on the hazy tableland would have thought himself alone in the vastness!

And then, in an instant, it was all over . . . a sudden wrenching apart, a few darting figures fleeing toward the hills. Kanaloa had been captured. A roar burst from the Maui troops, a shout of victory.

Back at Kawaihae that evening, by the flickering yellow light of torches, a terrible and exultant ceremony was held. A shaggy, fierce old priest, calling upon Maui's war-god, knelt on the chest of tightly bound Kanaloa and gouged out his eyes. An offering fit for the fleering god. But it was an unfortunate idea. Word of this offering reached the scattered remnants of the Hawaii army. Had

Maui chosen merely to sacrifice Kanaloa's body, it would have been in keeping with the war traditions; all warriors would have accepted it as such, albeit with rue and melancholy. But wanton, barbarous cruelty was unacceptable to any man with Hawaii's blood in his veins. Runners met Lono, marching overland from Hilo, and told the tale; Lono was grim. He had been able to gather more troops as he passed through Hamakua, and now his army was swelled to a formidable size. If the troops needed anything to fire their spirits—they had it! This time the battle was no slight fracas, but a holocaust. Lono swooped down and butchered the men of Maui. The king and his general were both captured and doomed to die for the vengeful Hawaii war-god, Kukailimoku.

Because of the importance of this victory, Lono decided to build a *heiau* for his war-god—the usual tribute at the end of a successful campaign. The site he selected was already the scene of many such monuments . . . but one more would not make a great difference. In times of peace these *heiaus* were neglected, only occasionally restored by itinerant monarchs to bring good fortune to their rule. The building or restoring of a *heiau* to the war-god, or even to others of the gods, was an act of reverence in itself; they did not necessarily remain temples of frequent use.

Temple architects were summoned to the king's presence. These were men of priestly affiliation whose profession it was to know every *heiau* in the islands—when and why each one was built, and whether or not it brought mana to the builder. These architects proposed several plans which Lono and his high priest considered. When they had made their tentative choice—with a few suggested changes—the architects made a small model of the *heiau* of sand and pebbles. A few more minor changes and the working plans were completed. The foremost *alii* of the island were summoned to conclave, and after the matter had been explained to them, actual construction began.

After the ground had been consecrated, there was a period of hard, sweating labor. Most of the available stones in Kahaluu had already been used for earlier temples; units of workmen were sent afield to bring in more. This laying of the foundations was the work of weeks, and at its conclusion—when the terraces were laid—the ceremonies began. There was a period of rest while the builders awaited a propitious day, a day when there should be no cloud in the sky, no wind, no rainbows, no smoke to be seen in all of Kona. On this day they set out in solemn procession and slowly toiled up the hot slopes to the heavily wooded forest far up on Hualalai. With them they carried provisions of roasted pigs, coconuts and bananas. In the cool shade of the forest they waited while Lono and his high priest sought out a tree for their needs, a *koa* tree, tall, straight, and of great girth. When the tree was found the priest intoned a prayer. No sound interrupted his chant; even the gray green leaves were still. The king's mind was occupied with the single thought of Kukailimoku. All was well: the spell was lifted, and the priest turned to Lono saying, *"Ola, ola! O Ku!"* The king answered, *"Elieli!"* (it is well), and taking a small live pig from one of his attendants he dashed it, squealing, to the ground. The priest picking up the twitching, bloody body buried it carefully at the foot of the tree. After this, all sat down to avail themselves of the ample feast brought with them.

When their hunger was appeased, the men lay down and each flung a bare brown arm carelessly over his eyes and rested or slept. After perhaps an hour the priest arose and approaching the tree once more commenced chanting. The men wakened one by one to his deep reverberant voice. Nothing disturbed the chant; the time was propitious. Lono approached the tree and touched it with a polished ceremonial adze. But before the chopping of the great trunk commenced, the executioner brought forth a Maui chief, a prisoner of war, and with symbolic violence slashed off the prisoner's head with one stroke of a long, shark's tooth knife; the remains, like those of the pig, were interred at the foot of the tree. Now the brave work began; the tree was surrounded and the men fell to, their adzes chopping rhythmically and steadily. After several hours, during which the cutters were replaced by several shifts to make the work more swift, there was a shattering crack!—and the tree, shuddering, toppled slowly over into the soft wet jungle beneath. It was the matter of a few minutes to lop off the boughs and trim the great trunk down to a thing of reasonable symmetry. With a chorus of grunts the men heaved it up on their shoulders and set off triumphantly for Kahaluu. As they marched in the pale coolness of the afternoon they chanted:

> "O Kuamu, O Kuamu, be silent,
> O Kuawa, O Kuawa, reflect . . .
> Shout forth the triumph, shout, shout!
> Confuse their defeat, flee, flee!"

On the day following, runners were sent throughout the province. All roads were to be cleared of brush and weeds, and stone markers replaced on the boundaries of the smaller land sections. This was a purification of the province, a necessary precaution for the solemnities to follow in which this whole wide sunny slope was to take part. At the new *heiau*, the chiefs who were to act in the ceremonies were themselves purified by the invocations of a company of priests. The tabu began at nightfall. No sound could be made, no fires built. Should there be any disturbance, even the bark of a dog, the ceremonies would be postponed until a night and day had passed without such blasphemy. The people of the district, each person aware that he might be included in the sacrifices if he was party to any such disturbances, muzzled dogs and pigs with tapa and placed their chickens under calabashes.

Once all the structures were complete, tribute was brought by the people of the province—robes, red *malos*, tapas to swathe the scaffold and decorate the wooden gargoyles, brightly colored leaves, flowers and evergreens for the offering tables; in lots of four hundred were contributed pigs, coconuts, bananas, bundles of tapa, *lauhala* mats, red fish and *kukui*-nut torches. Prior to the most formal ceremonials, a great feast was held in which all the laboring *alii* took part; this was followed by a short period of rest—under strict tabu.

The night before the final ritual, a company of priests, with their long hair and beards smeared with colored lime, sat within the sanctum and chanted away the hours of darkness. In the morning the gargoyles were dressed and feathered mask-symbols put in place; Lono took the red mask of Kukailimoku through the village of Kahaluu, and if any person had broken the tabu, the crest feathers of the god stood on end, and that person was marked for sacrifice. The silence was profound throughout the district; only the lapping and swishing of the surf and the rattle of palm fronds in the faint breeze failed to show respect for the awful Kukailimoku.

At dusk Lono and the high priest entered the temple alone. No other person in Kahaluu stirred out of his house; not a light showed except for the few torches within the sacred place. There was no moon: the sky was a brilliant carpet of stars. The priest was attired in a long robe of white tapa, and a white turban was wrapped around his venerable head; with a flowing mane of silky white hair and white beard reaching nearly to his knees, he was a figure of dignity. Lono was dressed in a robe of scarlet. Taking his place before the mask-symbol of Ku, he stood rapt and motionless while the priest began his chant. The rise and fall of his mournful, booming voice swelled through the palms and echoed in the still reaches of the mountainside. All the night through these men maintained a vigil and at last, when the western sky at the sloping rim of the volcano showed gray with dawn, the priest's voice died away. The world was hushed with the new morning. Lono spoke: "*Amama!*" ('tis ended).

This new day was held sacred to Kane, the god of nature and the ascendant god among the majority of the Hawaiian people. Chiefs and priests gathered on the *heiau* terraces. They knelt in two rows before Lono and the high priest, the right leg crossed over the left, the right hand crossed over the left.

"Put up your hands," the priest commanded. Each man extended his right hand, pointing toward the gods in the heavens; holding their hands thus they joined in with a chant led by the high priest. This prayer lasted for well over an hour, and the right arms of the assemblage grew stiff with pain, but none faltered. When at last Lono gave the *amama*, they were allowed to sit back on their haunches. Tribute was now heaped upon the altars, and finally the charred naked bodies of the Maui king and his general and other less important sacrifices were brought out (they had not been burnt alive, but had been strangled prior to cremation). These gruesome objects were brought before Lono. In the blackened, almost obliterated mouth of the king of Maui was a sacred fish hook and a length of line. Lono took the line in his hand and chanted:

"O ku, O Kuniakea, O Lononuiakea
O Kanenuiakea and Kanaloa,
Here is the offering, the sacrifice:
A noble tribute, a royal ornament,
An enemy to my country, a land-grabber.
O curse rebels without and within—
And the land-grabber, too!
Preserve me as the mainstay of my kingdom,
And all the chiefs,
And all the people,
And the kingdom from end to end!
Amama! 'tis free . . . 'tis finished!"

Palm leaves were brought in by two men, one representing a chief and the other a priest, who after fastening the leaves to the scaffolding, performed a slow, involved, sacred hula. The sacrificed bodies were then laid upon the altars face down, a pig in each right hand, coconuts and bananas in the left. All eyes turned to the feathered mask-symbol of Ku, and it was seen that the brilliant tuft of red feathers on the crest was standing up and fluttering in the breeze. The war-god had accepted the sacrifice. Great was the rejoicing, and another lavish feast was held which lasted for several days.

Although the temple was neglected for the palm grove and its heaps of food on the cloth of green leaves, there were two who stood guard at the sacred enclosure:—two little dogs, one white, the other blind and black, who howled and howled into the hollow loneliness of night. These dogs had been the pets of the Maui king and his general. Day after day they remained at the *heiau*, taking no food, and the emotional hearts of the villagers were touched. On the day when the weak cries were finally stilled, the people of Kahaluu buried the little dogs beneath the altars on which the bodies of their masters lay.

In further commemoration of the victory over the Maui army, an unknown Kahaluu artist added one more picture to the sea-washed gallery on the rocks near by. Cutting more deeply than was usual for the Kahaluu artists, he dug out a large, childish figure of a man, a portrait of the king of Maui. The bones of this king were retained for many years by Kona priests, but early in the Nineteenth Century they were returned to Maui.

ALAPAI

OR SEVERAL GENERATIONS AFTER LONO THE RULERS
of Hawaii lacked that bold incisiveness of deed
and vividness of personality which in the preced-
ing kings had so appealed to the imaginations of their people. Furthermore, to keep the royal dynasty pure, there
was much inter-breeding; the Hawaiians had no conception of incest, though it may be said that marriages between brother and sister were marriages of blood only
and cohabitation was infrequent. And so, competent
though these later kings may have been—popular even—
the bards are content with a mere recital of their names
and a weaving together of the complicated cross threads
of family histories. Early in the Eighteenth Century a
king named Keawe II allowed the government to get
somewhat out of hand, and on his death his sons brawled
among themselves. This left the whole kingdom in an
uproar, as most of the high chiefs of the various provinces
were his sons—or sons of his sister wife.

One of these high chiefs was Alapai-nui, governor of

Kohala. His name meant "Big Liar"; however, it did not necessarily reflect on his character. Hawaiians frequently bestowed deprecatory names on their offspring to assure the gods—at times when divine interest seemed to be falling off—that there was no false pride in the family. Indeed, some of the names bestowed by solicitous parents were so deprecatory as to be untranslatable.

Alapai was one of those grim warriors who, with tough hide and bold determination, frequently came to the fore when affairs of the kingdom were unsettled and, without regard for family ties, prerogative or violent opposition, carved out for themselves the position of *alii aimoku*—and held onto it. However, he had to ally himself with Time, and wars raged for many years. When finally he had established himself indisputably as king, he married a widow, who brought with her two children by former marriages—sons, ironically enough, of chiefs whom Alapai had killed to gain the throne. However, in the spirit of the times, no one chose to make an issue of this fact, and Alapai brought the boys up. As he devoted the rest of his life to unsuccessful attempts at the conquest of Maui, the young princes had intensive training in the arts of warfare, and in early manhood had so distinguished themselves that they held positions of high prominence in the kingdom. The elder of the two was called Ka-lani-opuu, and might have been heir to the kingdom had not Alapai killed his father to further his own interests. The other had the unmistakable name of Kalanikupuapaikalaninui Keoua, or, more simply, Keoua. While Alapai's court was established in Kohala, the most convenient place from which to launch campaigns against Maui, Keoua fell in love with a niece of the king and married her, a young girl named Ke-kui-a-poiwa.

In the higher circles of society a woman's first duty to her husband was to provide him with a son. That the first child might be indisputably the child of her husband it was the custom for the man and wife to be sequestered in separate establishments [1] and guarded by priests. When the woman gave natural evidence that she was not with child she was taken to bathe and then led to a tent of tapa which was set up at some prominent place in the village. The townspeople were informed and gathered about the tent, together with the priests from the *heiau*. Then the husband appeared bringing with him a wooden staff on the head of which was carved a representation of one of his family gods. This staff he set in the earth outside the tent and entered to his wife. The priests commenced invocations to the gods of fertility and their prayers continued until evening by which time it was hoped that the prince had *hoomau keiki* (sown a child);

[1] *Pa-lama:* a place fenced in with sacred lama wood. The name later came to be used to signify hospital—"caring for."

he came forth from the tent, priests and people departed, and the wife returned to her home where, if it was found that she was pregnant, she remained in a state of tabu until the child was born.

But despite this invocation of the assistance of the gods, Keoua's wife did not conceive him a child; her hair remained unshorn, a sign in Hawaiian society that a woman had not yet borne a child (the week after childbirth, the hair would be cut close to the head and worn thus thereafter throughout her life). After a time Kekuiapoiwa took a trip to Maui to visit at the court of King Kahekili, who, even though he was at war with Hawaii, was also her relative. Soon after she returned, she was discovered to be pregnant; now, of course, there was no proof that she carried Keoua's child, and indeed there is reason to suppose that Kahekili himself was the father as later incidents will show. Perhaps Alapai suspected her for when she had a strange yearning for the eyeball of a Maui chief the king called to his *kahunas* [2] to visit her and make a report to him; these mystics returned to him with the unanimous conviction the child would be a rebel, a child who would "slay the chiefs." Had he believed the child was Keoua's the king might not have been so alarmed by this prophecy; but, as it was, he called in his executioner and ordered

[2] *Kahuna*—professional man. Used without an attributive adjective it is generally taken to mean "priest."

him to keep watch over Kekuiapoiwa and as soon as the child was born to kill it. What Keoua's thoughts were on the matter is unknown.

The girl heard of the king's intentions soon enough and in her distress bethought herself of a childhood friend who was the granddaughter of the chief who governed the deep valleys and mountain jungles of the Hamakua cliff region. She sent for this friend and together they planned for the child to be hidden away in the mountains at a place called Awini. To help them they took into their confidence one of the king's runners, a man called Naeole. The girl from Hamakua then returned home and with her mother prepared the place where they would bring up the child; the older woman even started to weave a feather cloak for this great chief who was to be born.

Toward the end of October of the year 1753 [3] there was a night when suddenly the sky of stars was obscured by heavy clouds; a tempest swept in from the sea and deluged Kohala in leaden downpour. Thunder cracked and the clouds were ripped again and again by livid sheets of lightning. In the wet, cold darkness of the small thatched hut where she had been confined for these many months, Kekuiapoiwa was suffering steady and increasingly racking convulsions and her fingers dug into the

[3] According to the best estimates; the actual date is unknown.

thatch as she clenched her hands around one of the horizontal poles of the hut's framework. A powerful older woman, a chiefess, sat behind her pressing her knees into the small of Kekuiapoiwa's back and pulling at her shoulders to ease the pain. And then in one fainting moment of agony the child began to come. Other women assisted its delivery. The young mother groaned; the child, slapped by a plump brown hand, gave a piping wail. At that moment a torch flared in the doorway and a tall man appeared. Taking the child from the startled midwives, he wrapped it hastily in tapa lined with a soft woolly substance. As suddenly as he had appeared he was gone.

From the place where the child was born, to Awini was no great distance as the bird flies, but the trail was tortuous, winding down into valleys and up the steep, shaggy, rain-sodden walls of mountain. But Naeole was fleet of foot and his charge was infinitely precious. He reached the place in little more than two hours, and motherly hands took the child from him. An old priest washed the tiny body and put soothing herbs about it, praying to the gods to watch over this child of destiny. The foster mother still had milk in her breasts; she had only recently given birth to a daughter, and though it was against tradition for a man child to suckle after a female, it did not seem to harm this infant.

But scarcely had the child arrived when the old chief

of the mountains heard other runners approaching and warned the women to beware. Hastily the babe was placed beneath a pile of *olona* fibers which had been collected for the making of his feather cloak. When the runners appeared they looked into the hut and asked if a man carrying a bundle had passed this way. The women said "no" drowsily, affecting to have been awakened from sleep, and the runners passed on. When the dawn came up over the silent sea stretching far away below the mountain fastness, the priest prayed that the signs of a royal birth—the rainbow, the fleecy clouds touched with the colors of morning and the remnant veils of rain—would not betray the child's hiding place to the king's sharp-eyed *kahunas:* and the gods heard the prayer. The boy was called Paiea, but in later life he was to be known as Kamehameha ('The lonely one').

After five years the excitement of the kidnapping had died down at court, and Naeole, who had stayed on with the child at Awini, returned with him in triumph; the king allowed him to assume the position of *kahu.* He was a worthy man; probably there could have been no better choice for the young prince's *kahu* than one who believed so fanatically in his great future. They made a curious pair, Naeole and Kamehameha, for the child, like his protector, was somber and without laughter, and seated on Naeole's broad shoulders he was borne through the village crowds like some supernaturally severe child priest.

As the years went on, the king ostensibly continued to be as devoted to his two stepsons as he had always been. But it is probable that he had come to fear them also. They had grown, perhaps, too powerful. Kalaniopuu sensed this and stayed more and more in the province of Ka-u, which he had inherited from his father and which inheritance Alapai had graciously confirmed. Keoua, however, continued his career as a commander of the king's troops and an acknowledged court favorite. But in the year 1769, Keoua died under suspicious circumstances—at least, Kalaniopuu considered them suspicious; he was convinced that his half-brother and lifelong friend had been poisoned, or prayed to death, by the king. Kalaniopuu knew his stepfather well enough to believe that affection would never stand in his way when he deemed his own welfare imperiled. And Keoua's popularity was such that the king might well have feared him. . . .

The royal court was established at Waipio at the time, and the body of Keoua was laid out in a large thatched hall. Many of the chiefs had gathered there to mourn. The wailing and lamentation was frenzied; a few of the *alii* who had been particularly close to Keoua chanted through lips bloodied from the teeth they had knocked out. In this excess of grief it was scarcely noticed when Kalaniopuu appeared and joined in with the mourners.

Was it not proper for him who had been closest of all to the deceased? He made his way through the throng where the boy Kamehameha stood, dry-eyed and grave, looking on his father's body. He whispered to the boy, and the two of them after a moment began to make quickly for the door. But now there were eyes upon them. A hue and cry was set up; Kalaniopuu was trying to kidnap Kamehameha! In the tumult Kalaniopuu managed to escape; two war canoes were awaiting him at the shore and he made off, returning to Ka-u. This attempt of Kalaniopuu's was seen as an act of open rebellion, and he made ready his province for an attack by the king's army. But the attack never came. Alapai, who was now well on in years, maintained an apparent indifference to his stepson's defection. It may have been that he honestly loved the chief too well; but whatever the reason, he suffered Kalaniopuu to remain in Ka'u undisturbed. And the young Kamehameha continued to receive favor at court. A few years later the black tapa covered Alapai at Kawaihae.

Alapai's son succeeded to the throne as Keawe III, but his tenure was short-lived. He had only to proclaim the first of his land distributions when rebellion flared up, instigated by hot-headed Kee-au-moku, a warrior born, who would fight anybody on the least provocation. Keawe was able to defeat Keeaumoku in their first skirmish, but the rebel chief then threw his lot in with Kalaniopuu and the combination of the two was too much. Kalaniopuu, as dynastic heir to the throne, had never for a moment acknowledged Keawe, and as soon as he had heard of Alapai's death, he had set off with his armies for Kohala. Keawe met the forces of Keeaumoku and Kalaniopuu near Kealakekua Bay, and after a battle that lasted two days, he was killed and his army dispersed. Now, Kalaniopuu was king.

PART II

DISCOVERY AND RESOLUTION

KALANIOPUU

WORD OF KEAWE'S OVERTHROW WAS QUICKLY had—rumor outran the runners. In every village the *alii* gathered in the compound of their overlord, and the common people in the palm grove. Now that the irrepressible chief of Ka'u was *alii aimoku*, who were his friends? What were his whims? Those who had spoken scornfully of him in the past hoped that their audiences had been inattentive;—but against chances of the alternative they sought out well-hidden caves where they began to store their wealth—spears, fine tapas, feather capes, canoes:—one could never tell about the pre-emptive disposition of a new sovereign.

When Kalaniopuu finally made his royal tour he was met with an embarrassed display of generosity and pressing protestations of loyalty. He looked into the merits of claims—and hopes—put forward, and in the ultimate distributions of lands he had the genius to satisfy all;—at least, no one protested! As to his whims, it was soon apparent to the people of Hawaii that their new king gave little thought to the traditions of Lono, that god of peace and husbandry. His sacrifices were made on the altars of Kukailimoku, the dark god of war.

Having seen his spear pinning one writhing king to bloodstained earth, Kalaniopuu thought: Why not another? Why not Hawaii's long-time enemy, the king of Maui? Alapai had failed, but in Kalaniopuu's mind Alapai had failed in many things; he was contemptuous of the memory of his uncle and former patron. New fleets of canoes could be built, new weapons carved from the hard wood of the mountain forests, village pastimes subordinated once more to the artful practices of war games. *Ae!*—Maui could be conquered. And then, perhaps, the Dream—Oahu and Kauai! His blood quickened at the thought of himself as sovereign of the blue, wreathing seas and the seven island kingdoms of Hawaii. Violently Kalaniopuu swept down on Maui;—violently, many times. He dedicated more than twenty years to this effort, and innumerable warriors and promising young chiefs.

But the time would come. And chiefs enough remained.

In the last days of November, 1778, Kalaniopuu's armies were encamped in the province of Hana, one of the two Maui provinces which had fallen to his arms after all these years of battling. A few more skirmishes were necessary, a few more isolated rebels to put down, and then he would return home for the holidays, the glorious yearly four-month period when no work was done and a man could indulge himself to his heart's content in sports, *awa*-drinking, hulas, carousing. This festival was called the *makahiki* and was patronized by the god Lono; his banners would be carried in procession about the island as a signal to all to stop work and enjoy themselves.

While the king was lying on his mats one afternoon, relaxing under the soothing ministrations of his masseurs, a courtier burst in upon him with a startling message. Two huge *heiaus*, floating on the sea, had been sighted off the western shore:—the *heiaus* of Lono himself! Even now the god was receiving the king of Maui. Kalaniopuu's oiled body grew tense; he sat up, waving the masseurs away. *Heiaus?* Lono? Yes, said the messenger, unmistakably Lono:—they bore the *makahiki* banners vastly enlarged and hung on sky-raking poles.

The king's gnarled brown hand sought the piece of ivory about his neck; fingering it seemed to release his tension and allow his thoughts to run free. It all flooded back to him now, the news he had received the year before from his spy Moho who was stationed on Oahu. *Heiaus* had come to Kauai, said Moho, and had gone thence to Niihau. The gods had visited on shore and were described as "creatures with loose skins, angular heads—gods indeed. Small volcanoes were clamped between their teeth and there were openings in their sides for the stowing of property and into which they would thrust their hands bringing forth knives, iron, beads, tapa, nails and a hundred other miraculous things." The metals had made the greatest impression, for what little the Hawaiians had was salvaged from rare pieces of flotsam that had floated to their shores. Lono had stayed at the islands but a fortnight—just long enough to establish his divinity and exact payment for his miracles in the form of a dire sickness which his retinue had spread among the native women. The excitement his visit had caused had already passed into legend. A high priest on Oahu—who had not himself seen the marvelous evidence—had been dubious and prophetic: "Those people are *haole* (foreigners); they are surely the people who will come and dwell in the land." Another, supporting this theory, recalled: "These are the people of whom Kekiopilo, the seer, spoke when he said, 'Some day foreigners will come here, white people . . . and as for their dogs, people will ride upon them and they will bring dogs with very long ears.'" In spite of these utterances—if they were made at all and had the currency attributed them by native chronicles—the majority of the Hawaiians remained convinced that the phenomenon was the return of Lono, even as he had promised to return when he went off to Tahiti centuries before.

These were the thoughts that crowded into Kalaniopuu's mind as he sat in the thatched shade looking out across the dark blue waters toward the faintly visible outline of the island of Hawaii. Earnestly he prayed that Lono would abandon the Maui king and proceed on around the island; sacrifices were made in the temples, and the priests gave voice to the prayers of their king.

The prayers were answered, for on the following day —Sunday, the 30th of November, 1778—the fabulous *heiaus* (or floating islands, as some of the imaginative ones said) were seen approaching Hana, moving slowly and majestically, their numerous *makahiki* banners bellying out, splendid in the silvery morning sunlight. Hastily, Kalaniopuu ordered his sailing canoe to be prepared and a few pigs stowed aboard as an offering. The intimates of the royal court put on their finest capes and their gourd helmets which came down to their chins, with large holes cut out for the eyes; so arrayed they looked like a species of strange, huge birds.

As the royal company approached, paddling swiftly over the swells, the *heiaus* showed sign of having seen them; several of the banners were pulled down and the speed diminished. When the big canoe was alongside, ladders were unrolled, ladders of wondrous thick sennit, and a row of weird faces appeared at the fencing above— pale faces, the color of sickness, and oddly decorated with cloth caps. Hesitant, a little frightened, Kalaniopuu searched these faces for sign of recognizable emotion. They smiled; hands beckoned. Bravely the king caught hold of a ladder and climbed up the stained and barnacled wooden wall, followed by his eager men. Reaching the sunlit terrace, the Hawaiians resisted temptation to stare and prostrated themselves; they remembered they were in the presence of a god—only the king and one or two other chiefs of high tabu remained standing, for, after all, they were this god's representatives among the people. A tall, weatherbeaten figure, spare and with a slight stoop, approached the king; his eyes, beneath heavy brows, were small and bright, his face thinly austere. From the deference paid him by others of the assemblage, Kalaniopuu knew this to be Lono and accordingly addressed him with a reverent chant of greeting. The god promptly took him by the hand and, gripping it firmly, moved it up and down —undoubtedly a gesture of friendship and love; the prostrate warriors who had been peering up through the holes in their helmets groaned with awe and pleasure. Pronouncing the word *"aroha"* (aloha) in a kindly tone, though not relaxing his vigilant expression, Lono signaled for the Hawaiians to arise.

Now they could look about them. *"Tahaha!"* . . . *"He-ia!"* . . . *"Auwé!"* Mouths fell open; brown eyes stared. There was iron everywhere, and fat coils of sennit.

The order and design of things, the marvelous conception and carpentry—this was no *heiau* but a canoe, a canoe that would dazzle the most imaginative of seers. But no less exciting was the study of this host of superior beings crowding round the warriors, smiling, gesturing, pointing things out. These gods had a rough grayish skin, sometimes mottled to meaty red, and were swathed hotly about in cumbersome apparel—some sort of ceremonial dress, evidently. Hair covered their ears and was rolled or drawn up in a knot at the back of their necks—one might suppose them to be women but for the fact that many had grizzled hair, some of it bleached, growing not only where a man's beard should grow but high up on their jowls and cheekbones. Among themselves these gods chattered in gibberish, using odd hissing sounds:—they seemed to know but a few words, badly mispronounced, of the language of civilization. Lono was referred to by an abrupt ugly sound which the Hawaiians could only approximate as "*Kapena Kuke.*"

Kalaniopuu stayed aboard for several hours, extravagantly delighted with all he saw. Other canoes had come alongside by now and the simpler people, overcoming their awe more quickly than had their king, entered into trade with the newcomers; more and more they came, like fishermen to a place where the *aku* are running, for in one day they made greater profit than in years of ordinary living: they were paid for their profusion of bread-fruit, bananas and *poi* in the fabulous material, iron!

Before he left the vessel—for his dignity would not allow him to overstay his welcome—Kalaniopuu recommended to Lono his nephew Kamehameha who had come aboard with the young prince Keoua of the Red Cape (Keoua Ahuula) somewhat later. Lono nodded and smiled and, as a present for the king, brought out some pieces of beautiful red tapa, soft and luxurious, and some interesting necklets. The tall Hawaiian lord was well pleased.

And so, in the soft breeze of that Sunday evening, His Britannic Majesty's ships of war, the *Resolution* and *Discovery*, under the command of a farmer's son who had become the world's most famous navigator and explorer, coasted slowly down the Maui shore. Above the ships towered the awesome, purple mass of the volcano called House of the Sun (Hale-a-ka-la); the sun itself soon fell back into the mountain's shadow leaving the heavens brilliantly awash with scarlet and gold. Kamehameha's outrigger canoe, towed behind, made a tiny white wake in the wide, lazily churning path of the *Resolution;* he had been persuaded to spend the night aboard. When night descended and neither the young prince nor hero-chief had returned, an uneasy murmur swept through the camps of Kalaniopuu's people. Had Lono required a sacrifice? A few old women commenced a low wailing; the sound was taken up all down the shore, swelling mournfully in the night air. But at dawn boy and warrior returned—unscathed, excited by a night in another world.

The commander of the two vessels, Captain James Cook, was on his third voyage into the little-known, vaguely charted Pacific Ocean. His first two voyages had already accomplished much toward revealing its secrets and had made him one of the outstanding figures of his time. His company—though not his companionship —was sought by seafaring men and scientists alike for he was talented in both these lines. King George III himself had wistfully drawn him out on the beauties and enchantments of the sunny southern seas . . . that dull, sleepy, royal George who was "forever drawing maps" of far-off places. After his second voyage Cook had been given a snug berth as post-Captain at the Greenwich naval hospital. He might have expected more—and perhaps he did. Perhaps it was the hope of promotion to Admiral's rank, a knighthood even, that prompted him to give up his berth at Greenwich and accept the command of a third expedition to the Pacific. The purpose of this voyage was ostensibly to run to earth the persistent rumors of a navigable passage across the northern reaches of America; this was not the sole motive for the expedition, but the Admiralty was less frank about the others—the scouting of trade routes and the survey of lands of potential wealth which might need the protection of the British crown.

On his way to the northwest coast of America, Cook had sighted the Hawaiian Islands and had put in at Kauai to restock and refuel his ships. He had named these uncharted islands after his patron, the notorious and dissolute Earl of Sandwich, then first lord of the Admiralty and under whose management the British navy fared worse than at any time in its history. Cook's purpose in returning to "the Sandwich Islands" was to refit his ships after months in the north and at the same time to make a more thorough survey of his discovery.

Kamehameha told him that another island lay to the southeast and he decided to investigate it in the hope of finding better anchorage than Maui afforded; by making a leisurely circuit of the island he could chart the land and at the same time trade with the natives for supplies. Ten months in the northern latitude had been hard on the British sailors. Added to short rations and bitter cold there had been lack of any adventure to fire a sailor's imagination. After Tahiti, which they had visited on the voyage out, what had Alaska to offer? Thus Cook's one hundred and ninety men were overjoyed at the prospect of spending a few months in the tropics, which they had already discovered to contain islands of endless pleasures.

Lieutenant Rickman, one of the young officers aboard the *Discovery*, phrased it: "Fresh provisions and kind females are the sailors' sole delight; and when in possession of these, past hardships are instantly forgotten." Hawaii's kindly sun soon thawed out and melted away memories of the bitter months.

When the ships were nearing the island of Hawaii, the surgeons—of which there were only three now that old Anderson had died—submitted a report to Captain Cook. There were, according to this report, a number of men aboard both ships who had "the Venereal Disorder"— syphilis. The report was tardy; evidently no examination had been made prior to the squadron's visit to Tahiti and Kauai. However, if this thought occurred to Captain Cook, he said nothing about it. He merely gave orders that in the future no man afflicted with the disorder could go ashore and that none of the sailors were to be permitted to take girls aboard without the commander's express permission.

But what could the officers do to enforce this order? The Hawaiian girls were so forward. And so charming. The ships had scarcely sighted Hawaii before canoes came off in great number crowded with fresh provisions . . . and girls. As for the girls, could one blame them for their forwardness? They received bits of iron—fabulous payment in their eyes for the simple, natural gift which they had to offer, and surely they acquired powerful mana from associating with these divine beings? They had no way of knowing that they would also acquire a disease which would decimate their population within a few short years; there had never been such a thing as disease among Polynesians. And so the moral resistance of the Englishmen was short-lived. As the ships coasted down past the awesome windward cliffs and fertile green valleys Cook conveniently turned his back on the new trading which sprang up.

Seeking to ease their consciences, two of the surgeons, Samwell and Ellis, neither being of the celibate's turn of mind, examined native girls and discovered that many already suffered from the vicious disease. Profound observers!—they preferred to think the effects of their visit to Kauai in January could not have spread this far. It was a comforting thought and Ellis remarked that under the circumstances it would be impossible to leave the women in a worse condition. The report was forgotten, therefore, and the captain's orders as well. Surgeon Samwell's journal now read: "When any of us sees a handsome girl in a canoe that he has a mind to, upon waving his hand to her she immediately jumps overboard and swims to the ship where we receive her in our arms like another Venus rising from the waves."

The daily receptions were least reserved aboard the

smaller vessel, the *Discovery*. Captain Clerke was suffering from tuberculosis and kept to his cabin. As for the lieutenants, Jim Burney and Jack Rickman, and the master, Tom Edgar, they were all young men and did not fancy themselves as admirals yet. The officers could conduct themselves with reasonable privacy. Not so the men: they had only the fo'castle to retire to, a dingy place still redolent of their recent hardships. Under these circumstances standards were relaxed and the silver-blue moonlight of tropic night picked out many unwonted shadows on the decks of that very proper man King George III's ships of war. Surgeon Ellis struck the only harsh note in this idyll; as a man of science he was forced to note that when the ships encountered swells the unusual motion affected some of the guests at times not always the most fortunate.

The *Resolution* and *Discovery* kept close together along the northern coast, but on Christmas Eve they became separated in a slight gale and, each taking a different tack, did not sight each other again for several weeks. Both were out of sight of the island on Christmas Day and the occasion was celebrated in bachelor style according to naval tradition. Every man was given a double ration of grog; inasmuch as the normal daily ration was one gallon of beer for each man, or lacking beer, half a pint of rum, brandy or arak, there was no lack of gaiety aboard and the lads drank generous toasts to the wives awaiting them in Portsmouth or in London. Thus did "Lono" conduct his own religious festival unmindful that on those palm-lined shores just over the horizon, a reverent brown-skinned people were making sacrifices to him in their temples of stone.

In the first week of the new year, 1779, a series of gales sprang up which kept both crews active trying to prevent further damage to the already badly worn riggings. When the weather cleared, the captains decided leisurely progress was no longer practical; good anchorage must be found soon so that repairs could be effected. Boats were sent off to examine coves and bays along the southern shore and it was this coincidence of purpose that brought the two vessels within sight of each other once more. Having passed the southermost point of the island, they were proceeding together up the western coast when on Saturday, January 16th, they found themselves near the entrance to a large bay, cupped at the foot of the volcano Mauna Loa. It appeared ideal for their purposes, sheltered from all but the fiercest sou'westerly gales. The pinnace of the *Resolution* and the large cutter of the *Discovery* were dispatched to make soundings.

Meanwhile the sailors, idle aboard ship, entertained the friendly Hawaiians who had continued to come aboard as long as the ships were close to land. Cook was astonished at the multitudes which had come each day and the many more that stood curiously along the cliffs watching the ships' progress; he could not guess that he had led a procession around the island and, as a consequence, he estimated the population to be far greater than it actually was.

The sailors discovered that by cutting the metal buttons from their clothes and sewing them on strips of red cloth they had a popular form of jewelry. "Excellent *douceurs* for the girls," remarked Doctor Samwell. The sawbones was not unlearned in feminine psychology. On this warm Saturday morning he entertained "the most beautiful girl so far" by leading her before a full-length mirror. "*Wahine maikai au!*" she cried out (What a fine-looking girl I am!), and the surgeon assured her she spoke no less than the truth.

It was evening before the boats returned, but they brought word that the harbor was satisfactory. The natives called it Ke-ala-ke-kua ('The path of the gods'). Both vessels prepared to stand in at daybreak, but when the morning sun rose there was not a breath of air. Indeed the whole vista might have been under glass. Even the small boats ordered out to tow and their admiring convoy of outrigger canoes looked like many-legged bugs paralyzed on the water's surface. Progress was slow and sweaty work.

Once the ships were within the harbor and riding on the translucent cobalt waters, the still oppressiveness vanished. Word had spread on night wings up and down the Kona coast that Lono was coming home, for at the foot of a wide ribbon of earth swirling down from the volcano's summit stood a massive temple of gray stone, the foremost shrine to Lono in all the islands.

Ten thousand people came to Kealakekua this morning, ten thousand ardent, shouting people, chests and shoulders and big friendly faces glowing in the sunlight like figurines of burnished copper, incredibly animate. The bay swarmed with outriggers; those who could find no place in a canoe came on surfboards, or even swam out to plunge like schools of porpoises in the clear sparkling blue water about the ships; and the more daring swarmed up the stout oaken sides. Girls, their naked golden bodies gleaming wet with salt water, found the way below. The tall, loose-jointed men stayed on deck to watch the sailors, crowding about so that many a sweating, red-faced tar had to shoulder his way to the ropes, pushing as many as he could of his laughing, dripping admirers overboard. Down, down they would plummet and a moment later would be climbing the ropes again.

If the clamor, the crowding, the laughing and jostling made confusion aboard the ships, it was multiplied tenfold in the bay and on shore. Canoes were upset and

their cargoes of coconuts, breadfruit, bananas, sent bobbing through the water, tangling with paddles, bumping
surfboards;—occasionally a boatload of pigs would join
them, squealing frightened protest, adding pandemonium
to the roar of human voices. Every palm along the shore
had a bloated, fantastic look with the innumerable men
clinging to its trunk, and dark heads projected like so
many more coconuts from its feathery tufts; the roofs of
the houses were covered with people; people milled along
the shore in uneven, wavering rows; they clung from
ledges on the cliff.

Meanwhile, the god whom they had come to welcome
stood forth calmly in full view on the afterdeck of the
Resolution; a few of his officers were gathered around
him, very proper in their velveteen pantaloons, white
waistcoats, spade-shaped coats of blue broadcloth, and
cocked hats. From time to time the god, unconscious of
his divinity, put a brass spyglass to his eye and scanned
the shore.

Just off the head of the bay rose its most dominant
feature, a reddish cliff, pocked with lava bubbles, perhaps
800 feet high at its eminence, and declining away on the
left behind a well-populated village on the north arm of
the bay. Where the cliff shelved off abruptly on the right,
cut by the flowing ribbon of land from above, there was
a fine strip of beach ending in a promontory of rock.

Behind this promontory was the *heiau*, and about it and spreading off under the palms and pandanus another big village. Over the cliff face there was only the most hazardous path to connect these two villages. Communication obviously was by sea. Captain Cook shrewdly discovered this fact, and decided that the most satisfactory anchorage would be in a position forming a triangle with the villages, the cliff being the base; so situated his guns could command either source of potential trouble and at the same time force the lines of communication. Thoughtfully he tapped the spyglass in his open hand.

While he was thus considering his prospects, two of the Hawaiian king's representatives came aboard and presented themselves. They were young *alii* named Palea and Kanaina and served Kalaniopuu in the capacity of aides-de-camp. From them Cook learned that the king was still engaged on Maui but was expected to return very shortly. With the assistance of several of his officers who had learned some Tahitian, and with his own smattering of that language, Captain Cook found it not too difficult to converse with these young men whose looks he appraised and found very much to his satisfaction. They were both well over six feet tall and of muscular physique, carrying themselves proudly and with an unexpected litheness of movement; in features they might have compared to many Englishmen except for the dark, smooth, reddish hue of their skins. They offered to serve in any way they could, and their quick understanding—as well as their influence among the Hawaiians—was soon demonstrated.

While conversing with them, the captain's eyes suddenly narrowed with anger as he observed one of the natives on the forward deck pick up a belaying pin and start to make off with it; Palea, following his glance, at once ran forward, and, seizing the thief, made him return the pin, at the same time ordering all the Hawaiians off the ships and to keep clear with their small craft. Returning to the captain he then offered his services and Kanaina's to police the ships, an offer which was promptly accepted; thereafter, the two men came aboard at dawn each day—Palea on the *Discovery*, Kanaina on the *Resolution*—and drove out all girls with orders not to return till nightfall; among the men only chiefs were allowed to come aboard.

When the ships had come to anchor shortly before noon, Palea and Kanaina went ashore and returned with an old priest known as Kuaha. He was a shriveled ugly little man with a scurf-ridden skin—a common complaint among the higher class Hawaiians as a result of over-indulgence in the lotus-like *awa*. His small, pouched eyes were bleary, yet there was in them a spark of shrewdness and Captain Cook was willing to accept the fact—as explained by Palea—that he was the high priest of the district. The officers promptly dubbed him "The Bishop." The old man, despite his disreputable looks, was solemn and formal in his greeting. Putting a square of red tapa about the captain's shoulders, he stepped back and held out a small pig before him while he intoned this chant:

> "O Lono of the boundless universe,
>   Thou of countless forms—
>   The flying cloud,
>   The puffy cloud,
>   The cloud barely seen on the horizon,
>   The billowing cloud,
>   The terrible thunder-cloud of heaven—
>   From Uliuli,
>   From Melemele,
>   From Tahiti,
>   From Ulunui,
>   From Hakalauai,
>   From the land of Lono on high,
>   In the infinite,
>   In the divine guise of Laka . . .
>   O Lalohama,
>   O Olepuu-the-refuge,
>   E Ku!
>   E Lono!
>   E Kane!
>   E Kanaloa!
>   E god from Apapalani of Apapanuu
>   From Tahiti east,
>   From Tahiti west,
>   Behold this sacrifice . . . !

Behold this offering . . . !
Preserve the chiefs,
Preserve the worshipers,
And establish the luminous day o'er the floating earth!
Amama . . . ua noa!"

He held out the pig to Captain Cook. With a bow the tall Englishman accepted it, looked at it uncertainly for a moment, and then handed it ceremoniously to one of his officers who found a platter to set it upon. The momentary confusion was fortuitous as it suggested to the captain a way of returning a compliment to the raffish old priest. He invited him to dine.

At the stout table of polished oak strange dishes were set before Kuaha on immaculate crockery. He was not deterred by the wonder of these things; he knew food when he saw it, and he was hungry. Greedily he dipped in with his fingers, popping large morsels into his mouth and sucking at the straggle ends of his mustache. Only when he tasted a goblet of wine did a startled look pass over his face; he choked, sputtered, and set the glass down hastily. Was this poison? he wondered; but no, the others were drinking it with apparent relish, those men with faces the color of fish belly. *Auwé!*—what barbarous tastes, no wonder their skins were pallid. When his appetite had been satisfied, Kuaha began to look about him; his eyes were suspicious, as though they sought some clue that would reveal his host's hypocrisy. It was not instinctive wit that prompted his suspicions—rather, it was jealousy. Next to the king's high priest he, Kuaha, was the prelate to whom greatest respect was paid, and, as entrepreneur between man and god, he had fallen into the habit of thinking the entrepreneur more important than either.

It was a somewhat awkward meal, but Captain Cook had been in such situations before and behaved graciously toward his guest. Kuaha could find no obvious fault. Lulled by the pleasantness of being the center of attention, the priest's doubting mind was forced reluctantly to accept this man as Lono—at least, for the time being. The fellow obviously had strong mana. Being by profession a spell-caster and oracle, Kuaha had no great respect for his ancestral gods as gods: he himself was largely responsible for their material manifestations. But he was Polynesian and he did believe in mana, the mystic power "that rolls through all things." Furthermore his livelihood depended on his giving a convincing performance of the priestly duties, and he felt that it would be not only wise from a personal standpoint but also extremely politic to maintain a reverent attitude before this peculiarly endowed man;—or god, if he chose to call himself that.

In the village at the head of the bay there had been great preparations under way all morning for the reception of Lono, and when the lunch was over Kuaha asked the captain to come ashore with him and be inducted into the ceremonies of the *heiau*. Cook was agreeable to this and asked his protégé, Lieutenant King, and the astronomer, Mr. Bayly, to keep him company. It was after three and growing somewhat cooler when they set out in the pinnace for the beach.

A sudden hush spread over bay and shore when it was seen that Lono was coming. The people in canoes and on surfboards covered their faces with their hands; it was blasphemy to look upon a god, but there were few who could restrain themselves from peeking between slightly parted fingers. A crowd had gathered at the beach, but as the pinnace came in closer, the curious onlookers fled to their houses or crouched down behind rocks and trees. By the time the boat's prow slid into the wet gray sand, there were none in sight but four bearded priests holding before them long sticks tipped with dog fur; these were to be Lono's heralds. Captain Cook saw no cause for alarm in the behavior of the Hawaiians; he was used to being an object of awe—even his own sailors often slipped quietly down a hatchway when they saw him coming. Giving orders for the men to stand by the pinnace, he set out for the *heiau* with his two officers and Kuaha, the heralds walking on ahead.

But the Hawaiians could not stay long hidden; they

began to emerge in large groups from their hiding places and creep along after the small procession. If Captain Cook turned his head slightly to look around him, they all fell flat on their faces; the moment he returned his attention to the priest, they would be up again and stealing along after him. Those who were slow to rise were trampled in the sand. Soon tiring of this procedure, a number of the leaders hit on a sort of compromise between their curiosity and the tabus, and began to crawl along after the priests and the three Englishmen. By the time the party had reached the *heiau* nearly a thousand people were crawling silently behind them.

The *heiau* seen from the ships had appeared to be but part of the village. Now it loomed as a massive gray citadel, self-contained, and built in terraces; a fence ran around the outside edge from which tall fleering images glared down, and human skulls; some small thatched huts were visible, various walled enclosures, loggias made of palm-frond, and more images of a different type. The little company was greeted ceremoniously at the entrance by a tall, heavily-bearded young man, high priest of the temple.

Mr. Bayly nudged Lieutenant King and whispered, "I'll wager this lad's the local curate."

After "the Curate" had intoned a chant of welcome, he led the way to the upper section of the *heiau* where stood a high wooden scaffolding, wrapped about with tapa. Below this were twelve god-symbols ranged in a staggered semi-circle—basketwork faces, cleverly inter-woven with scarlet and yellow feathers, with big con-torted mouths and staring mother-of-pearl eyes. The cen-tral forward image was Ke-akua-o-Laka ('The spirit of Laka'—progenitor of the universe). Numerous offerings were piled up before this in an advanced stage of decay—sugar cane, coconuts, breadfruit, plantains, and a hog, all giving forth a strong septic stench.

"Whew," said Mr. Bayly, discreetly holding a hand-kerchief to his nose as though he had taken a pinch of snuff.

Kuaha presented Captain Cook to each of these idols, and then indicated that he was to stand before the central one for an invocation of the Laka spirit. The old man then calmly picked up the putrid hog from the heap and began to chant; when the prayer was over he dropped the hog and led Cook to the scaffolding where he set the example by climbing up the shaky structure with surpris-ing agility. Gravely Captain Cook followed him. The posts creaked and shook beneath his weight; reaching the first of the three levels, he turned to face into the temple and stood, holding on with both hands.

His two officers precariously maintained sober expres-sions while inwardly convulsed at the sight of their humorless and austere captain swaying above them on the scaffolding.

A procession of ten more priests now made its appearance, bearing a large square of red tapa and a small, live pig. "The Curate" relieved them of these things, and, after handing the cloth up to Kuaha, held out the pig and chanted over it; a moment later he dashed it violently to the ground to kill it. The piteous shriek let out by the creature startled Captain Cook so that he very nearly fell off his perch. Then Kuaha draped the tapa about his shoulders and allowed him to descend, which the captain did with more haste than grace.

Now they approached the idols once more and as he passed before each one Kuaha snapped his fingers contemptuously until he came to the symbol of Laka. This he kissed reverently and prostrated himself before it. Captain Cook, although growing exasperated by this mumbo-jumbo, conscientiously followed his mentor's example. He had forgotten, perhaps, that in his own country priests bowed before a holy symbol and kissed it reverently.

The serious business was concluded. Now they could eat. The young temple priest led the way to a lower terrace where a feast was laid out. Before two twelve-foot idols, draped in red tapa, Captain Cook was enthroned; one of his arms was supported by Kuaha, the other by James King (thoroughly mystified, but enjoying himself hugely). The priests quickly set about brewing *awa* by chewing up roots [1] and spitting the juice out in a bowl to be strained through a piece of tapa and then handed round for all to enjoy.

While this process was taking place, "the Curate" masticated some coconut meat and made a pasty oil which, wrapped in a piece of tapa, he used to anoint the shrinking captain's face, head, arms and shoulders. When the *awa* had been passed, all fell to at the heaps of rich, fragrant food set before them. Palea, who was on the other side of King, tore off choice pieces from a tender, roasted hog, and offered them to his friend, feeding him courteously with his fingers. The lieutenant had no strong objection to this for Palea, like most of the Hawaiians, was scrupulously clean. But Captain Cook was not equally fortunate with his Ganymede. It was "the Bishop's" lot to feed Lono, and Captain Cook, by nature exceedingly fastidious, could not rid himself of the memory of the old priest handling the putrid hog a few minutes before. Shuddering inwardly, he politely refused the proffered morsels. Kuaha immediately realized the enormity of his error; this personage would naturally be above menial tasks. He hastened to chew up a piece of the meat and offer it to the captain nicely masticated. Cook turned very pale and pushed the food gently away with the

[1] Piper methysticum.

back of his hand. Seeing his discomfort, the two officers shifted their positions and began to reach into their pockets for trinkets they had brought along as gifts. The priests were regretful that such a delightful party should be brought to this early close, but the pleasure at the gifts they received made up for any disappointment. Cook gave them all a gracious farewell but was more than usually taciturn as the pinnace was rowed back to the *Resolution*.

That night, the first in Kealakekua, was a gala one aboard the two ships. Samwell, the sawbones, summed it up when he wrote in his journal the next day: ". . . as to the choice and number of fine women, there is hardly one among us that may not vie with the Grand Turk himself." Presumably the two captains had no wish to set themselves against this nabob and kept to their cabins.

Monday morning the crews set about the business of getting the equipment on shore. Tents, masts, sails, rigging, water casks, the bread, the flour, the powder—"in short, every article that wanted either to be reviewed or repaired"—was made ready to go. Taking along a guard of marines, Lieutenant King went ashore early to find a suitable camp. Palea met him, and together the two walked about the village. What the Englishman hoped to find was a clearing of some sort which would give the carpenters and sailmakers plenty of room and at the same time allow for the setting up of an astronomical observatory where Mr. Bayly could work; he explained these things as best he could to Palea. The young chief suggested that some of the houses be torn down and space cleared in the heart of the village, but King would not hear of it. The location which appeared most suitable was a large field adjoining the *heiau;* being just off the beach it would be convenient for landing the gear, and was close to the big spring of brackish water. Though surrounded by a stone wall the plot was vacant, being given over to a few patches of sweet potatoes. He had only to ask for it and it was promptly allocated. The friendly "Curate," informed of this, came down from the *heiau* and put up sticks with little bags of black and white tapa dangling from them, signifying that the area was tabu to all villagers. Having done this he asked Lieutenant King to make it tabu for the Englishmen to leave the site after sunset—Kalaniopuu had sent word to the priests to take every measure to prevent the spreading of the "Lono sickness." Unhappily, prevention was not in the natives' power.

During these first few days a busy trade sprang up between the Hawaiian villages and the English ships. By the third day so much pork had been taken aboard that the sailors had already begun to salt it and stow it in large casks in the hold. The fresh fruit and vegetables which would not keep were added to the daily rations of the crews and the beneficial effect was soon noticeable.

A general overhaul of the ships disclosed the fact that the metal eyes which held the *Resolution's* rudder in place were nearly eaten through with rust; the bolts were ready to fall out. Perhaps a week more at sea would have seen her at the mercy of wind and current. Arrangements were made to take off and repair the rudder as soon as possible. On both ships calkers were swung out on platforms to work the seams. These calkers were a source of great interest to the Hawaiians, who would paddle out from the shore and spend hours watching. But one ingenious fellow eventually caused the entertainment to be outlawed. It occurred to him that it would be interesting to see what would happen if he should heave a few rocks at the calkers. He thereupon did so, and was frightened nearly to death by the results. A group of marines from the *Resolution* were sent out after him. Captured, he was taken on deck, suspended by his hands from the shrouds and given fifty lashes with the cat-o'-nine-tails. As the incident took place in full view of all the canoes on the bay, trading slacked off thereafter and was only resumed —with considerable hesitation—after several days.

Once the observatory had been set up on shore, Mr. Bayly went to work making the astronomical studies that were to be used for future charts of "the Sandwich Islands." Captain Cook took an interest in the work, being a scientist at heart; indeed, the purpose of his first voyage to the Pacific had been to observe the transit of Venus over the sun, and his observations, made at Tahiti, had been his stepping stone to fame.

With the work going on at the observatory and squads of sailmakers and carpenters busy there during the day, a permanent camp had been established in the potato patch. But it was not popular at first. The men chafed at the rule which forbade them to go out after sunset; no restraint had been placed on their evening hours aboard ship. The first night they had tried to bribe "the Curate" into relaxing his vigil and closing his eyes to a girl or two, but while friendly and sympathetic the young priest was inflexible. On the following night, therefore, the sailors took matters into their own hands. Stealing out under the cover of darkness, they succeeded in proving to several girls that the tabu could be broken without fatal results. From that time on, this particular tabu fell into disrepute.

The priests lived in an isolated part of the village back of the *heiau*. They had their own palm grove and fish pond, and the sequestered spot was well suited to their calling. On Tuesday afternoon Captain Cook was invited to a ceremony there, performed before one of the priests' sacred houses near the corner of the *heiau*. Offerings were made and the captain was formally invested with the title of Lono. It must have been clear to him now that he was an object of veneration among the Hawaiians;—even the sailors recognized this, calling the place of his investure "Cook's Altar." The captain, however, would not take warmly to this folderol. He was quite dispassionate in his observations and cared not whether the Hawaiians considered him a god but only how tractable they were to his requirements. Discovering that a few enterprising ones had found a treasure-trove in the sheathings of the ships and were trying to remove them, Captain Cook had two or three muskets loaded with small shot fired into their midst. This barrage startled and offended the Hawaiians who had no idea of doing wrong. Seeing that they were not particularly frightened, Cook experimented further by having several cannon fired over the large concourse of canoes which was gathered about the *Resolution*. In a moment the canoes were empty and hundreds of heads bobbed in the water with frightened eyes turned toward the ship; no canoes ventured near for the rest of the day.

Cases of outright theft were very few. On one occasion Palea observed a man snatch up a belaying pin from the deck of the *Discovery*. The young chief was after him in an instant and both men plunged over the side. Deep down in the translucent blue depths a commotion became visible. A circle of canoes formed around the spot. After nearly

two minutes Palea emerged, but of the thief there was no
sign. Dr. Law was of the opinion that Palea had given his
victim "a deadly squeeze" under water.

On Sunday, January 24th, the men on the ships awoke
to an odd sensation: there was no sound of any sort on
the bay. Kanaina and another chief, a stranger, came
aboard while it was still dark and drove out the girls.
They explained that the bay was under tabu for the immi-
nent return of the king: Palea had already gone to meet
him. This made Captain Cook exceedingly angry. Was
his supply of provisions to be cut off merely because the
king was coming? A lieutenant was sent ashore in the
Resolution's jolly boat to see if something could not be
done. It couldn't. He brought back word that the village
people were all confined to their houses and trade was
at a standstill. The Hawaiians might respect their god, but
they also respected their king—who, after all, was more
familiar to them. Captain Cook's lips were depressed in
a thin line of anger, but there was nothing he could do
and so he took the occasion to discipline his men. Two
sailors were given twelve lashes apiece for absenting themselves from the boats while on shore; a third was given
twelve for the same offense plus twelve more "for having
connections with the women knowing himself to have the
venereal disorder on him." Thus did Captain Cook ap-
pease both his wrath and his conscience.

Shortly before noon the king arrived. He came in a war canoe, followed by a fleet of some hundred and fifty others. But he took no notice of the British ships; instead he headed straight for the beach. From the royal canoe warriors took down the four wooden images, dressed in feather cloaks, which had been set in each corner; the whole company, carrying their weapons, then marched to the *heiau*. After some minutes Kalaniopuu emerged and now seemed ready to turn his attention to his guests. With his favorite wife, Kanekapolei, and his two young sons, he was paddled out to the *Resolution*. Coming aboard he greeted Cook warmly and presented him with three freshly roasted pigs; the visit was merely an informal gesture to renew their friendship. Ceremonies would be held on the morrow. Captain Cook, however, rose to the occasion and gave the royal family gifts of bead necklaces, two looking glasses, a large glass bowl, some nails and other trifles. To the king himself he gave a nightshirt of flowered linen which tickled the old monarch inordinately. He quickly put it on, and with his ponderous rolling gait marched up and down before the company, chuckling with delight. Captain Cook urged the royal family to partake of some food with him, but Kalaniopuu could not be persuaded to eat anything but cooked breadfruit which he had brought along. After about an hour the royalty took their leave well pleased with their reception and leaving among the Englishmen an agreeable impression of their friendliness and intuitive good manners.

Monday morning was quiet enough. The tabu continued to be enforced. It was not until midday that the king made his appearance. He was paddled out in one of the big canoes and accompanied by the foremost chiefs .of the kingdom, all wearing capes and helmets. Behind came another canoe bearing Kuaha, the priests, and a group of chiefesses. Behind this canoe came yet a third, its central platform heaped with innumerable foodstuffs —hogs, fruits, vegetables. While the priests chanted and beat upon their sharkskin drums the three canoes were paddled in a circle about the English ships; then, abruptly, they turned toward the shore. Captain Cook, who had been standing at the rail watching the maneuvers, rightly interpreted this as an invitation for him to follow. The canoes had hardly pushed their prows into the soft sand before Cook, in his big cutter with Lieutenant King and a guard of marines, came riding in on a long, low wave and stepped out on the sand to greet the king. The old man was very solemn on this hot morning and gravely acknowledged Captain Cook's salute. They walked together toward the enclosure where the carpenters and sailmakers were at work; seeing Captain Cook with the king, these men promptly withdrew to a respectful distance and watched while the procession filed in and was seated around in a circle. When all were silent, Kalaniopuu stood up and, taking off his splendid cape, approached Captain Cook and put it around his shoulders; then, removing a helmet from the head of one of the chiefs, he put it on Cook's head, at the same time pressing into his hand a beautifully woven fan.

Other chiefs now came forward and laid before the captain six more capes, superb in color and pattern, each representing, in all probability, at least a hundred years in the collecting and weaving into pattern of its delicate, tiny feathers. While Cook was acknowledging these gifts, attendants entered the circle bearing four fat hogs, stalks of sugar cane, bunches of coconuts and breadfruit, which were heaped up before the guest. Then, as the highest compliment of all, the king formally exchanged names with this man whom he called "Lono" (however, the exchange was not one of popular usage as it was in the case of Palea and Lieutenant King—Palea was frequently referred to as "Tini," the Hawaiian pronunciation of "king"). At the conclusion of these courtesies, Kalaniopuu's high priest Holoae chanted a blessing, entering at the head of a procession of priests and bearing the usual scarlet tapa and small pig.

It was now Captain Cook's turn to be the host, and he invited the king and as many of his courtiers as the cutter could hold to go aboard the *Resolution* for dinner. Once on board ship he emulated the Hawaiian ceremonial by presenting Kalaniopuu with his own hangar and a completely fitted tool chest; this was hardly in the spirit of the Polynesian who always feels that he must give better than he receives, but the king seemed pleased.

While the Hawaiians were on board an incident developed between Kamehameha and Palea. The warrior-chief refused to allow Palea to enter the great cabin with the other chiefs and behaved in a surly manner toward him. A group of midshipmen were preparing to go ashore at this moment and Palea begged them to take him along; he was trembling and obviously very frightened, explaining that Kamehameha might very likely have him killed. But the small boat had scarcely pulled away from the ship's side when Kalaniopuu came out on deck and called out "Tini!" The midshipmen, at Palea's request, returned and the young chief, still trembling, went aboard to speak with the king. They had exchanged but a few words when the old man began to laugh heartily and Palea's frightened look vanished. The middies were intrigued by this incident, and, as boys will, discussed it for days thereafter, building up Kamehameha—who certainly looked the part—into a sort of ogre.

Anxious to learn as much as possible about the formation of the island and the character of its inhabitants, Captain Cook sent out an expedition to explore. The party was composed of Mr. Nelson, the botanist; young George Vancouver, a midshipman from the *Discovery*; and Jack Ledyard, a corporal of marines. Although eager to ascend to the summit of Mauna Loa, they discovered the volcano to be far larger and far higher (13,680 feet) than they had believed possible and quite beyond their abilities to climb in a short time; they had to be contented therefore with exploring the great Kona slope and having a few glimpses into the mountain forests.

The Hawaiians continued to be hospitable and friendly with their guests, though by the end of January the cost of living on such a lavish scale began to be felt in the rural areas. Cargo after cargo of the best foodstuffs the island provided seemed to be swallowed up by the fabulous ships. At first there had been enough excitement to repay the farmers for the increased tribute demanded by their overlords; canoes had come from all parts of Kona filled with people eager for a sight of Lono and his wonderful canoes. But now the novelty was wearing off. Many of the Hawaiian men, too, resented the treatment of their women—and their women's preference for the diseased white sailors. Added to these economic and social troubles was the growing undercurrent of opinion that this "Kapena Kuke" was not Lono at all, but merely some king from a foreign land who had come to Hawaii because of

a food shortage in his own country. Certainly the Englishmen had been gaunt and pale when they arrived; now
they were fat and sleek—the Hawaiians would pat the
Englishmen's stomachs and laugh, saying that now the
gods were fattened up might it not be better if they went
home and returned to Hawaii next breadfruit season?

Captain Cook had no wish to outstay his welcome. The
men were growing soft and he knew it was time to resume
the voyage. When the *Resolution's* rudder had been hung
again and the sails and rigging and other gear began to
go aboard, Kalaniopuu realized that his guests would soon
be leaving and felt genuine regret at losing them. Certainly his lifetime had known no more fascinating days
than those spent in this company.

On Sunday afternoon, January 31st, Captain Cook sent
Lieutenant King ashore to treat with the priests for the
purchase of some wood; both ships needed fuel. The wood
Captain Cook had in mind was the fencing of the *heiau*
and a few of its idols, and he had instructed King to offer
two hatchets in payment. The young officer had been on
good terms with the priests and knew the enormity of this
request, but he had no choice in the matter and presented
himself to the friendly "Curate." The priest explained
that both fence and idols were held deeply sacred and
were not subject to barter; but, of course, the *heiau* was
dedicated to Lono and if the god himself chose . . . !

The lieutenant, ordering his group of marines to collect the wood, held out the two hatchets to the priest. The grave, bearded young Hawaiian declined them, but King thrust them into his hands and retired quickly to the cutter.

The following morning, William Watman, a gunner on the *Resolution*, was found dead in his hammock. He was an old man and had long been ailing. Captain Cook had no reason to conceal his death from the Hawaiians, and, on being informed of it, Kalaniopuu asked that he be buried in the *heiau*. There was some murmuring among the chiefs. This seemed to confirm the rumor. If one of the company of gods was mortal, how many more might be? Even . . . ?

The temple priests assembled for the burial ceremony on Tuesday morning. They had made a hole in one of the stone terraces about four feet deep, covering the bottom with green leaves. When the body of the old seaman had been laid to rest, one of the king's henchmen came forward and put a roasted pig at the head and another at the feet, together with a quantity of breadfruit and plantains. More foodstuffs were about to be added when Captain Cook abruptly ordered the grave to be covered. Although the commander had read the Christian burial service over the grave—listened to with great interest by the priests—instead of a headstone William Watman had a wooden idol to watch over his spirit; the Englishmen affixed to the base of this idol a sign reading:

"GEORGIUS TERTIUS REX, 1779
Hic jacet Gulielmus Waterman" (sic)

It was held in place by wooden pegs, lest the natives, coveting nails, take it down. The crowd departed, but the priests stayed on, and for several days thereafter conducted their own ceremonies over the grave.

On Wednesday morning on the king's invitation, Captain Cook went ashore to witness a festival being held in the grove of the priests. On his arrival he found the ground littered with bundles of tapa, packets of feathers, and a variety of the trinkets which the Englishmen had given in trade. Likewise, a prodigal display of foodstuffs of every description. Captain Cook at first imagined these things to be intended as a farewell gift to himself, but Kalaniopuu disillusioned him by explaining that this was part of the annual *hookupu* (giving of gifts) to the king from the people of the province. However, he had not invited his guest ashore merely to view his wealth. With a gesture of the hand he indicated a huge pile of tapa, packets of feathers, and all of the hogs and vegetables; these were to be his farewell gift to Captain Cook. Although accustomed to Kalaniopuu's generosity, the Englishman was genuinely impressed by the magnitude of this gift. Rejecting the feathers, he accepted all the rest and quietly expressed his gratitude.

As it was known that the ships were to sail the following morning an exhibition of boxing was held that afternoon followed by hulas, and in the evening the royal family was invited on board the *Resolution*. Captain Cook's first contribution to the festive spirit of the evening was a band concert during dinner. It was a sensation. This was the first time that any music other than chanting and the undisciplined warbling of the nose flute had been heard by Hawaiians and the whole company was enthralled, many of them forgetting to eat. Captain Cook observing their enthusiasm ordered the band to play without pause. It was only by a promise of something even more dazzling that the guests could be persuaded to leave this place of enchantment and go out on deck. When the company was seated, a sudden whirr and explosion came from amidship and a brilliant rocket soared up, arching against the cliff and breaking into a shower of tiny jewels. At the first sight of it the king was out of his chair and down the hatch, accompanied by several others of his party. The laughter and assurances of the English officers recalled him and he was persuaded to sit down once more, laughing himself—albeit somewhat nervously. The succeeding fireworks were enthusiastically received.

It was now the 4th of February, 1779, and Captain

Cook's little squadron was leaving Kealakekua Bay after a visit which had been satisfactory to the explorer in every way. His ships were laden down with foodstuffs, fresh and salted pork, breadfruit, bananas, taro, plantains and coconuts enough to keep his men healthy for many months;—but more than that, his observations had been careful and detailed and he had a new and valuable group of islands to bring home to England as a prize. He had not demanded their cession to the empire, nor had he set up the flag on Hawaii's soil; he was more subtle than that. He had secured the friendship of the king and the Hawaiian people; it would be the task of those coming later to convert this friendship to their own uses. And so, with this feather in his hat, he was prepared to sail north once more and finish the survey which had been the main purpose of his trip.

There were many on board both ships who looked back on the gracious scene of serene blue water and palm-lined shore with regret. These men brought up in the cold and squalor of the back streets of London or Portsmouth or other English towns had never known such generous friendliness and such simple freedom of living; they had never been treated as individuals before—or admired for their homely looks. These few weeks at Kealakekua were something out of a dream. During the party on the night before one of the chiefs had drawn Lieutenant King aside and urged him to stay on in Hawaii; if he should find it difficult breaking away from Captain Cook (who the Hawaiians thought was King's father) they promised to take him to a secret hiding place in the hills and conceal him there until the ships sailed. The young officer had been touched, and was even more so when he saw the obvious disappointment among the Hawaiians when he turned down their offer. As he stood on the afterdeck gazing with kindly eyes on the throng of canoes that followed after to escort the ships out of the bay, he wondered if he would ever again meet such kind-hearted and lovable people.

The winds were desultory and by noon of the following day the ships had only moved as far as Holua-loa, a dozen miles from Kealakekua. It was to this place Kalaniopuu had retired after laying a tabu over the bay, and on seeing the ships close to shore he came out once more for another farewell, bringing with him coconuts, taro, hogs and some fine fresh fish. In return he asked a favor. With him in his canoe were an old priest and several girls who were anxious to go to Maui. Captain Cook consented to take them aboard. The priest, however, was not so anxious to reach Maui that an opportunity for gain would leave him indifferent; during the night he stole a large piece of Russian silk from the captain's cabin and dropping silently overboard swam ashore with it. He saw no

necessity of concealing the theft from his fellow countrymen, and the king, hearing of it, promptly took him into
custody and returned him to the *Resolution*. Captain Cook
was surprised to see Kalaniopuu again. On discovering the
cause for this visit he elected to be generous, asking that
the priest be forgiven and his bonds removed; as for the
silk—that he gave to the king for being so honest with
him.

Later that night flashes of lightning were seen on the
horizon and before long a sharp gale bore down on the
ships, deluging them in heavy sheets of rain. It was a typical *kona* (southerly) storm and, increasing in its fury,
drove both ships before it far out into the channel to the
lee of Maui. All the following day it continued and the
ships were separated. On Monday night the *Resolution*
sprung the head of its foremast; almost at the same time a
leak was discovered in one of the holds through which
water was pouring at the rate of ten inches an hour, neces-
sitating night-long shifts at bailing and pumping. The gale
had abated somewhat the following day and both ships
made their way to the wide, unsheltered bay of Kawaihae
at the foot of the great central tableland of Hawaii. But
as the day progressed the wind began to box the compass
and no further progress could be made. Not until late that
night was the *Discovery* close enough to be hailed from
the flagship and hear the tale of its disasters. Captain Cook

mistrusted the anchorage at Kawaihae and saw nothing for it but to return to Kealakekua. Although the main force of the gale was abated, the weather was still dirty and the sea was running a short, heavy swell. One big wave broke full over the *Discovery* and washing through the great cabin nearly carried everything away with it.

But by Friday the last vestiges of the storm had disappeared and in a sparkling dawn the ships re-entered Kealakekua Bay. The summit of Mauna Loa was capped with freshly fallen snow.

This time there was no tumultuous reception. Indeed, the bay seemed deserted. At Holualoa the king's council had observed the ships and guessed at their destination; a meeting had been held to determine the attitude which they should adopt in this unwelcome circumstance. Most of the people had had enough of Captain Cook for the time being. The produce of Kona was nearly exhausted. Many chiefs spoke out with the opinion that Captain Cook should be denied any further assistance. But there was a strong faction—among them, Kamehameha—who felt that their tradition of hospitality required them to resume their earlier offices and receive the strangers courteously whenever, and as often as, they should return. In the end this faction prevailed and the court readjourned to the village of Ka-awa-loa ('The long bay') which lay across the water from the English camp and the *heiau*.

Anxious to effect the necessary repairs as quickly as possible, Captain Cook ordered his men to take over the *heiau*. The broad stone terraces were much easier to work upon than the uneven ground of the potato patch, and the small houses would serve as sail lofts and as a hospital for the sailors who had been injured during the storm. The priests showed no surprise and once more took over the responsibility of maintaining the "Lono" tabu by setting up tabu sticks around the *heiau* and offering themselves as heralds whenever the captain came ashore.

During the morning carpenters from both ships worked at getting the *Resolution's* damaged mast ashore. Lieutenant King with a guard of eight marines supervised the landing party. A few canoes came off to trade, but the attitude of the majority of the natives seemed somewhat hostile. They demanded much higher payment for their goods and showed a propensity for thieving.

On Saturday the king arrived and was received cordially by Captain Cook. His arrival somewhat alleviated the awkward situation and trading recommenced more briskly. But all was far from well.

The next morning one of the natives making free on the deck of the *Discovery* suddenly seized up the armorer's tongs; but before he could make his escape he was captured and given a severe flogging. Seeking revenge for this treatment he stole aboard again in the afternoon and awaiting his chance managed to seize both tongs and a chisel and, diving overboard, was picked up by a passing canoe. Tom Edgar, the master, taking two midshipmen with him, set out after the thief in the small cutter.

Palea had also observed the incident. Hastily paddling ashore in his canoe he intercepted the thief and recovered the articles—as well as the top of a water cask which had not been missed—and when Edgar arrived presented them to him apologizing for his less honest countryman. The officer, somewhat mollified, was about to return when he saw the pinnace of the *Resolution* coming to assist and rather than have the men from the other ship see how easily he was passing off the affair, he decided to take the thief's canoe as a punishment. Having no way of recognizing this particular canoe among the many drawn up on the shore, he picked out one that showed signs of having been in the water recently and was about to take it along when Palea interposed. It was his canoe. Edgar was not very familiar with the language and the pinnace was close now; he could not afford to have this young Hawaiian argue him out of what he conceived to be his duty. Paying no attention to Palea, he ordered the midshipman to launch the canoe and tie it to the stern of the cutter. Palea flared up at this and seized the officer's arm, twisting it up behind his back, and at the same time catching hold of the Englishman's queue with his other hand. One of the middies, a plucky youngster, rushed to his aid and beat Palea over the head with an oar. Letting go of Edgar, the Hawaiian snatched the oar from the boy and snapped it over his knee.

By this time a crowd of natives had gathered and when Palea broke the oar they let out a roar of mingled rage and delight. Picking up some loose stones they began to fling these at the boats' crews, and closing in, seized the *Discovery's* boat while the midshipmen fled into the water. Palea's act having caught their imagination, the Hawaiians then broke all the oars over their knees and were turning to the boat itself to break it up when the young chief interposed. After his first surge of temper he had calmed down and was distressed at the turn things had taken. The assisting pinnace had been upset in the commotion and three or four of the men in it, unable to swim, had taken cringing refuge on top of a rock a short distance from the shore; these offered such a tempting target for stones that Palea had a hard time dissuading his friends from their sport. Finally, however, he drove them back and coming down alone to the water's edge made signs to Edgar that he might return and receive his boat with impunity. Thinking to take some sort of vengeance for the indignities he had suffered, the officer asked Palea to come with him to the ship as a sign of good faith, but the chief was not to be tricked and, refusing courteously, walked off through the crowd.

Edgar was seething with rage. Damning the Hawaiians and his bedraggled midshipmen indiscriminately, he made for the shore, and instead of rescuing the cutter, left a few of the boys to guard it while he himself set off on foot with one of the middies to seek help from the group at the *heiau*. As soon as he had disappeared, the crowd grew bolder again and closing in drove the boys into the water and were just about to have another go at breaking up the cutter when Palea returned, Mr. Edgar and his midshipman walking sheepishly before him. This time the Englishman decided that he had had enough and was willing to make his escape but, he pointed out, there were no oars. Palea picked up a few that were not too badly broken and silently handed them to him. Edgar did not protest and made off as best he could.

He had not gone far, however, when Palea in his canoe caught up. He had brought one of the midshipmen's hats which had been knocked off in the scuffle. This he presented courteously and with a return to his usual deferent manner said that he hoped Captain Cook would not hold this incident against him. Edgar, who, by now, had also recovered his wits, replied that Palea had no need to worry and that on the whole he had conducted himself honestly and well.

But when tne captain was informed of all this he frowned and remarked grimly, "I am afraid these people will oblige me to use some violent measures. They must not be left to imagine they have gained any advantage over us." He was familiar with the art of face-saving.

The mood was definitely changing. Those chiefs who had disagreed with Kalaniopuu and Kamehameha concerning the new attitude toward Cook had not accepted their defeat in council; nor had many of the common people been pleased by the return. On this Sunday afternoon, a few daring ones had begun to roll stones down from the cliff on the sailors who were drawing water below, and in the evening a group of chiefs had appeared and driven off the natives hired to roll the water-casks to the shore. Only the appearance of Lieutenant King prevented trouble. King's firmness, added to his popularity with the majority of the Hawaiians, prevailed on the chiefs to throw away their stones and allow the work to proceed unmolested.

During the night some warriors paddled out and, without being overheard by the sailor on watch, managed to cut loose the *Discovery's* six-oared cutter from an anchor buoy and make off with it. The loss was not discovered until dawn. Captain Clerke immediately went over to the *Resolution* to discuss the matter with Captain Cook. They agreed that this was a theft which could not be overlooked. Cook's method of dealing with affairs of this nature was not an original one, but one which had proved effective elsewhere on his voyages. He proposed that Captain Clerke should go ashore and persuade the king to come aboard ship where he would be held hostage until the cutter was brought back.

Clerke had been suffering much from his tuberculosis and said that he did not feel up to such an expedition. Thereupon Captain Cook said he would go himself, and set about loading his double-barreled gun. The launch and small cutter of each ship were ordered out under the command of two lieutenants, each to patrol one side of the entrance to the harbor and prevent any canoe from entering or leaving; they had orders to fire if necessary.

The captain went ashore in the pinnace, accompanied by Lieutenant Molesworth Phillips of the marines, Sergeant Gibson, Corporals Ledyard and Thomas and six privates. He was followed by the launch under the command of Lieutenant Williamson, and a four-oared cutter under the master's mate, Henry Roberts. There were altogether about thirty-eight men, each with a musket, a cutlass, and a cartridge box.

The arid, rocky promontory on which the village of Kaawaloa lay was a torrid blaze of sunshine when, about a quarter past eight, Captain Cook arrived with his formidable party. Only the marines went ashore with him. Lieutenant Williamson was ordered to lie off at a little distance with both the other boats and wait for him. The Hawaiians at the landing place showed their usual courtesy and respect. Cook asked to see his two young friends, the king's sons, and when they came forth eagerly to greet him, he inquired where their father was. They offered to lead the way. Drawing up the marines along the shore and leaving them in charge of Sergeant Gibson, the captain accompanied by Lieutenant Phillips followed the two boys.

The king's house was about a hundred yards from the shore, and on arriving there, Cook ordered Phillips to go in and bring the king to him. Kalaniopuu had just waked up, his white hair was tousled and he sat perfectly naked on his pile of mats blinking his red eyes and smiling at his visitor. Informed that Captain Cook was outside, he hastily donned a *malo* and taking Phillip's hand walked out with him. Captain Cook, going straight to the point, told the king of the theft of the cutter. The tall, old Hawaiian listened with obvious concern, and Cook was convinced that he had had no previous knowledge of the incident. Therefore, changing his tone, the captain invited Kalaniopuu and the two young princes to come aboard the *Resolution* and spend the day. The youngest boy, hardly waiting for his father's answer, gave a whoop of joy and running down to the shore, swam to the launch where he was hoisted aboard by one of the friendly midshipmen.

The king had given his hand to Cook who held it in friendly fashion while he talked, urging him to come along with him. Now, they walked slowly down toward the shore. But suddenly the queen, Kanekapolei—mother of the two princes and Kalaniopuu's favorite wife—came running heavily down the path. She had heard of what was happening and was unaccountably frightened. Tears were coursing down her big cheeks and she took the king pleadingly by the arm. Being weak and unsteady on his feet, this unexpected gesture caused Kalaniopuu to lose his balance and sit down awkwardly on the ground. His mind jarred out of drowsiness, he looked up at his wife's tear-stained face and then at the great crowd of chiefs which had suddenly closed in around him. Their expressions brought a sudden fear upon him.

At this moment Lieutenant Phillips approached Captain Cook and said, "Shall I draw up the marines close to the water's edge in order to secure a retreat? I see plainly by the Indians' actions that it will become necessary." The captain was not particularly alarmed, but he allowed Phillips to go ahead, and the marines were ranged along the white, pebbly shallows. Cook's situation was now somewhat awkward; it seemed useless to urge the old king to come with him in the face of the crowd's hostility, but for the moment the usually resourceful captain could think of nothing else to do and continued to talk to Kalaniopuu. It was hard to give his invitation the proper note of casual friendliness; but the king, at least, was taken in. He was genuinely fond of Captain Cook and he finally rose to his feet to go along. At this point, several of the chiefs, guessing his intentions, came up behind him and seized his arms, and Kanekapolei began to wail aloud. Cook saw that the situation was hopelessly out of hand and turned to Lieutenant Phillips to tell him so.

Meanwhile, at the harbor mouth a canoe had run the blockade. In it were two men: a son-in-law of "the Archbishop" and one of Palea's brothers. The boats had opened fire and Palea's brother was killed, but the other chief escaped. He arrived at Kaawaloa just as Cook was turning away and told the crowd what had happened. Cook was walking toward the marines when he observed that all the women and children who had been in the crowd had suddenly disappeared; he saw, too, that many of the chiefs had begun to put on rude *lauhala* guards over their chests.

A man stepped forth from the crowd, and Captain Cook recognized him as Palea's oldest brother; this man held a rock in one hand and in the other a long steel spike, such as those the ships' blacksmiths had been striking off to barter with the Hawaiians. "You have killed my brother. I shall be revenged," the Hawaiian shouted at Cook and at the same time he hurled the rock with all his force. The captain ducked. Holding in his temper, he quietly told the man to desist. But the chief advanced closer, contorting his face into a ferocious scowl and brandishing the dagger.

Coolly, then, Cook aimed his gun and fired a barrel of bird shot at the warrior's mat-shield; the shot failed to penetrate the thick *lauhala*, but the explosion set off the temper of the mob and with yells of fury they began to hurl their stones. A Hawaiian warrior rushing at Lieutenant Phillips attempted to stab him, but the marine knocked him down with the butt of his rifle. The man who had first provoked the attack continued to advance toward Captain Cook, and the captain fired at him once more—this time with ball. The shot went wild and entered the groin of another chief near by.

Now the battle became general. The marines fired a volley into the crowd expecting to drive them back, but the action only served to incite them more and they surged forward before the marines had a chance to reload. Four of the Englishmen were cut off from the rest and immediately slain; the others were forced into the water. The lieutenant, stabbed through the shoulder, managed to shoot one of his assailants in the belly before the attack could be repeated.

Captain Cook meanwhile had gone to the water's edge and shouted to the boats to pull in. Mr. Roberts quickly brought the pinnace in as close as possible to the shore, but Lieutenant Williamson unaccountably withdrew further off; the men in his boat raged at this and were for pulling in and getting into the fight, but Williamson reminded them that his orders had been to lay on the oars offshore and he said grimly that he would shoot the first man who disobeyed him. This left the rescue of the marines entirely to the men in the pinnace, and prevented them from using their muskets effectively.

Captain Cook was now the only Englishman left on the shore. Holding one hand at the back of his head to ward off stones, and with his musket under his other arm, he turned his back on the crowd and walked hastily out into the shallow water toward the pinnace. One of the Hawaiians braver than the rest followed him and struck him with a club. Cook staggered and fell on one hand and one knee, dropping his gun. As he tried to get to his feet, another native stabbed him in the back with an oiled wooden dagger. He fell forward in the shallows. Notwithstanding the fact that a number of Hawaiians quickly leaped upon him, he managed once to get his head up and throw a look of anguish toward the men in the pinnace before the life flowed from him. Seizing his feet the

Hawaiians dragged him up on shore where they stabbed him repeatedly with their daggers.

The men in the pinnace were wholly unable to come to his aid in these crucial moments; everything had happened too quickly. Three of the marines had struggled out to the boat and were clambering into it amid a hail of stones and spears; it was neither possible to get the pinnace farther inshore because of the shallows and the rocks nor for the men in the boat to get to Cook's assistance.

Phillips was the last to reach the pinnace, and scarcely had he been pulled in when he observed one of the marines, an old man named Jackson, who had received a spear in the eye, floundering in the deeper water, bleeding horribly. Phillips dove after him without a moment's hesitation and, despite his own wound, managed to pull the old man to the boat.

The men in the launch kept up a brisk fire, as did the men in the cutter, Lieutenant Williamson having given the order, and the Hawaiians soon dispersed, but although they left many of their own warriors lying dead, they took with them Cook's body. Some of them were seen running up the slope back of Kaawaloa, and Lieutenant Gore who had observed something of the fray through his telescope, caused the great guns of the *Resolution* to be brought to bear and fired into the village for several minutes.

When the boats returned to the *Resolution* and *Discovery* with the news of Cook's death a deep silence reigned over both ships. The men were given a ration of grog and those who were unwounded ordered to the observatory to reinforce Lieutenant King who, with a small party, had been stationed there to guard the vital materials at the *heiau*.

King had seen the commotion across the bay, heard the firing and could only guess at what had happened. The Hawaiians with him were perturbed, and as easily as he could, King assured them that whatever had happened he was anxious to remain on peaceable terms. His assurances had the desired effect temporarily. But as he stood on the soft gray sand of the beach, watching the pinnace make its way to the *Resolution* and, in a few minutes, pass and repass between the two British vessels, he knew in his heart that the climax had come. It seemed unbelievable, standing there in the warm friendly sun on such a languid, peaceful day, that the passions of either side could be so aroused as to create any real hostility.

Captain Clerke, on the *Discovery*, had been on deck with a spyglass to his eye and after watching the rout of the natives and the return of the boats, he had now turned the glass to the other shore, and seeing King surrounded by a number of natives, assumed that the next attack would be made there. Immediately he had two of the ship's four-pounders trained at the beach and fired. They had been skillfully aimed—one ball severed a coconut palm beneath which many of the natives had been sitting and the other shattered a rock directly behind the main crowd. It was convincing proof of the quality of the ships' weapons. Lieutenant King, however, wished that this proof had not come. He had only just succeeded in pacifying the Hawaiians, and now they were all far more alarmed than they had been previously. He dispatched a boat to Captain Clerke to tell him that all was well and that he would make a signal if any aid were needed. Repeatedly reassuring the crowd, he awaited the return of the boat. Finally it came, in charge of Mr. Bligh (afterward Captain Bligh of the *Bounty*) who brought word of Cook's death and orders from Captain Clerke to strike the tents and send all equipment immediately on board.

King had scarcely received this news when the Hawaiians heard the story on their side. A friendly chief approached King and asked him if the news were true: his face showed honest and profound sorrow. In the precariousness of the situation, King feared that even these proven friends of his might catch something of the passion of the moment; therefore, he affected to disbelieve the report. As naturally as he could, he ranged his marines at the top of the *heiau*, putting them in charge of Mr.

Bligh, and then set out himself to consult with Clerke about their new strategy.

Once King had departed the Hawaiians began to heave stones at the sailors who were attempting to fill water casks. Mr. Bligh was not troubled by any doubts as to what to do in such a situation; he promptly ordered the marines to open fire. Hearing the firing, King ordered his boat to be turned back and found the natives putting on their mat-shields and arming themselves with obvious intent. Looking along the cliff, he could see several groups of Hawaiian warriors making their way hastily over the precarious trail that led from Kaawaloa. The seeds of violence had been sown and were germinating quickly.

King's return had no marked effect among the Hawaiians on the shore. A few, from entrenched positions behind their stone walls, began to throw more stones; on the far side, a group of warriors who had crept up behind sheltering rocks, suddenly stood forth at the foot of the *heiau* with the intention of storming it. Mr. Bligh's marines fired once more, but it took several volleys before all the warriors had been dislodged. Fortunately, Captain Clerke had taken the first volley as a signal and had sent a reinforcement of marines to the shore which arrived just at this time, and the Hawaiians were forced to retire to more sheltered positions.

The priests, who had come down from their retreat,

were the calmest of any on this troubled field, and Lieutenant King begged them to approach the embattled warriors and attempt appeasement. In this mission they were successful. The repeated volleys from the marines had taken a heavy toll, and the deadly effect of the Englishmen's weapons had surprised them; the warriors were ready enough to make a truce. The sailors and marines, thereupon, working with all possible haste, managed to get the sails and other apparatus into the boats.

King now felt that he could safely return to the ship. As soon as he was aboard the *Discovery*, he went with Clerke to his cabin and heard the whole melancholy tale. King being better acquainted with the Hawaiians, it was decided that he should go ashore and demand the return of Cook's body immediately. Taking with him a few midshipmen, he ordered a boatload of marines to follow, but as the boats drew close to shore he saw that the Hawaiians appeared very uneasy and that the men were taking up their arms; therefore, with an unspoken prayer to Lady Luck, he ordered the marines to lie on their oars while he proceeded on alone with the midshipmen. Standing up in the prow of the boat, he showed himself to be unarmed, and as further assurance, held up his white pocket handkerchief.

The moment the Hawaiians perceived this gesture, they set up a shout of joy, and presently the women and children began returning from the cliffside where they had taken refuge; as though indicative of their own non-belligerency, all of them sat down on the rocky shore and extended their arms in a gesture of friendliness and good faith.

They had found themselves entering in a state of war with a force whose methods and weapons were far beyond their imagination; the discovery had raised a panic of uncertainty among them in which their only decision was to defend themselves and their homes as fiercely as they knew how. Beneath this attitude their feelings for the Englishmen remained unchanged; they were distressed at the uncontrolled events which had led to the violation of the friendship which they had had with these beings from another world. At this moment, then, their cry of joy when they guessed at Lieutenant King's mission, was a cry full from the heart. Still, King hesitated to land. Could he really trust them? He had thought them simple and affectionate and had trusted them before, but had they not committed a deed whose savageness would send a wave of horror round the world? Seeing this eleventh-hour hesitation, the old priest Kuaha guessed its cause and himself made a gesture: diving into the sea, he swam toward the small boat holding up a piece of white tapa. Mr. Vancouver helped him aboard. The old man's manner was conciliating, but far from humble; and there was a glint in his murky eyes that might have been taken for a sly feeling of triumph. Lieutenant King informed him that the body of Captain Cook was to be returned immediately, or the two ships would open fire on the villages with all the deadliness they possessed. Kuaha agreed readily to these terms, and with assurances of lasting friendliness and good faith, swam in to the shore once more.

While waiting his return, King was persuaded by the obvious cordiality of the crowd to draw in closer. A group of young chiefs who had been his friends entered into a conversation with him. From them he learned that eight or ten chiefs and about twenty common people had been killed and others badly wounded. As for the body of Captain Cook, the young men informed him that it had been taken up-country and there cut up and divided among the great chiefs; it seemed incredible that Kuaha could hope to gather together all these bits of bone and flesh. Lieutenant King agreed that it seemed unlikely and, after a few more minutes when Kuaha had not reappeared, he reluctantly returned to the ship.

The command of the expedition had now evolved upon Captain Charles Clerke who removed to the *Resolution*, promoting Lieutenant Gore to the command of the *Discovery*. This made King first lieutenant on the *Resolution*, and the logical man with whom Clerke would consult. They dined together and spent the evening in gloomy conversation.

About eight o'clock, they were aroused by the sound of a gunshot from the deck. Hurrying out, they heard a voice in the darkness call in guarded tones, "Tini!"—the Hawaiian's name for Lieutenant King. Captain Clerke ordered the sentry to cease firing and allow the native to come aboard. There were two of them, "the Curate" and another priest. They had paddled out secretly to bring something which had belonged to Captain Cook. The sentry's aim had been good; one of the priests had been wounded in the shoulder. "The Curate," who had been a self-appointed bodyguard to Cook whenever the captain went ashore, now wept honest tears as he lamented, in the curious stylized wail of mourning, the loss of his great friend "Lono"; although the speech was rhetorical, it was none the less moving for its obvious sincerity. When he had ceased this lamentation, he presented King with a small bundle wrapped in tapa. While Captain Clerke looked on with apprehensive eyes, the lieutenant undid the wrappings.

Within was a section of human flesh.

The officers stared at it in dreadful silence. They scarcely heard as the priest went on to explain that except for the head and bones which had been divided up among the high chiefs, the rest of the body had been burned.

This unhappy piece of flesh had been allotted to Kuaha for ceremonial purposes and the old priest had sent it to the Englishmen as a sign of good faith.

In a moment, both King and Clerke were possessed of the same hideous thought. King turned to the Hawaiian.

"Are you perfectly sure that the rest of the body has not been . . . eaten?"

The man's dark eyes widened with horror. He looked first at Clerke and then at King. "Is that the custom among white people?" he asked.

The question was so innocent. Both officers felt the weight lifted from their hearts. King smiled and shook his head ironically.

When Dr. Samwell took the wounded priest into the surgery to dress his shoulder, the man asked him when Lono would come again, and what would he do to the Hawaiians for this blasphemy? Many of the people on shore expected him to return in two or three months. In the days thereafter, the Englishmen found this question everywhere repeated to them. It was only among the high chiefs and a few of the priests that there existed a doubt of Cook's being the prodigal god; he had gone away once before to return—why, thought the common people, would he not return again?

The two visitors were invited to stay aboard the ship that night—an invitation which might have had sinister connotations to men more subtle than they; but the priests were trusting. They refused, however, with the explanation that their actions were sanctioned only by a small group of the priests and that if word of their clandestine errand reached the ears of the king or any of the high chiefs it would have disastrous consequences. There were still many influential chiefs opposed to the Englishmen for what they considered the wanton murder of their people; and, in this connection, "the Curate" warned King and Clerke against placing too much trust in the crafty old Kuaha.

On board the two ships careful precautions were taken, all the guns and swivels being loaded, and sentries posted forward aloft and on the gangways. Likewise, a third of the sailors were to maintain their arms, and a four-oared cutter patrolled the waters about both the ships. All during that night, the sweet warm air was filled with piteous wailing and lamentation drifting down on the breeze from both shores.

Early the following morning, which was Monday, Kuaha came out in a small canoe, bringing a small pig and repeated his assurances of entire sympathy and good faith. After the conversation of the night before, the Englishmen could scarcely conceal their antipathy toward him. Later in the morning another lone paddler appeared; passing before the two vessels he crowed triumphantly and waved Captain Cook's cocked hat. This was too much for the sailors. A representation was made to Lieutenant King asking him to use his influence to prevail on Captain Clerke to send out a revenge party. Clerke himself was enraged by the insult, but restrained his temper and only allowed the gunners to fire one or two shots into Kaawaloa. He pacified the men by telling them that the ships were in a defenseless state, but that as soon as the gear could be put in order, he would allow them to go ashore; if he knew his men, their rage would die down in two or three days' time. Meanwhile, they had the problem on their hands of repairing the foremast of the *Resolution* which, after the action at the *heiau*, had been brought aboard and slung on the booms where the carpenters of both ships were hard at work upon it.

The random shots fired into Kaawaloa took some effect, even though the Hawaiians, seeing the action aboard the ship, had anticipated the move and had taken cover before the shots were fired. Kuaha made another trip out, pleading with the Englishmen to cease their attacks. Several more high chiefs had been killed, he said, and among them, Kamehameha. This last bit of news had the effect on Lieutenant King that crafty Kuaha intended; he knew that King had been drawn to the savage young warrior chief, and the priest thought that a small lie of this sort might show the Englishmen how difficult it was to bring punishment on those who deserved it without hurting those who had been their friends.

About noon three girls swam out to the *Discovery* from near the *heiau*. Shortly thereafter a canoe came from the same place in an attempt to do some trading. The canoe was ordered to return to the shore.

Under the cover of darkness, the two friendly priests visited the ships that night. They told Clerke that while the shots had thoroughly frightened the chiefs for the moment, the long range effect had been merely to anger them more. Proof of this was had Tuesday morning when some sailors were sent in for water. The Hawaiians had taken up positions in the most inaccessible places, but also, thanks to the curious formation of the shore, potentially the most harassing. They had moved their house walls to make barriers against the water hole; and men were concealed in caves along the cliff. From every side the sailors were met with a hail of rocks, and, although the *Discovery* had been warped close to the shore to afford protection, it was unable to cope with the guerrilla opposition. Cannon shots could only dislodge the most vulnerable; the others kept up their hampering barrage. In the course of the morning, only one cask of water was filled.

In the afternoon, therefore, Clerke gave permission to the watering party to burn down a few of the near-by huts in the hope of discouraging the hidden assailants. The

men, maddened by the persistent attacks and armed now
with their commander's permission, carried out their own
schemes. Before long the whole village was in flames.
Among the first houses to go were those belonging to the
priests. The Europeans had gone savage in their own turn.
Without mercy they shot Hawaiians fleeing from their
burning houses. One unhappy native trying to fill his
calabash from the well in order to put out the flames, had
the calabash shot out of his hand and in a panic retreated
to a cave in the cliff where he held two marines at bay
for a considerable time; they only penetrated his defense
after they had literally riddled his body with bullets. Mr.
Hergest, one of the young midshipmen, took a shot at
Kuaha as the old man was escaping from the flames of
his house but the pistol missed fire.

The veneer of civilization does not lie very deep. When
the men returned to the ships, two of the marines carried
poles each with a Hawaiian head impaled upon it.

As the flames began to die down, a man appeared in
the upper reaches of the village walking slowly through
the drifting ash and smoking ruins, attended by fifteen or
twenty young boys. When the ships fired at them, they
threw themselves to the ground, and when the firing
ceased, got to their feet once more holding up bits of
white tapa, palm boughs, everything they could think of
to suggest their peaceable mission. The leader was "the

Curate." They were allowed to advance to the shore, and at his own request, "the Curate" was brought aboard the *Resolution*. Captain Clerke and Lieutenant King welcomed him.

They tried to make him understand how they had been driven to this last enormity by the actions of his countrymen. The tall young man was respectful but exceedingly grave. He expostulated with the Englishmen for their lack of trust. He explained that the priests, believing in their word, had not retreated to the hills with the majority of the villagers, but had instead gathered together all the sacred objects and stored them in "Cook's Altar" beside the *heiau*. This house was among the first to be burned. Furthermore, the priests had been tirelessly working to collect the remains of Captain Cook.

"The Curate's" large soft eyes were sad and reproachful as he talked. Now they strayed to the deck and discovered the two gruesome blood-clotted heads of his countrymen lying on a coil of ropes in the sun. He said nothing for a moment, and then quietly asked Captain Clerke if he would have these thrown overboard. Clerke's pale face was suffused with color as he hastily gave the order.

That night a huge moon rose over the shoulder of the volcano and shone down with serene radiance on Kealakekua Bay, tipping the palms with silver and making a trembling path across the dark waters. But earth and sky were alone in their serenity. Between, the night air was filled with the melancholy wailing and lamentation of Hawaiian men and women, mourning their lost ones. Nor was the sleep of the one hundred and eighty-six Englishmen untroubled.

The body of Captain Cook had been carried to a place on the cliff above Kaawaloa. A few of the chiefs had wailed over it. Others recalled that in dying he had groaned, something a god would never do; these were less interested in lamentation and urged that the body be scraped and the flesh burned. When this was done, the bones were divided among the great chiefs—the head to one Kahu-o-peonu, the hair to Kamehameha, the bones of legs, arms and thighs to Kalaniopuu, and so on. The bodies of the marines killed on the first day of fighting, Corporal Thomas, Theophilus Hinks, John Allen and Thomas Flabchett, had been wholly burned except for the limb bones which were divided among the lesser chiefs. Only a few bits of flesh had been saved from the body of Captain Cook to be used in religious ceremony. One portion had been sent by Kuaha to Lieutenant King and Captain Clerke. The other? . . . Two children wandering along the slope had come across something hanging on a tree which they took to be the heart of a dog, a great delicacy; the temptation was too much—they had stolen it and eaten it. This fact, fortunately, was never made known to the Englishmen.

Thursday and Friday passed uneventfully. The watering parties sent on shore were unmolested and no natives were anywhere to be seen. On Saturday, February 20th, a procession appeared, marching down the steep roadway from the cliff back of Kaawaloa. Two priests were in the lead, beating sharkskin drums and chanting; all others in the company carried pieces of sugar cane, taro roots, or other offerings. Reaching the water's edge they all sat themselves down, a sign of truce, and a large piece of white tapa was brought forth while the priests increased the loud rhythm of their drums. Then from the crowd, a chief stood forth, clad in his finest regalia. In his hands he held a bulky package. Walking out upon a jutting rock he seated himself and signaled for a boat to be sent him.

Captain Clerke himself went ashore in the pinnace and received the package. The chief went with him aboard the *Resolution*, but tactfully withdrew to the other side of the ship when the officers prepared to undo his gift.

Within it, wrapped in several layers of black and white tapa, were the bones of Captain Cook. All the officers recognized the two hands, for Cook had had unmistakable scars on each thumb; an attempt had been made to preserve the hands by coating them with coarse salt. The skull was less recognizable. The jawbone had been removed, and the scalp taken off, although it was included separately with the ears still dangling from it. The bones of arms, thigh, and legs were intact; only the feet were missing. The chief informed Captain Clerke that the jaw-bone and feet had been seized by irresponsible chiefs and that Kalaniopuu was making every effort to recover them. All these gruesome objects bore the blackening smudges of fire and it was evident that the body had indeed been burned as the Hawaiians had said.

Hiapo, the chief who had returned these things, came aboard the following morning with the king's eldest son. They brought with them the jawbone and feet, as well as the barrel of Cook's gun which had been flattened out, his shoes, and a few other trifles which had belonged to him. Hiapo then made an earnest speech, saying that the king, Kamehameha and himself would do all in their power to preserve the peace, and that they had only been prevented in doing so before by the hostility of some of the other chiefs. The cutter, whose theft had precipitated the catastrophe, had been broken up, he said, and was quite beyond recovery. Captain Clerke accepted his solicitations and asked him to have a tabu put upon the bay while the squadron paid its last respects to the dead commander.

The bones were placed in a wooden coffin which was then weighted down with stone and carefully nailed, before being wrapped in the British flag. Both ships' companies were mustered on deck, and stood at solemn attention. The drums rolled. Captain Clerke's slight voice intoned the service tenderly, and then, while a volley of cannon thundered and rolled up against the cliff and echoed back from the slopes and ravines of the towering volcano, Captain Cook was committed to the deep.

There was nothing left now but for the Englishmen to bid a sad farewell to the solicitous chiefs and priests who had stood by them through all the sorry events of the last five weeks. About eight o'clock in the evening of February 22, 1779, the *Resolution* and the *Discovery* put out to sea again, and passing slowly by the shores of the bay lit with the flickering light of many torches, acclaimed by a welling chorus of *aloha*, left behind them the mortal remains of their commander Captain James Cook, born a farmer's son and died one of the most famous of those who pushed back the horizons and joined the world together with the unity of common knowledge.

And so it had come: History in a cocked hat and blue broadcloth had pulled aside the green mists that veiled Hawaii from the world and disclosed beauty and wealth of which future travelers might make what they would. In those last years before the foreigner came to stay, the king of Hawaii danced . . . big, cumbrous body in the torchlight, bloodshot, haunted eyes, but in the broad brown hands a suppleness and vitality. Restless, demanding feasts, dancing, games every night, the old man found the Kona province could no longer support him. There was no food. And so he moved on to Kohala and representatives were sent to all parts of the kingdom demanding tribute for him.

But there were chiefs in the kingdom who had not been at Kealakekua, who viewed the Cook incident with little interest—and surely, they felt, it was no reason to dispense with the ethics of government. The governor of the province of Puna, one Imaka-kaloa ('Tall watchtower'), was organizer and leader of a faction of these discontented chiefs and quite openly defied the king's assessors.

However, there was yet a spark of wit in the darkening mind of the king. He felt himself unable to cope with these new troubles, but there was no reason why he should not proclaim his heir and give the boy a chance to show the stuff of which he was made. The spark had been flickering in his mind for some time, and to make his proclamation he convened the traditional assembly of chiefs in Waipio at the famous old *heiau* and place of refuge overlooking the sea. Here in the ancient sepulcher still reposed the bones of Liloa, first *alii aimoku* of the island. And although Kalaniopuu with his Polynesian sense of the dramatic appreciated the historical effect of what he was about to proclaim, he could not know how curiously it was to round out a cycle.

In his brilliant cloak of *mamo* feathers he stepped out on the stone terrace before his loyal followers; the paving, gray with sun and sea spray, was hot under his bare brown feet. His voice shook somewhat as he spoke and his blurred eyes were squinted. His successor as *alii nui aimoku* (great chief possessor of the lands) would be his son Kiwalao, who would combine in his aristocratic person both the passive and active attributes of royalty, sacred blood and sovereignty; son of the tabu chiefess Kalola the prince was of the highest blood in the land. But in view of the high standing and military achievements of another, the new king would not be custodian of the hereditary war-god, Ku-kaili-moku; the guardianship of this sacred symbol would fall to Kamehameha.

The chiefs there assembled recalled the precedent for such a delegation of authority. They remembered too what the outcome had been—how the royal prince had been eventually overthrown by the lesser-born favorite. And they wondered how well Kalaniopuu recalled these things; it was hard to tell. The king had appeared so fatuous and incapable of late—odd that he should have chosen this particular temple!

As for Kiwalao, he had cause enough already to be envious of his savage-looking cousin. The latter was a national hero and had long been active in an advisory capacity to the king, whereas the young prince had always been in the background, sheltered under the aegis of his sacred mother. He felt it in his bones that this pronouncement of his father's boded ill for himself. However, his character was quite unlike that of the traditional victim, Hakau; he was a kindly and impressionable young man and determined to keep on good terms with Kamehameha—if the latter allowed it. Indeed, it is possible that, like the other young bloods of the kingdom, he felt an honest admiration for that stern warrior chief.

But in the emergency that followed, these matters were momentarily forgotten. The two cousins had a first class campaign on their hands, for the rebellious governor of Puna was no easy conquest for their arms. Indeed, though his forces were numerically less than the royal army, he successfully defended his province for a period of many months; familiar with the terrain and touched with a genius for guerrilla warfare, he darted about the cumbersome troops of Kamehameha and Kiwalao, striking sharply and unexpectedly and then quite as suddenly vanishing from view. Kamehameha was furious, and day by day grew more sullen and obstinate. But finally the renegade could keep it up no longer; the men lost—which would have been but slight disadvantage to the royal forces— were serious defeats for him, and eventually he was forced

King Kamehameha I

to take to the hills and hide in a secret subterranean cave. But unhappily he was betrayed, and ferreted out, and his body destined as a sacrifice to the once more victorious Ku-kaili-moku.

The ceremonies took place in Kalaniopuu's ancestral province of Ka'u at the major *heiau* Pakini. Representing his father—for the old king was still *alii aimoku,* in spite of proclaiming his heir—Kiwalao was in charge of the ritual. He was nervous. At no time was the king's role an easy one, but the first time was surely the worst. After the chanting had been concluded, the prince walked forward as steadily as his shaky knees would allow him and heaped up the hogs, coconuts and bananas on the altars. Suddenly, he heard a gasp of surprise from the crowd of nobles and priests, and half turning to see what the commotion was about, he felt himself pushed rudely aside. It was Kamehameha, holding out in his arms the charred corpse of the vanquished chieftain. Was he not custodian of the war-god?—he would make the sacrifice. In a loud, firm voice he began to chant, and Kiwalao was left standing helplessly beside him. At the conclusion of the chant he placed the body on the altars, putting pigs and coconuts in either seared hand, and turning to face the audience, signified its dismissal. Kiwalao was pale and could find no tongue for the anger which burned within him. His cousin's word and gesture were commanding:—as though mesmerized, the crowd obeyed him and moved out of the temple. Even Kalaniopuu smiling somewhat stupidly to himself followed after. Kamehameha did not look at Kiwalao, but stood, his back to the altars, staring proudly after the retreating assemblage. Kiwalao did not habitually think quickly. He hesitated for a long moment, and then with bowed head walked off the stone terrace while Kamehameha's eyes burned into his back.

Outside the villagers were as tumultuous as a yard of dogs at feeding time. Knots of people were gathered at every shady spot talking excitedly, each man giving his version of the affair, each chief and priest trying to explain to his neighbor why he had obeyed Kamehameha's order to leave the *heiau;* and the explanations were far from satisfactory. Kiwalao quickly retired to his own establishment and did not appear at the court. The great majority of the *alii* felt that the prince had been grossly insulted and expressed this opinion with furious words in order to cover up their secret shame at having been so coerced. Kalaniopuu, listening and nodding to the talk, was alarmed at the attitude so freely expressed and feared for the safety of his favorite. After nightfall he slipped out of his sleeping house and sought out the tactless chief.

"You must leave here at once," he said, and his voice was clear and forceful. "Go to your lands in Kohala and take with you the war-god. Stay there; call no attention to yourself until the resentment of the chiefs has died down."

Kamehameha was moved by the old man's concern, and at the same time elated to discover that his action had not alienated the royal favor. He had a mystic confidence in the rightness of his action, but he also had his simple faith in the mana of Kalaniopuu, and it might have weakened his own case for himself if he had lost the king's friendship. There was nothing to be gained by brazening the matter out among the chiefs, and he agreed to the king's command. As he touched his broad nose affectionately to the wrinkled cheek of his uncle, his thick lips which were habitually turned grimly down, curved into a warm and understanding smile. And that night, accompanied by his wife and his elder brother, he set out in a small outrigger for his patrimonial estate at Halawa in Kohala.

A few months thereafter Kalaniopuu died, an exhausted and unsuccessful old man. His life had been one of action, and as a powerful chief he had been able to maintain a reasonable control over the people he governed, but he was not the conqueror he had dreamed of being and many years of his life had been wasted in proving this to him. As an added blow, just before his death he learned that the king of Maui had recovered the provinces of Hana and Kipahulu which had been all the success his conquering arms had known. And he died, too, troubled with an unhappy conscience, feeling himself in some way to blame for the death of Captain Cook;—be it said for Kalaniopuu that he had no reason for self-reproach in this matter, but it is a credit to his character that he himself assumed the blame for his people's failure to understand a strange, semi-religious phenomenon.

A prince called Keawe-mauhili ('Keawe-the-perpetual-wanderer'), through the dispensation of Kalaniopuu, had inherited Hilo and was one of the most influential chiefs of his time; to his advantage was the fact that he was born of sacred blood—on the death of the king he shared with Kiwalao the prestige of the highest social rank in the kingdom—but he was more than prince, he was a politician as well. Not satisfied with his vast holdings on the windward side, he coveted the rich lands of Kona, and as parceling out of the lands was the royal prerogative, he carefully wooed the favor of his nephew Kiwalao. Success was practically assured him, for the young prince as heir-apparent had had little attention paid him. Logically then, it was to his charming, well-born uncle that he turned for advice when he assumed sovereignty of the kingdom. The Kona chiefs saw the game too late. They knew of Keawe's interest in Kona and realized now that he stood in good chance of gaining their lands. For a moment they regretted their long-time devotion to Kamehameha which had caused them to overlook Kiwalao, but then a solution presented itself, suggested by the canny old warrior Keku-haupio who had been military tutor to Kamehameha. Let them not regret their allegiance to Kamehameha. Was he not the strong man in the kingdom? Was not strength of achievement nearly as important in the eyes of the gods as sacred blood? A rift already existed between the new king and his cousin:—very well, such a rift could be employed to the advantage of the Kona chiefs. He, Keku-haupio, would go to Kamehameha and sound him out.

Arriving in Kohala he sought the chief out at Hapuu ('Tree fern'), a pretty little cove shaggy with pandanus trees which was Kamehameha's favorite estate; no, he was not there, said the women, but a little way down the shore body-surfing with his brother. The waves were high that day and the two big men were shouting and vying with each other as to who could ride the farthest in the churning white foam; Kamehameha appeared to have forgotten that there was anything in the world beside enjoying himself and tilling the land. Farther up on his lands were the taro fields which he himself cultivated with his own hands. Thus had he been living—as farmer, fisherman, athlete— since he had abandoned the royal court. But on the sight of his old companion-in-arms, Kekuhaupio, his manner changed. At once he was alert, eager for news of the court; his quick mind summing up and proposing a hundred questions before the older man had time to finish his story. Of course he would come to their assistance.

Such was the state of affairs within the nation when Kiwalao, accompanied by his uncle, set out for the royal sepulcher at Honaunau in which the body of Kalaniopuu was to be placed. Once the formalities of the burial were over, Kiwalao proposed to announce his new partition of lands.

Reaching the City of Refuge at Honaunau he was informed that his cousin Kamehameha had come from Kohala to be present at the ceremonies and was staying with the high chief of the Kealakekua district a few miles away. Kiwalao was aware of the formidable coalition of the Kona chiefs, but as yet they had done nothing of a rebellious nature and he was assured by his uncle that the royal forces were equal to any emergency. But the young king secretly dreaded an emergency and, hoping to solve the situation through diplomacy, paid a call on his cousin.

He was received with all the courtesy traditionally due to an *alii kapu* (tabu chief), and the cousins saluted each other by touching noses to cheeks, wailing together and shedding tears over the memory of Kalaniopuu. Then the king spoke of the matters that had troubled him.

"Where do you stand? There is a chance that both of us may die. Here is our relative inciting us to battle. Perhaps only the two of us will be slain. What tragedy for us!"

Kamehameha could make nothing out of this:—he had no fear of being killed! Where did he stand on the matter?—well, he answered evasively, he would come to view the body on the morrow and they could talk further then. Kiwalao saw that he could gain nothing by pressing the point, and, feeling that once again he had been affronted by his cousin, angrily took his departure.

The next day Kamehameha went with Kekuhaupio to the royal court and paid his respects to the dead body of his uncle. Although the attitude toward him was fairly hostile, he greeted old acquaintances affectionately. In the evening he was invited by Kiwalao to an *awa* party, a gesture of courtesy which would have been unthinkable to avoid. In the torchlit darkness of a spacious thatched council chamber, the court *alii* were seated in a circle passing the *awa* root from one to another to be chewed. Kekuhaupio leaned toward the king.

"Pass some to this one to be chewed." He nodded toward Kamehameha.

"And why should he be invited to chew?" asked Kiwalao.

"It was so ordained by your father that the one should be prime minister to the other."

Grudgingly the king handed a piece of the root to his cousin. Accepting it, Kamehameha chewed it thoroughly and then taking a bit of tapa strained the liquid pulp through into a calabash. This he handed to the king. On Kiwalao's right was seated one of his particular favorites; after a moment's hesitation he handed the bowl to this man who took it with a smile and raised it to his lips. Kekuhaupio sprang forward. Dashing the bowl from the courtier's hand he turned a furious face on Kiwalao, saying, "You are in error, majesty. Your 'brother' has not prepared the *awa* for such a one as this, but for yourself alone." Forthwith he took Kamehameha by the arm and, like a mother who does not want her child contaminated, pushed him before him out of the house. "Let's take to the canoes and leave this place," he muttered angrily.

On the following day Kiwalao made his proclamation. Runners were unnecessary; the Kona chiefs knew what the judgment would be. Not only was wily Keawe-mau-hili affirmed in his governorship of Hilo, but he received a good portion of the lands of Kona; indeed, little was left to the Kona chiefs but their hereditary estates, the titles to which were respected by the king.

Oddly enough, the king's half-brother had likewise been shabbily treated, and in his anger staged a riot. Presumably the riot was directed against the king, but the outcome of it was the burning down of a coconut plantation belonging to one of the Kona chiefs. This was all the provocation they needed to start a rebellion. The king and his uncle came to the aid of the fractious younger brother, much to his chagrin, and a full dress battle took place, lasting for eight days. The tide was turned when Kiwalao, seeing Keeaumoku fall, attempted to remove that chief's feather cloak and ivory pendant. But Keeaumoku was not dead, and grappling with the king, managed to hold onto him until Kamehameha arrived and finished him off. With Kiwalao slain, the spirit of victory pervaded the Kona troops and, renewing the onslaught with redoubled fury, they soon had the field to themselves.

Keoua, the dead king's brother, escaped to Ka-u with some of the royal troops; others took refuge at Honaunau where, according to tradition, they were inviolate. But Keawe-mauhili, wounded in the thigh by a spear, was captured. The greatest prize of all! The Kona chiefs had good reason to congratulate themselves and laud their warrior leader, Kamehameha. But unhappily for the kingdom such a prize was virtually untenable. Keawe-mauhili, because of his sacred blood, was almost a mythical figure come to life in the eyes of his guards. Their whole concept of society was turned topsy-turvy by their orders to stand guard over a man on whom they had been taught

their shadows must never fall, a man in whose presence
to be in any position other than prostrate meant death.
Their fear of his mana was great, their traditions strong
in their hearts:—they let him go free!

PART III

BROWN MAN AND WHITE

KAMEHAMEHA I

THE FIRST TWELVE YEARS

THE ORIGINAL PURPOSE OF THE ALLIED CHIEFS IN
defying Kiwalao had been merely to secure their
own lands from the encroachments of the contriv-
ing governor of Hilo, Keawe the Wanderer. Not that
they had no further ambitions, but it is possible that had
the king heeded the implications of their coalition and
been less eager to flatter his uncle an open breach might
not have come—at least, not so soon as this. But now the
king was dead. He had appointed no successor and the
Kona chiefs knew themselves to have a most likely candi-
date in Kamehameha, favorite of Kalaniopuu and the appointed military head of state.

Kamehameha, fresh from the casual life of country
gentleman, slipped into his new role easily; he had known
the time would come. Now he was prepared to give all
his thought and energy to the building up of a kingdom
such as Hawaii had never known. Wise enough to know

that one man's judgment can never be unerring, he appointed the Kona chiefs as his counselors and seldom acted on any major problem without first seeking their opinions; the ultimate decision, however, was his alone. But in these first years of his struggle for supremacy, major problems were plentiful, and it was a long time before this compact team of warrior chiefs began to function incisively. The opposition was strong.

Immediate antagonists were two: Keawe the Wanderer and Keoua of the Red Cape, who controlled between them the provinces of Hilo, Puna and Ka-u. In their opposition to Kamehameha, they were mutually supporting, but had Kamehameha not pressed his aggression with such immediacy they might have fallen out with each other; however, Kamehameha had to learn his lesson.

Judging that the mature Keawe was the more dangerous of the two, Kamehameha made his first thrust at Hilo, but the crafty prince anticipated him. Not caring to fall into blasphemous hands again, Keawe solicited armed assistance from the one man in the islands whose blood was as noble as his own, the king of Maui and archenemy of the kings of Hawaii. Kamehameha, expecting to snare the lobster in its hole, ran into a nest of eels. His plan called for a land attack and an attack by sea to be delivered at the same time, but Keawe's spies were sharp and brought him news of this plan. Instead of building two defenses, Keawe concentrated on a powerful offensive against Kamehameha's land forces, and was so successful that the naval force was unable to land its troops before it was commandeered to help the land army escape.

Kamehameha retreated to Laupahoehoe and remained there for some weeks before he came reluctantly to the conclusion that he would be wiser to return to Kohala and put his own kingdom in order before he embarked on a series of wars. He had hoped to triumph over Keawe by the sheer surprise of a sudden, reckless attack, but he had not the troops to push forward a long campaign.

While in Laupahoehoe he was moody and restless; his defeat at Hilo, result of mistaken judgment, hurt his pride, and he sought to distract himself out of self-criticism by seeking a dangerous adventure. Trumping up an excuse, he decided that the province of Puna must be a doubtful stronghold, being controlled as it was half by Keawe and half by Keoua, and he determined to sound out the true sentiments of the Puna people. For this undertaking he prevailed on his chief navigator to man a canoe in secret and be ready to sail after the court had retired for the night. The night chosen was unpropitious; a violent storm lashed the sea into a heaving, churning mass of white foam, and lightning flashed intermittently. But Kamehameha was undeterred; he had faith in the intuitive skill of his navigator. Into the fury of the night the little outrigger made its determined way, tossed and flung about on the mountainous waves, but the sea never once wet Kamehameha who sat unperturbed in the stern with a cloak wrapped about him. Toward dawn the storm abated and the canoe drew in swiftly toward the Puna shore.

Many people were already abroad. They were bringing out nets to be dried and mended. One man, who had been born in Kona, shaded his eyes against the silver glare of the sunrise and squinted curiously at the approaching canoe.

"*Tahuhu!*" he cried in surprise. "It's Paiea!"

"And who is Paiea?" asked the others.

"Paiea? You don't know? That's what we called Kamehameha when he was a boy."

Kamehameha!—the name struck its hearers like a flung stone. In a moment they were seizing up their nets and running to the nearest shelter—a dense grove of pandanus trees. The man from Kona remembered then that Puna people were taught to fear Kamehameha, and rather than face the warrior alone, uncertain of his own status, he followed them.

Seeing the people flee from him distressed Kamehameha and he was determined they should know he came on a friendly mission. While the canoe was still standing off, he dove into the sea and swam with hasty, powerful strokes to the shore and ran toward the shaggy, mass of pandanus. But on his approach the Puna people once more fled.

Two fishermen who were carrying between them a particularly heavy net became exhausted, and rather than leave the valuable net to the prey of Kamehameha, turned to defend themselves against him. But he was no longer after them. They saw him standing helplessly on a shelf of lava, one foot caught in a crevice of the rock. With an exultant shout, the men dropped their net and ran back and with their heavy canoe paddles began to strike at his head. They might have killed him there had not their overeager blows broken the paddles. Then they abandoned the torture and went to summon the others. Kamehameha, so angry that he scarcely felt the cruel bruises and the hot blood trickling down over his cheeks, picked up a rock and hurled it with all his strength after the retreating men, but his aim was wild and the rock shattered the trunk of a *noni* tree and lodged itself in a ledge of earth. The crowd quickly returned and, standing a little way off, stared with awe at the helpless warrior, quailing a little under his ferocious glare. At this moment the navigator came running up breathlessly, and seeing his prince's plight, immediately sought to release him. The spell was broken. With an angry shout one of the men of Puna hurled a spear which struck with a sickening sound into the navigator's naked side. Kamehameha swiftly bent and broke off the spear at its head that he might have something with which to parry others; he was none too soon, for the sight of the stricken man writhing at Kamehameha's feet impelled the others to attack, each eager for the glory of having killed Kamehameha. But this was an art Kamehameha knew of old, and no crowd of fishermen was any match for him. Snatching their spears from the air, he hurled them back with sure and terrible aim and routed everyone except those eight or nine who lay pinned to the earth to move no more. Left alone he was finally able to extricate himself from the crevice, and picking up his wounded friend, carried him back to the canoe.

In Laupahoehoe he told the story to his *alii*. With much emotion he dwelt on the skill and bravery of the unfortunate navigator. He knew that this loyal officer faced harsh judgment from the chiefs for allowing him to undertake such a foolhardy venture, but he was determined that the man should be protected. Apparently his words took effect. The *alii* listened sympathetically, and when he was through, offered their medical skill in healing the man's wound. "Any doctoring must be done in my presence," warned Kamehameha. But that night the navigator was taken to a distant house and confronted with his crime, and the spearhead was twisted cruelly in the gash until he died in agony.

Kamehameha wept when he heard what had happened. Furiously he faced the people of his court.

"When I returned from Puna I told you to doctor this man in my presence. But you persisted in treating him according to your own barbarous and distorted judgment. And thus my comrade is dead. I now proclaim before you all that henceforth the *Mamalahoe* [1] is the law of the land. Let the aged man go and sleep by the roadside. Let the aged woman go and sleep by the roadside. And let no one injure or molest them."

This rhetorical speech established the first great law of Kamehameha, a revolutionary law in the annals of Polynesia. Thereafter it was a crime punishable by death to set upon any person incapable of defending himself. For the courtiers who listened to this speech there was no doubt as to Kamehameha's feeling in the matter, for he had referred to the navigator as *hoapili* (comrade) and he had never been known to call any man by such an affectionate name.

The court of the king of West Hawaii was now established in Kohala at Kamehameha's patrimonial estate. The king himself lived at his favorite cove, Hapuu ('Tree fern'); there he built a *heiau* on the cliff for his war-god,

[1] *Mamalahoe:* The exact name has been subject to discussion. *Mamala* means "splinter" or "break off"; *hoe* means "paddle"; while *hoa* means "comrade." The name could refer to either the incident of the helpless king or the murder of the helpless navigator—*Mamalahoe* or *Mamalahoa*.

Kukailimoku, who was to rest awhile that *mana* might accrue to him while the king set about building up the resources of his lands. And perhaps it was symbolic that old Kekuhaupio—the king's military tutor and counselor —should die shortly thereafter from a wound received accidentally in a spear-throwing contest.

In the year 1785 Kamehameha took a new wife. She was the seventeen-year-old Ka-ahu-manu ('The feather cape'), daughter of Keeaumoku, who was born in the time when this intractable warrior was living in poverty on the island of Maui. It was Kamehameha's marriage for love. That Kaahumanu also loved him may be seen in the fact that they were constantly and warringly jealous of each other, an emotion which under the free standards of ancient Hawaii was somewhat superfluous.

A story is told of them that at one time Kaahumanu suspected him of philandering and swam all the way from Kailua to Honaunau—a matter of some eighteen miles— to spy on him. In the City of Refuge she hid herself in a dark recess beneath a huge rock which stood at the entrance to the central *heiau*. When Kamehameha came by this way, unaccompanied but for a pet dog, she kept silent, but the dog recognized the scent she wore—a perfume made of mountain herbs—and commenced to bark excitedly. The king stopped. Stooping over he peered beneath the rock, and to his huge delight, his eyes met those of his wife looking sheepishly out at him.

In this year Kamehameha made another attempt to dislodge Keawe, but the Hilo prince was reinforced by Keoua's troops, and again fought off the attack. But Kamehameha was not discouraged; he recognized by this time that he was dealing with a shrewd warrior. And furthermore other matters were demanding his attention. Kahekili, the enterprising king of Maui, had engaged in a series of battles on the other islands from which he was to emerge as sovereign of both Maui and Oahu, with control over Kauai and Niihau which were nominally ruled by his brother. He had already shown an interest in the affairs of Hawaii, and it was reasonable to suppose that he would soon take action to overthrow Kamehameha and set up his friend Keawe as puppet ruler of the island. Kamehameha was aware of this threat, and at the same time secretly jealous of Kahekili's successes. On the pretext of an expedition to recapture the lost Maui provinces of Hana and Kipahulu, he made a foray against Maui and met with some success; but he had not come with men enough to support an effectual large-scale invasion, nor could he manage to strike directly at Kahekili who was a crafty warrior and believed in conserving the strength of his troops, eluding the vicious blows of Hawaii's compact, reckless little army. Kamehameha was now forced to the conclusion that war-like exuberance and vaulting ambition were not enough to build him the empire he wanted. He realized that there was another weapon besides that of an army—the weapon of diplomacy and intrigue, and if he wielded that well he might secure greater advantage than he had by the force of arms.

But these green islands in their peaceful summer sea were no longer isolated from the rest of the world; kings and chiefs were no longer to be allowed to work out their own destinies. News of Captain Cook's death had shocked the world, but the shock was not of long duration—not long enough, at least, to prevent the curious westerners, in the birth pains of imperialism, to follow down the suggestions implicit in the published reports of Cook's discovery. In 1786 the islands were visited briefly by another British squadron, under the command of Captains Portlock and Dixon who had been on Cook's expedition. In the same year a famous French navigator, La Perouse, looked in at Maui. Thereafter, scarcely a year passed that one or more ships did not call.

With the establishment of trans-Pacific trade routes and the increasing demand for furs from the Pacific northwest, Hawaii became an established rendezvous and supply station. Here were ample fuel, refuge from the cold northern winter, fruits and vegetables in abundance (and, of course, the other requisite of "the sailor's sole delight").

Naturally such commerce was not unprofitable for the Hawaiians, though few captains scrupled not to take advantage of their innocence. Still, if a transaction may be valued in the terms of mental attitude, the balance was fair enough at first: what the westerner offered in underpayment, the Hawaiians received with secret delight as overpayment. Among the first to have any comprehension of the westerners' scale of values was Kamehameha: he made it his business to discover the fine points of the game and, once learned, played it in his turn. Before long even the bargaining Yankees found a match for their wits in the king of Hawaii.

Once a Yankee trader offered Kamehameha twenty quarts of rum in exchange for some hogs. The king accepted and insisted on being present when the rum was measured out (in a quart pot). "But there are only nineteen!" he said when the supercargo had finished. Sure that he had made no mistake, the Yankee offered to take the measure again. "Well, it's no matter. Let's just split the difference," suggested the king. But the supercargo was not to be tricked, and started to measure the rum for the second time. Kamehameha laughed and said that rather than put him to all that trouble he would accept the first measure. He had no desire to cheat; he was merely playing the Yankee game.

Among the pioneers of the trans-Pacific trade route

was an Englishman, Captain John Meares, who acted for a company of British merchants operating from Bombay. He was one of the first to perceive the advantages of Hawaii and wrote: "The situation, climate and produce of these islands may be made to answer very important commercial purposes; besides, the inhabitants are a brave and generous race of people, susceptible to the highest mental cultivation, and worthy of sharing, as they are already ambitious to share, the fate enjoyed by British subjects. The well-directed industry and assured fidelity of half a million people would surely add to the grandeur and prosperity of the British Empire."

Captain Meares acquired first-hand knowledge of Hawaiians by taking with him to China a young chief of the island of Kauai who had begged to accompany him. His name was Kaiana, and he was a half brother of the kings of Maui and Kauai (Kahekili and Kaeo), hence of very high rank. Six and a half feet tall, magnificently built, he had a sensitive, strong face with sharp-cut features and large intelligent eyes. Dressed in the flamboyant cape of Hawaiian nobility and with a warrior's casque set on his curly black hair, he brought business to a standstill as he walked down the crowded China streets. And he gave it a jolt of life again when he stopped to purchase an orange or a piece of cloth that caught his fancy and offered, as the highest payment he knew, a handful of iron nails. Captain Meares, himself a somewhat mousy little man, took delight in this prize exhibit and became genuinely fond and proud of him. Other British merchants in China were equally fascinated; one, a captain in the East India Company, wanted to take Kaiana to England, but Captain Meares would not hear of it—he already saw the advantage in having a prominent chief working for his interests in Hawaii, and was anxious to get the Hawaiian home as soon as possible. Before they sailed for the northwest coast again, one Mr. Cox—"a commercial gentleman of China"—presented Kaiana with cattle, sheep and other animals and gave him a sum of money "to be expended as his own untutored choice or wayward preference should direct." The cattle did not survive the journey, but Meares superintended the young Hawaiian's expenditures, seeing to it that he bought useful things that would stand him in good stead in the islands.

While at Nootka Sound Captain Meares learned from the captain of another vessel that since Kaiana's departure, his brother, the king of Kauai, had become jealous of him and would probably make an attempt at his life if he returned. In order to investigate this story, Meares went on ahead to the islands, leaving Kaiana with Captain Douglas, who commanded the second vessel of the expedition, the *Iphigenia*. Reaching the island of Hawaii in October, 1788, Meares diplomatically sent gifts to Kamehameha in Kaiana's name. At Kauai, he discovered the prevailing sentiment to be against Kaiana and sent a message to be delivered to Captain Douglas when he should arrive at Kealakekua; he then returned to China.

Two months later the *Iphigenia* sailed into Kealakekua, accompanied by a small schooner, the *North West America*, which the ships' carpenters had built at Nootka. Kamehameha, informed that Kaiana was aboard, came off to greet him, and the two chiefs embraced with lavish affection, tears streaming down their cheeks. Captain Douglas was greeted courteously by the king and presented with two feather capes and a *lauhala* fan. He was the first white man to go ashore at Kealakekua since Captain Cook, and was accorded much ceremony, being met by priests who intoned a chant and presented him with hogs; wherever he went, crowds of villagers paid him marked respect. Nevertheless, Douglas was suspicious and feared for the safety of his new schooner. She had a complement of but a few men and might be easily surprised and captured. To impress Kamehameha with the schooner's armaments, Douglas arranged an inspection tour for the king; he was helped in the scheme by Kaiana, who had watched the vessel a-building with keen interest and was anxious to have Kamehameha see it. When the king came aboard he was given a salute of seven guns and was sufficiently impressed.

Several days after the arrival, the schooner parted one of her anchor cables and the anchor was given up for lost. The king, hearing of the accident, immediately sent expert divers to the Englishmen's assistance. The divers were six, directed by a petty chief. Before going to work they sat in their canoe and consumed bowl after bowl of *poi* to give them strength. Then at a signal from the chief they plunged in, plummeting down through the blue waters till they were lost from sight in smoky depths. Three, four, five minutes passed, and finally four of the divers emerged. Another came up a minute later. But the sixth continued to stay under. At last he was sighted, floating unconscious near the surface, and his fellows hauled him out. Blood was flowing from nose and mouth, but he was alive, and when he regained consciousness told Douglas that he had been able to clear the cable, but that the anchor was too deep to be recovered. The captain of the schooner had kept a watch on the man and swore that he had been under for seven and a half minutes.

Impressive! But a few days later Captain Douglas was annoyed to find that the anchor cable of the *Iphigenia* had parted—with the aid of a knife. He at once sent word to Kamehameha that unless the anchor were recovered he would level the village with his guns. The king was distressed; he had not been party to this sabotage, and willingly provided divers who, this time, were able to recover the anchor without further incident.

Douglas allowed the king and queen to sleep aboard the *Iphigenia* on several occasions, offering them the use of his own cot, which they considered "a luxury of no common description." He describes Kamehameha as "rather an object of fear among his people . . . of tyrannic disposition" and "with few of those qualities which gain a sovereign that first of all titles, father of his people." But Kamehameha was young yet. What man ever won such a title at thirty-five? He was perhaps a little self-conscious of his power, and conscious already of the greater power that would one day be his. Some of the *alii* who had watched Captain Douglas shaving suggested to the king that he try it. For an answer Kamehameha gave each one of them a kick where it would do him the most good and teach him not to make flippant remarks.

Kaiana, apprised of the situation on Kauai, had come to the decision to throw in his lot with Kamehameha. By so doing he was assured of a grant of lands and an important position in the government. He was a man of spirit; furthermore, as a result of his travels, he felt himself to be an equal of the Englishmen and hence a man to be treated with respect among his own. To impress the king and court he made quite a show of sending his things ashore, and indeed his collection was well calculated to impress, consisting of "saws of different kinds, gimblets, hatchets, adzes, knives and choppers, cloth of various fabrics, carpets of several colors, a considerable quantity of chinaware and ten bars of iron."

Kamehameha pressed Captain Douglas to leave carpenters with him that he might have a schooner built. This was a favor the captain could not grant, but he did present the king with something of almost comparable value—a swivel gun, which he had his carpenters affix to the platform of one of the war canoes.

The following year Captain Douglas put in at Kealakekua again and an attempt was made to capture his ship— at least, so he was led to believe by Kaiana, who was not above playing a trick on his patron Kamehameha on the chance that it would forward his own cause. Fortunately, however, Captain Douglas learned the truth of the matter and was thoughtful enough to leave a letter for future shipmasters stating that Kamehameha could be fully trusted.

During this year (1789) a Captain Mortimer visited Hawaii and supplied Kamehameha with more arms. He describes the king as "one of the most savage-looking men I ever beheld, and very wild and extravagant in his actions and behavior." A hint of Kamehameha's blossoming personality is found in the word "extravagant," though more apt description would have been "exuberant."

The shipmasters of the early days in the trans-Pacific trade were as a whole a decent lot, but there is one who stands out from the others in a particularly ugly light. He was a Boston man named Simon Metcalfe. With his son Tom, Captain Metcalfe had skirted the Pacific Coast of America on a trading expedition. Curiosity prompted him to turn the prow of his snow, the *Eleanora*, toward Hawaii, and he left his son in charge of their schooner, the *Fair American*, to finish their business in the northwest and join him in the islands later.

The *Eleanora's* first port of call was a tiny village on the island of Maui. Captain Simon was anxious to take aboard fresh fruit and vegetables. During the night, a rowboat which had been riding at the stern of the snow, was stolen. Captain Simon was not an incautious man—he had stationed a sailor in the boat, and of the sailor there was no sign. Drawing his own conclusions, he ordered the ship's cannon to be fired point-blank into the village, reducing it to a shambles and killing many inhabitants. Somewhat later he learned that the people who had stolen the boat were from another village a few miles down the shore; sailing on to this place, he discovered that the sailor had been killed and the boat broken up. The natives who brought the news were most apologetic. Maintaining outward calm, Captain Simon accepted their apologies and suggested that the village send provisions to trade with him; for the sake of order, he asked that all canoes approach the vessel on the starboard side. The Hawaiians, greatly relieved that they were not all to suffer for the crime of a reckless few, came out in great numbers and swarmed about the starboard of the *Eleanora*. Captain Metcalfe stood at the rail and looked down on them, smiling a bleak New England smile. Then he raised his hand. The ship heeled over from the concentrated force of a broadside; he had had all his guns brought to the starboard for greater effect. The slaughter was ghastly; even Captain Simon, who would have liked to enjoy his vengeance, was constrained to go below where the screams and moans could be heard but faintly. Well over a hundred Hawaiians were killed, and many others fatally wounded.

Then the *Eleanora* sailed for Hawaii. Cruising down the leeward shore, Captain Simon engaged in desultory trade. Off Laemano ('Shark's head') one of Kamehameha's counselors came aboard, one of the twin chiefs, Kameeiamoku. For some petty offense or other, Captain Simon, still in a dirty mood from the incident at Maui, struck this chief across the face with a rope's end. Kameeiamoku, tense with fury, would have killed the Yankee on the spot, but his warrior's eye saw that he and his men were far outnumbered. He immediately left the ship and vowed that he would have his revenge on the next foreign ship that came his way.

As fate would have it, the next ship was the *Fair American* under the command of Captain Tom Metcalfe. Tom had run into a Spanish squadron in the northwest—Spain was then intent upon keeping the Pacific Coast in her own control—and was taken captive to San Blas in Mexico; he was released eventually, but by this time was long overdue at the rendezvous with his father. Kameeiamoku went aboard the schooner on the pretext of offering hogs and vegetables in trade. After the long voyage from Mexico, Tom Metcalfe was overjoyed at the prospect of decent food again, and, with the four members of his crew, gave the Hawaiians a hearty welcome. But his joy was short-lived. Once the warriors were aboard they fell on the hapless seamen and threw them into the sea;—none could swim. Only one was spared, and he by the merest chance—an ignorant Boston sailor named Isaac Davis; he was found later bound up in an abandoned canoe. His rescuer was a man named Ridler, carpenter's mate on the ship *Columbia,* who had been left at Hawaii to collect sandalwood. Ridler took him to Kamehameha.

Hearing of the incident, the king became very angry. Still, he preferred to mete out punishment to Kameeiamoku in his own fashion. The *Eleanora* was then anchored in Kealakekua, and, lest the captain (his connection with the captain of the *Fair American* was not known) hear of this act of piracy and take his own measures, Kamehameha gave the order that any man who came ashore from the snow was to be forcibly detained. Only one did—the bos'n, John Young. When the bos'n did not return, Captain Metcalfe assumed he had deserted, and sailed off to China without him; he had already given up his son as lost.

Thus did Kamehameha, by a curious train of circumstances, acquire for his court two white men who, above all others, white or brown, were to be his guiding stars. Simple, uneducated sailors—yet, as though the gods had willed it, men of a peculiar genius. Their knowledge was instinctive and sure; they knew the white man's ways and had an intuitive wit for playing the game with destiny. Davis—known as Ikake, the Hawaiian pronunciation of Isaac—was given the king's protection and, with John Young—called Olohana, from his favorite phrase "all hands"—was accorded privilege in the court. The two men became friends, but more important, both came to love Kamehameha sincerely and devotedly, sensing, one must suppose, his essential greatness, and feeling, after the manner of their own, that God had willed they be counselors and friends to this huge, brown man, the king of Hawaii. Firm in this belief, they reconciled themselves to the strange life they had entered on, married into the royal family, and became high chiefs of the realm.

By 1790, Kamehameha's forces were strong. He had guns, white men to advise him, and a powerful reserve of warriors and war material. He was strong politically as well, for he had wisely appeased Keawe the Wanderer, and now there was only the lord of Ka-u, Keoua, to oppose him. But Keoua was small fish: Kamehameha was planning to go after the wily black marlin, his old enemy Kahekili, king of Maui, whose vaunted empire of the central islands rankled in Kamehameha's breast. When he prepared for the momentous expedition his matured wisdom stood him in good stead; Keawe sent him valuable reinforcements.

And so in the full glory of arms Kamehameha swept down on Maui. But Kahekili was absent. Enjoying fruitful years, he had set up his court on Oahu—at Waikiki, for he liked the graceful palm groves, the long beach of ivory sand, and the incomparable waves that would carry a man on a surfboard for nearly half a mile. To rule over Maui Kahekili had left his son, Ka-lani-kupule ('The heavenly prayer of Ku'). Kupule was far from weak, but he lacked the military genius of his father, and the sudden invasion by powerful Hawaii troops caught him off guard. Across the barren sun-scorched central plain Kamehameha's warriors flowed like a crimson tide, driving all resistance before them. The Maui army had little choice but to take to the valleys, but the western Maui valleys are cut clean and end against sheer walls of mountain. Into one of these Kupule's troops retreated, fighting, running, struggling through the wet jungle that coiled around them. Herded before the relentless tide of crimson-cloaked warriors they backed up against the cliffs and were cut down. The mountain stream was choked with bodies and the water ran red down to the sea, giving the battle the name of Ka-pani-wai ('The damming of the waters'). Kupule, with a handful of his retainers, managed to escape, scrambling up the wet green cliffs, clinging to the few bushes and twisted vines that offered themselves to hand.

With comparative ease Kamehameha next invaded the small island of Lanai and then girded himself for an encounter which for him was probably more difficult than any armed strife. He was an *alii aimoku*, a chief who takes possession of the lands, but he was not an *alii kapu*, a sacred chief; in other words he did not incorporate in himself both the active and passive powers of sovereignty and hence would not be likely to found a dynasty. Indeed, a dynasty already existed which had yielded to the temporal might of Kamehameha as *alii aimoku* but which might be expected to revert to power on his death. This dynasty was represented by Keawe the Wanderer and three women who had taken refuge on Molokai. These women were Kalola, the widow of Kalaniopuu (his "sacred wife") and mother of the late king Kiwalao; Kalola's daughter who had been wife of her half-brother Kiwalao; and their little girl Keopuolani ('The swelling clouds of heaven'). Kamehameha felt assured that his succession to rule would be lasting, and therefore sought to reconcile himself to the older branch of the Keawenui dynasty by incorporating their tabu into his own line; to do this he wished to take as his "sacred wife" the girl Keopuolani. Kalola, white-haired, wrinkled, and weak with age, had fled from Maui with her charges but she could not avoid Kamehameha forever and at last agreed to meet with him in her refuge on Molokai. She was ill; her mind was no longer sharp and willful and she told the conqueror that on her death her daughter and granddaughter should be his. When she died, shortly thereafter, Kamehameha knocked out two of his front teeth as a sign of respect for her, and took into his court the two women. When Keopuolani was old enough he married her and she bore him the two sons that were to follow him to the throne.

While encamped on Molokai, Kamehameha flung down the gauge to Kahekili by sending him two bowling stones —one white and the other black; peaceful invasion or war. "The Thunderer" replied: "Wait . . . wait until the black tapa covers me and the hog has been placed at my head. Then Hawaii shall be the bowling stone that will sweep the course from here to Tahiti. Let him then come and possess my land." How Kamehameha might have treated this response is unknown, for affairs on his own island took a turn for the bad and diverted him.

Keoua—*alii aimoku* of the province of Ka-u and part of Puna—had not looked with pleasure on his uncle's assistance to Kamehameha; they had been allies—now it looked as though they were enemies. The prince waited until Kamehameha and his armies were far away and then marched on Hilo. Keawe The Wanderer was caught—and in a trap of his own setting, for his best warriors were off with Kamehameha. Keoua showed him no pity:— there was cold satisfaction in his voice as he offered the charred corpse up to his vengeful war-god. This business attended to, he marched into Kamehameha's lands sacking and laying waste to the country.

As soon as Kamehameha received word of these events he returned to Hawaii and promptly engaged Keoua in battle. But the warriors of Ka-u were fresh; they were able to hold off the greater, but war-scarred, troops of Kamehameha. As a consequence, by the curious code of Hawaiian warfare, the struggle was abandoned by both sides. Returning to Hilo, Keoua set up his government there, established as *alii aimoku* of East Hawaii. These matters attended to he set out for Ka-u attended by a company of twelve hundred warriors and their wives. The trail to Ka-u led up over the slope of Mauna Loa.

The second night, while they were encamped on the mountain, Pele—the volcano goddess—had a spasm. The crater of Kilauea exploded; stones, ashes, smoke and sulfurous gases vomited heavenward and showered down on the surrounding company. With the earth trembling and shaking beneath his feet Keoua gave heart to his panic-stricken people; they were to form three divisions and each make for home by a different route—in that way some might escape. Hardly had they separated when the most terrifying explosion of all occurred. The very fibers of the earth seemed to split apart as though the whole island would crumble into the sea. One of Keoua's divisions was caught; in a deadly hail of rock they were swallowed up by an impenetrable vapor of volcanic gases; all were killed down to the last frightened child. The prince himself escaped with the two other divisions, and reached Ka-u safely. But what to most Hawaiians would have been a catastrophic omen left Keoua undaunted, and he was able successfully to fight off two attacks by Kamehameha's forces that followed soon after, one led by Kaiana into Ka-u and the other by Keeaumoku into Hilo.

Some months before this event Kamehameha had sent a messenger to consult with a famous prophet on Oahu; he wished to find out by what means he could finally bring the whole of the island under his control. The answer was that he must build a *heiau* on the brow of a hill [2] which rises back of Kawaihae and commands the sweep of that green sparkling coast. Construction of the temple was now underway and the flat-lands and slopes of Kawaihae were crowded with the camps of people come from every part of Kamehameha's realm to join in the labor. The king himself carried many a boulder up the dusty, sun-scorched hill. He had made his half-brother Ke'lii-maikai ('The good chief') his religious proxy and forbidden him part in the labor so that he might remain ceremonially clean for the ultimate services of dedication. But the work was interrupted by new war.

Kahekili was far from pleased at the ascendant power of the king of West Hawaii; it was a challenge to his own greatness. So he had persuaded his brother Ka-eo ('The victorious one'), king of Kauai, to join him in an attempt to crush Kamehameha. Together they had re-taken Kamehameha's outposts on Maui. Before embarking for Hawaii, Kaeo stood up at the top of the fortified hill Kauwiki which had long been the rallying point of Hawaii's armies. Throwing his spear heavenward with all his strength, Kaeo watched it fall, and then addressed the assembly of warriors: "It is said of old that the sky comes close down to Hana, but I find it high enough; I have

[2] Kohala Hill—Puukohala.

thrown my spear and it did not pierce heaven, neither, I suppose, will it pierce Kamehameha. But this thing I promise you, O chiefs and warriors of Kauai, be strong and be valiant and we shall drink the waters of Waipio and eat the taro of Kunaka." He was true to his promise; while one fleet of warriors landed at and ravaged Kohala, Kaeo descended upon Waipio, destroyed the ancient *heiaus*, the place of refuge, and even laid blasphemous hands on the sepulcher of Liloa before Kamehameha could rally his warriors and make a counter-attack.

On the advice of Young and Davis, Kamehameha prepared to meet the invaders by sea that he might use the swivel gun, gift of Captain Douglas. The two Englishmen took charge of the armed canoe. Kaeo and Kahekili were willing to meet the challenge; they too had guns and a few foreigners to man them. In the shadow of the towering red Hamakua cliffs the fleets met. Roar of gunfire replaced the shouts and insults inaugurating Hawaiian warfare of old:—and the sharks, impartial raiders of the ancient sea battles, now paid for their victories as mortally as the sweating, brown-skinned men. The sound of cannon and musket-fire, the hoarse-throated yells of men, rolled up against the cliffs and drowned out the roar of surf and the drumming boom of waterfalls crashing into the sea. The battle was long drawn out; the slaughter was so general and so terrible in this new type of warfare that the basic savagery of men habitually hidden under the sportsmanlike code of ancient Hawaiian battles burst out ferociously, and a mutual acceptance of defeat under the old code was no longer possible . . . one side would have victory. That in the end was Kamehameha's. The kings of the northern islands returned to their lands and hastily prepared for the return engagement with which they were sure Kamehameha would favor them.

But the young king had learned patience; he was not ready yet. The problem of the divided loyalty of his own island was one which must be solved now and for all. Kamehameha returned to Kawaihae and continued with the building of the *heiau*. By the end of the summer of 1791 it was completed. Perhaps its slow building had given Kamehameha time for reflection, for on its completion he sent the most statesmenlike of his counselors as emissaries to Keoua. They spoke friendly words and invited the embattled prince to meet with Kamehameha at Kawaihae and discuss grounds for a mutual understanding.

Keoua had not been alarmed by the omen of the volcanic eruption, but there was in him, nonetheless, a good deal of the Hawaiian mystic. He was a fatalist and felt impelled now to accept Kamehameha's invitation, come what might. Before his canoes reached the calm, sand-green waters of Kawaihae, he shifted his men about so that he had with him in one canoe his most loyal chiefs and friends—suitable companions for diplomacy . . . or death. Addressing himself to Kamehameha's emissary, he said: "It looks ominous ashore—the clouds are flying wildly."

Surprised, the older chief asked: "From whom should evil come on so calm a day?" But Keoua only answered again: "The clouds are flying wildly."

The canoes approached through sparkling, light-shot waters the broad beach of mustard-color sand. Here Keeaumoku had his home, close by hot springs in which he liked to bathe; the chief was at the beach with his retainers to greet Keoua. Kamehameha, coming down the hill from the *heiau*, was still a little distance off, and Keoua shouted to him, "Here I am!" to which Kamehameha replied, shouting likewise, "Rise and come here that we may know each other."

Keoua was about to step out of his canoe when suddenly Keeaumoku struck at him with a spear, running him through. With a cry of anguish, the prince endeavored to pull the spear out by its shaft, but in a moment fell dead. The ripples glittered red with blood.

Hard-headed, hot of impulse, there was in Keeaumoku no sympathy for compromise; let others play the game of politics, his was the fighter's code—and any who opposed the one fated king was a mortal enemy. Had this been planned treachery? It might seem likely; but if it was planned, it was done with infinite cunning to defend Kamehameha's name. The king arrived on the scene in time to save Keoua's brother, Kaoleioku, from the spear of Keeaumoku, but the important deed had been done. None now stood in Kamehameha's way as *alii aimoku* of the island of Hawaii. The body of Keoua and those of his followers who had been killed were immolated on the altars of the new temple, and thus the prophecy came true; completion of this *heiau* saw Kamehameha's mastery over Hawaii, albeit more through human means than divine.

In March, 1792, Hawaii was visited by another squadron of British warships, a visit second in importance only to that of Captain Cook. The commander was George Vancouver who as a lad of seventeen had been a midshipman on the *Discovery* under Cook. Now he was a man of importance in the royal navy and his flagship was another *Discovery*. On this first visit Vancouver did not see Kamehameha but on two subsequent calls the two became very friendly.

George Vancouver had entered the navy at 13. Now at 34 he had a smooth pleasant face with candid, almost lashless, eyes, a double chin and was a little inclined to stoutness; like his hero Cook, he flew into occasional rages, but none could be compared, as Cook's were, to the barbarous war dances of the southern islands; and, unlike Cook, Vancouver could unbend easily and be wholly charming and affable toward his men and the Hawaiians alike.

Next to Vancouver the man who did the most for Hawaii on this expedition was the "Naturalist," Archibald Menzies, who had visited Hawaii in 1787 as surgeon aboard the *Prince of Wales*. He was a clever, middle-aged Scot with a cheerful, shining, red face and bright blue eyes. In the exercise of his profession Menzies not only examined and classified the flora of lands visited, he supplemented Nature's bounty by introducing to these small isolated worlds new fruits and vegetables which would enhance their commercial importance. Among other things he had acquired some orange seeds (at the Cape of Good Hope) which he cultivated in a lath house on the deck of the *Discovery* and on reaching Hawaii had a number of flourishing young plants to be distributed among the chiefs. (In the middle of the Nineteenth Century Kona oranges were the largest and most important island export.) Vancouver himself purchased cattle in California and brought them to the islands, thus, in the early years, founding another important industry.[3]

The main purpose of Vancouver's expedition was to

[3] Descendants of these cattle now roam the central tablelands of Hawaii on what is the second largest cattle ranch in the United States.

complete the exploration of the northern Pacific and to receive from the Spaniards certain lands which they had seized and which they were now impelled to return to Britain. But there is no question that its humanitarian secondary purpose, even though commercially prompted, was an important achievement of the voyage.

Kamehameha was in Hilo putting his newly acquired lands in order when the *Discovery* and *Chatham* first reached Kealakekua in March, 1792, but Captain Vancouver was well pleased to receive a visit from Kaiana, a man of whom he had heard many favorable things—as indeed had most the shipmasters in the Pacific. In appearance at least Kaiana had not been overestimated even though he had grown heavier in the years since he had traveled abroad; his manner was courteous and agreeable, but the only English he could remember was the word "wine" . . . which was provided him and which he consumed in quantity.

Vancouver had brought from England a Molokai boy who had been taken there by an English trader. In Tahiti the boy—he was only sixteen—had fallen in love with a slumbrous-eyed belle of Papeete, and had attempted to jump ship but was apprehended by the Tahitians and returned to the friendly charge of Captain Vancouver who felt it his duty to take the lad home; the decision seemed justified, for although Kualelo languished in melancholy at first, he had no sooner sighted the purple summit of Haleakala lying on the horizon than the melancholy vanished and he became caperingly gay. At Kealakekua his spirit had its second great uplift; meeting Kaiana he decided that this lordly chief was the most admirable person his eyes had ever beheld. He was glad to be a Hawaiian then and wanted only a chance to serve his hero. Kaiana, seeing the patronage the boy enjoyed, acted kindly toward him; Kaiana was nothing if not an opportunist. He knew how to make an impression, bringing many gifts of hogs and vegetables to the English ships, and acting in a thoroughly princely manner. In turn Vancouver gave him grape vines, orange plants and an assortment of garden seeds, and on a Sunday morning allowed him to review the ships' companies. The Hawaiian found naval courtesy and naval etiquette far more impressive than on merchant ships, and at last overcome by the glamour of his position betrayed himself by overtalking; expansively he embarked on a dramatic story of how he had shot Keawe the Wanderer and as a result of this daring had divided the kingdom with Kamehameha, he ruling the southern half of the island and Kamehameha the north. It was a little too good to be true and Captain Vancouver, not to be caught, made a point of sending a gift of red cloth, axes and other tools to Kamehameha at Hilo.

As for Kualelo, the boy was encouraged by Kaiana to stay on at Kealakekua. Vancouver approved of this and had his young friend's things sent ashore, together with a gift of goats, tools, seed and household articles so that he might start out his life as a rich man. But once the ships had sailed Kaiana called on his youthful disciple and coolly appropriated most of these things.

In gray dusk the squadron reached Kawaihae and shortened sail to meet a double canoe which came out swiftly from the shore. Surprisingly the hail was made in English—asking what ships these were, the captain's name and whither bound. The man was invited on board and proved to be a Hawaiian; he called himself Jack Ingraham, having traded names with a Boston captain who had taken him on an eighteen-month voyage to New England and back. Captain Vancouver was delighted with the man's candor and humor and when he asked modestly if he might bring his "master" aboard, all were curious to see what sort of chief the fellow served. It was, of course, old Keeaumoku, the governor of South Kohala. Presented to Vancouver, Keeaumoku held out a letter signed by another captain stating that the chief was honest and civil and might be trusted by mariners as an influential man in the kingdom (this was an oblique slur on Kaiana's reputation). Jack treated his master with affectionate good humor, amusing the Englishmen with his facetious remarks—in English—relative to Keeaumoku's fondness for wine. The old man soon disabused Vancouver of the story which Kaiana had told and gave him accurate information as to the state of the kingdom. The captain was grateful for the impulse that had prompted him to send gifts to Kamehameha, and thereafter refused to allow Kaiana to board either of the ships.

When he sailed again for the northwest coast, Vancouver invited Jack to come along. The Hawaiian sought Keeaumoku's permission, and the chief was so upset at losing him that he burst into tears—but gave the permission. Thinking the American name somewhat incongruous, Vancouver asked Jack to revert to his Hawaiian name, Ka-lehua ('The Lehua'—a native tree with extravagant crimson flowers).

The squadron spent ten months along the coast of America. On its return the first port of call was Kawaihae but one of the periodic tabus was then in force and on the first day no natives came out except Keeaumoku, who brought a gift of hogs and explained the situation. His greeting of Lehua was as effusive as his farewell had been. Trading commenced the next day, but women were still under the tabu which forbade them from going out in canoes; this problem they solved by swimming out to the ships in the evening.

The first demand of all native traders was for firearms;

however, Vancouver had resolved not to contribute to this dangerous commerce and steadfastly refused;—the Hawaiians had to resign themselves to accepting cloth for their hogs—a yard and a half of scarlet cotton goods for five fat hogs being the ratio of exchange.

In California, Vancouver had taken aboard four cows and two bulls which he intended as a gift to Kamehameha; one bull had died in passage and the other cattle badly needed fresh pasturage, but he did not quite dare entrust them to Keeaumoku—despite the latter's urging and his statement that Kamehameha had lands close by offering excellent feed (lands which were, in fact, to become incorporated in Hawaii's largest ranch in later years). Not to affront the friendly chief, Vancouver said the cattle must be delivered to Kamehameha personally, and, on finding that Keeaumoku had taken good care of goats presented him the previous year, he further assuaged the old man's feelings by giving him a ram, two ewes and a ewe lamb.

While at Kawaihae the captain went ashore to call on Keeaumoku's wives who had professed a great eagerness to see him. With him went Mr. Menzies, the naturalist, and a guard of marines (though neither officer took arms). The bay shimmered in silver heat and the aisles of tall palms along the shore offered grateful shade to the Englishmen in their uniforms of heavy broadcloth. With

Keeaumoku they strolled leisurely down the palm-fringed roadway, baked hard, cracking in the sun and sprinkled over, as if with gems, by millions of twinkling salt crystals. The semi-naked villagers, their smooth skins burned a red black from long days on the sea, lined the way and reverently prostrated themselves before the little company. The marines winked at each other and made comments under their breath at the sight of pretty flower-bedecked girls smiling archly up at them. Keeaumoku's wives, however, were no longer the sylph-like, golden-skinned creatures they might have been as girls; they were extravagantly fat, and, with hair cropped short and serious demeanor, had a somewhat masculine look. The captain gave them—with what secret amusement—scissors, beads and other trinkets of adornment and, at their request, had his marines go through a drill which pleased them much more than their gifts. After refreshing themselves with coconut milk, the Englishmen wandered about viewing the chief's estate, and found that he had quite a collection of guns all kept in excellent order. Among them were a double-barreled fowling piece, two swivels and a carronade—the small cannon were to be placed on the platform of a double canoe which was building in the near-by shipyard. Vancouver promised Keeaumoku a canvas sail for this canoe and the old man was as delighted as a child.

Both Englishmen were impressed with the considerable

ingenuity of the saltern which was a prominent feature of the village. It was a series of small pools, carefully banked and dammed, into which sea water was conducted to evaporate in the sun, leaving a quantity of fine salt. Menzies took a botanical trip inland as far as Waimea, gathering plants to be studied and classified; on asking if he might see the inside of Kamehameha's *heiau* which loomed tawny and gray on the hill overlooking the village, he was told that it was tabu and that five *kahunas* (priests) lived in it; twelve skulls (one of them Keoua's) were ranged along the top wall.

When Vancouver left Kawaihae for Kealakekua he took along Keeaumoku and his wife who were anxious to be present at the meeting with Kamehameha and who were also taking this opportunity of visiting their daughter, Kaahumanu, who was Kamehameha's favorite queen. Because of a treacherous gusty wind from the Waimea plain, the progress southward was slow; two days later the *Chatham* was sighted off Kealakekua in company with a trading ship, the *Jackall,* which had just come from there (Vancouver had sent the *Chatham* around the island from the other way, and she had been lying off Kealakekua for four days awaiting him). Lieutenant Broughton of the *Chatham* sent word that he had already received Kamehameha—who had come aboard dressed in a Chinese dressing gown of blue silk, had warmly shaken hands with all the officers and had asked after his friend "George" (King George III). The Hawaiian king sent frequent gifts of food, but the master of the *Jackall* had warned Broughton that Kealakekua was strongly fortified and a dangerous harbor for small vessels. The English navy was not likely to take such warnings seriously. Vancouver ordered both ships to put in to the harbor, but for several days they were becalmed. In the interim the captain decided the bull and one of the cows which was ailing would have to be sent ashore, but the cow died in passage.

When Kamehameha finally came aboard the *Discovery* Vancouver was surprised to see how the years had changed him; there was no longer any trace of sullenness in the big wrinkled face, and his squinted eyes were warm and intelligent. He laughed readily and conducted himself generally with high good humor. After he had shaken hands with the captain, he asked if he might bring aboard his wife and a few others of his family who had come out with him; this was typical of the concern he always showed to do the right thing—before sitting down even he would ask where Vancouver would like him to sit. When the royal family came aboard, the captain was a ready victim to the charms of pretty young Kaahumanu; as he wrote—"she did credit to the choice and taste of Kamehameha, being one of the finest women we had yet seen on any of the islands." After her introduction to the captain and his officers, she turned to Keeaumoku and threw herself weeping with joy into his arms, and a moment later embraced her mother as affectionately. "It was pleasing to observe the kindness and fond attention with which on all occasions they seemed to regard each other; and though this . . . behavior would be considered as extravagant in the polished circles of society, yet to us . . . the profusion of tenderness . . . could not be regarded without a warmth of satisfaction at thus witnessing the happiness of our fellow creatures." So wrote kindly George Vancouver.

Learning from John Young that Kamehameha never thought of receiving gifts before he himself set the example, Vancouver decided to surprise him by offering a few presents to his company. Inviting them to his cabin, he took from a chest a red cloak which he had had tailored by his sailmaker and threw it about Kamehameha's shoulders; it was a showy thing with ribbons and borders of lace and gold braid.[4] The king was speechless with delight. Then, catching sight of himself in a full-length mirror, he began to chuckle and crow, dancing before the mirror to see the red folds swirl about him. "The cabin could scarcely contain him" and he burst out on deck,—adopting

---

[4] Vancouver presented Kamehameha with two such cloaks and, after the Hawaiian fashion of naming everything from spears to clothes, these were called Ke-akua-lapu ('The ghostly spirit') and Ke-kuku-ohe ('The bamboo plant').

a more dignified gait, however, as soon as he was within view of his assembled people on the blue waters below. With affected casualness he strolled by the rail, turning and posing, so that all might feast their eyes on his splendor. Murmurous admiration and applause fell like music on his ears. When he had calmed down a bit he returned to the cabin and asked Vancouver if he intended giving any more presents. On the captain's laughing assurance that he did, the king asked to be allowed to take over; he would not have his English friend giving much where little was due. Indeed he was so economical with the gifts which he took from the sea chest and handed to his retinue, that the captain several times felt impelled to supplement his offers. To the ladies of the party the king gave scarcely anything at all and when the gallant English officers made up for this deficiency it caused uproarious laughter in which Kamehameha himself took a larger part than any.

Later the captain conducted his guests on a tour of the ships, first leading the king to see the three remaining cows which were to be his. Kamehameha was fascinated, but a little afraid lest these "large hogs" should bite him. When he was finally prevailed upon to approach more closely, one of the cows chose the moment to turn its head and regard the brilliant new cloak with an expression of bewildered surprise; interpreting this as a look of active hatred, Kamehameha leapt backwards and ran into the crowd, upsetting several of his more portly courtiers. His uneasiness vanished, however, as soon as he saw one of his men go up to the cow and take it by the horns. Vancouver was then overwhelmed by a flood of eager—and intelligent—questions about cattle and cattle-raising which even an experienced rancher must have been hard put to it to answer; he did the best he could, however, which led Kamehameha to suggest that it would be wise to put a tabu on the cattle for a period of ten years to give them a chance to multiply.

After being becalmed for several days, the captain grew impatient and ordered out the boats to tow his ships into the harbor; Kamehameha sent a number of canoes to help out. Arriving at the anchorage between the two villages, Vancouver saw that, as he had suspected, the rumor of fortifications was highly exaggerated; it is possible that the master of the *Jackall* had mistaken the big *heiau* for a fortress. Actually there were little more than a few small cannon on the shore, one or two on canoe platforms.

When the ships had come to anchor in the clear dark blue waters of the bay Vancouver remembered so vividly, Kamehameha paid a formal visit. The shore was crowded with people, just as it had been on a similar day almost exactly fourteen years before; but there was a new young king in Kealakekua now—a king who knew white men, and a new young captain aboard the British warship *Discovery*—a captain who knew Hawaiians. The king appeared at the head of a fleet of fourteen of his largest canoes, his own having a complement of forty-six men at the paddles. Clad in a flowing cape of soft, lemon-yellow feathers, a helmet of red, yellow and black on his head, he stood on the long narrow platform in classic pose, straight and proud, a big brown hand negligently holding a polished spear upright before him. The fleet came out swiftly and circled the ships three times, while smaller outriggers were swamped and overturned in the scramble to get out of the king's way. But then, instead of turning in toward the shore as Kalaniopuu had done, Kamehameha came aboard and greeted Vancouver, touching his nose solemnly to the captain's cheek. Retainers were signaled to come forward and lay at the captain's feet heaps of feathered cloaks and casques. Then, taking him by the hand, Kamehameha said he had ordered ten canoes loaded down with hogs and would the captain have these brought aboard;—in all there were some ninety or more. But the most important gift of all was the cloak he wore. Earnestly asking the careful attention of all the officers Kamehameha told them that this was his gift to his brother "George" across the sea. It was the most valuable present he had in his power to give, being made of sacred *mamo* feathers collected and painstakingly woven into the foun-

dation mesh of sennit over a period of perhaps several
hundred years; it sometimes took that long to gather
enough feathers, and this cloak was the only one of its
kind in the islands. No king of Hawaii had ever had one
like it, said Kamehameha proudly, and because of its great
value he would not leave it aboard until the ship sailed;
then he would supervise the packing of it and exact a
promise from the officers that no man should put it about
his shoulders until King George of "Beretani" had worn it.

When the hogs had been taken aboard, the canoes that
had brought them were used to convey the cattle ashore,
as well as two ewes and a ram. Crowds converged about
the beach on which they were to be landed. Scarcely had
the first cow felt solid ground beneath her hooves when
she gave the Hawaiians a taste of excitement; with a bel-
low of joy she kicked up her heels and dashed wildly
down the beach, spraying frightened people before her
like the prow of a ship—some dove into the water, some
climbed palms, others just ran.

Left aboard ship as emissaries and interpreters for the
king were his two white friends, John Young and Isaac
Davis. From them Vancouver learned much about the
state of the kingdom and Kamehameha the king. He
learned that Kaiana in recent years had several times tried
to organize the natives to pirate ships that had anchored
in the bay, but each time his plans had been discovered

by Kamehameha and thwarted; as a result, a marked coolness had sprung up between the two. But what interested Vancouver the most was the tale the Englishmen told of their own treatment by Kamehameha; each expressed a deep and sincere loyalty to him, and while admitting they sometimes missed the lives they had known they were on the whole contented with their lot, nor would they consider leaving the islands.

Among the officers on the *Chatham* was a merry fellow named Thomas Manby. He kept a journal, not so much as a record of the lands he visited, but as a record of his own prankish and amorous adventures; on Kauai he claimed to have been left ashore as hostage in company with a number of the king's wives while the nervous monarch went aboard ship with other wives—on the king's return the first group of wives went aboard while Tom, still hostage, dallied among the second complement. Incidents such as this occupy most of his writings, and one would think he had never a care in the world; however, sometime later when almost swamped in a small boat on a heavy sea, he apostrophizes to one Kate, saying the only thing in his mind at that awful moment was the desire to get a command so that he could afford to marry her and that he would make her the most faithful of husbands.

An observatory was set up at the old site near the *heiau* and this time, remembering former difficulties and resigned to what fate seemed to force upon his race, Kamehameha designated a large house near by where, as Manby poetically expressed it, "the astronomers might entertain their female friends and observe the beauties of Venus whilst the other planets were obscured by clouds." Thus Manby. It is not surprising therefore that he should stray into the royal compound and seek the society of one of the queens. The girl, Keopuolani—the "Captive Queen" and sacred wife of Kamehameha—was seated at the foot of a tree stringing beads, attended by some twenty maidens. Tom Manby, smiling his most charming smile, sat down beside her and to refresh him she ordered fruit and coconuts. Neither could speak the language of the other, but both were equally adept at the language of flirtation. The girl was amused by Tom's hair and he allowed her to tie and untie the short queue which he wore after the fashion of the times; tiring of this, she decorated his hair with feathers, flowers, and other things that came to hand. After a time she wanted to see the color of his skin and half undressed him in her curiosity while her handmaidens peeked and giggled.

Then she discovered his tattoo. While in Tahiti Tom had allowed one of the local skin artists to decorate his leg above the knee; the artist knowing Tom's "disposition and the way I was circumstanced at the moment" did a very imaginative job. The girl-queen was fascinated by this and summoned an old man who examined the design for fifteen minutes, commenting the meanwhile on the symbols and causing unrestrained laughter among the ladies. "After passing an hour in flirtation with this generous queen," said Tom, "some little particulars were exchanged—tho' by no means criminal—that occasioned her majesty to be called to order by a little deformed wretch who I was afterwards informed held a situation of high honors in the royal household"; this "deformed wretch" was a guardian of the queen, so chosen because his deformity left him unsusceptible to any blandishments.

It would seem that the days when travelers had anything to fear from the natives of these islands through their own or the Hawaiian's ignorance were over; Kamehameha knew how to treat visitors cordially and in such a manner that no misunderstanding would arise—in such event he had two valuable counselors in Young and Davis. There would be unpleasant incidents yet, but none under the regime of Kamehameha. These days spent by Vancouver in Kealakekua were filled with incident, agreeable to both sides, and beneficial to the king's better understanding of people to come.

Vancouver had his marines go through their "manual exercise" and taught a few of Kamehameha's men the fundamentals of drilling. He found that the king had some two dozen muskets which he "said he had lately procured in the way of traffic from Mr. Brown, master of the ship *Butterworth* of London, and added that they were so very bad that some of them burst on the first firing, on which account they were now afraid to fire any of them." The English officer rigged up the royal canoe with English colors, sail and pennant. . . . Ashore another Englishman was encountered, a man named John Smith who had left an American fur ship here three months before because of ill usage; he had lived since then with Kamehameha who had made him a chief and given him lands . . . A special expedition was arranged to view the spot where Captain Cook had fallen. . . . A girl stole some things off one of the ships; apprehended, she was punished by being forbidden ever again to go out on the water, and her father was required to pay a fine in hogs. . . . Menzies made a six-day expedition inland, collecting plants . . . Kaiana, bringing a present of hogs and vegetables, was refused entrance to the ships and departed in a huff. . . . Vancouver was informed that the *Fair American* was at Keauhou and would be returned to Captain Simon Metcalfe if that dour old man ever came back to the islands. . . . Keawe-aheulu showed the orange plants landed the year before to be in flourishing condition. . . . A few days before the squadron was to leave, Kamehameha came aboard nearly in tears with news that the bull had died; however, there was still hope for island cattle as one of the cows was with calf.

But the most important event of Vancouver's stay occurred on a day when Kamehameha had prepared entertainment in the form of a mock battle. It was a good show, and the king's younger brother—Keliimaikai ('The good chief')—impressed the Englishmen by being able to hit a mark with his spear at thirty yards. Afterwards there were fireworks aboard the ships, and much toasting in bumpers of grog. Then Menzies writes, "As a great number of chiefs and natives were collected to see these entertainments, Captain Vancouver was very urgent with Kamehameha to take this opportunity of declaring himself and his subjects, together with the whole island, under the dominion of the king of Great Britain, but this he positively declined doing unless Captain Vancouver would promise to leave one of the vessels behind at the islands to assist in defending him and his people from the inroads of their enemies which was certainly a very strong and reasonable argument!" The inevitable question, shrewdly parried.

As the squadron was preparing to leave once more on a continuation of its survey of the American coast, there was a further exchange of gifts. Kamehameha had his heart set on having a plate, a knife and a fork (his cook had been allowed to observe the methods of the *Resolu-*

"The King's younger brother hit a mark at thirty yards."

tion's galley) and these were given him, together with a few choice articles from the wonderfully stocked sea chest in Vancouver's cabin. To Young and Davis the captain gave cooking utensils, carpenters' tools and a variety of garden seeds; he knew they would be in worthy hands. As for the king and his people, they had only food to give, but gave of their finest, sugar-fattened hogs in prodigality; these were, to western palates, the most desirable of the islands' produce.

On his return in January, 1794, Vancouver approached Hawaii from the windward in order to judge the possibilities of Hilo harbor as a suitable anchorage. He was pleased, on nearing the coast, to see a double canoe flying an English pennon from its masthead, putting off to greet him; it was Kamehameha. The big, cheerful, scantily clad king was aboard a few minutes later, overjoyed at the return of his friend. He must put into Hilo harbor, and stay for a month or so; here the king could provide any quantity of foodstuffs, for the fertile uplands could sustain the whole island with their varied produce. An investigation of the harbor, however, convinced Captain Vancouver that he would do better to return to Kealakekua and he urged Kamehameha to come along. At this the king's expression became dubious:—it was the season of the *makahiki*, the yearly Lono festival, and he was bound to stay in Hilo for the duration of the rites. Vancouver did not like to dissuade the king from such a tradition; still, the advantage of having the king to run things at Kealakekua was so great that he determined to try "a sort of artifice" and see if he could not get him to come of his own volition.

One morning at breakfast—a meal which Kamehameha and his favorites delighted to attend—Vancouver announced in a disappointed voice that he judged the king's refusal to go to Kealakekua as a sign that he no longer valued their friendship. Such an accusation brought tears to Kamehameha's eyes; dropping his fork, he sat in stunned silence. The officers pressed food upon him, but he seemed not to notice them. Nothing Vancouver might have said could have affected him more deeply. Friendship in his code was as important as any of his traditions: more important, indeed, for at length he called his brother to him and begged him to go ashore and seek permission from the priests for him to go. He told Vancouver that as king he considered himself the last person to violate his country's laws. The other *alii*, however, eager to take the voyage, laughed at his concern and said that of course the priests would make the exception under these circumstances. Comforted at last, he detained his brother to give him minute instructions as to the conduct of the government, and, this done, fell to his breakfast with a return of appetite and a lively good humor.

Windy weather prevented the ships from further communication with the shore, and after a short wait for the priests' consent it was decided by the king's counselors that this consent was but a matter of form and they might set sail for Kealakekua. Off the coast of Puna the weather cleared, and all gathered at the rails to view the magnificent prospect of the volcano Mauna Loa, capped with a fresh fall of snow at its summit, and spouting forth pillars of smoke from eminences lower down. Aboard the *Discovery* were seven Hawaiian chiefs, three of whom had brought with them their favorite wives. Captain Vancouver was disappointed not to have the pretty young queen Kaahumanu in the company, and upon asking the king about her learned that she had been suspected of infidelity with Kaiana and as a consequence had been banished, and was living somewhere near Kealakekua. The captain could see that the king was distressed by the incident, and was sentimentally moved to proffer his services towards effecting a reconcilation. Thanking him courteously Kamehameha replied that while he was "happy to receive any advice on state affairs, or any public matters, especially where peace or war might be concerned," he considered that "such differences as might occur in, or respect, his domestic happiness" were none of the good captain's business. And so for the time being the matter was dropped.

The squadron arrived off Kealakekua in semi-darkness, and Kamehameha went ashore to see that torches were lit to guide the ships in. There was already a vessel in the harbor, the *Lady Washington*, John Kendricks, and the *Discovery* came to anchor close by. Even at this late hour, many Hawaiians came aboard to bid Vancouver welcome. One of these brought him a courteous letter from an Englishman named Howell who had arrived as clerk on the *Lady Washington* and had decided to remain in the islands. He had been given lands by the local governor. This Howell was a curious sort of adventurer:—he had once been a clergyman in the Church of England, and was generally known as Padre Howell. At one time, it is said, he worked seriously on Kamehameha trying to convert him to Christianity. After listening to his arguments, Kamehameha said: "If I am to believe in your God, I must have proof of His power. You say He is wise and good and will shield from harm those who truly worship and adore Him. Give me proof of this by leaping from the Kealakekua cliff, and if you are unharmed I will embrace your God." Howell lost some of his missionary zeal after this.

The king announced the next day that inasmuch as he felt the usual bartering stirred up a competitive feeling among the chiefs it would be better if he himself was solely responsible for the victualing of the squadron; he could make himself compensation later in the form of taxes. Therefore he requested Captain Vancouver to make known directly to him all the squadron's needs and these would be supplied. Such an arrangement was far more satisfactory than the old methods of barter. Now Vancouver could make his presents as he wanted to—in the spirit of largesse from the paternal government of His Majesty George III. Among the first of these gifts were a young bull, two bull calves and two cows, as well as five rams and five ewes, which he had acquired in California and had had better luck in transporting than he had had with the first. Inquiry as to how the expectant cow of the previous voyage had fared brought forth this story. The calf had been born, a bull calf, and Keeaumoku was so elated that he ordered runners to carry it to Kamehameha in Hilo that he might see the miracle for himself. The little creature was carried overland on a man's back and fed upon fish and water; three days later he was in Hilo, hale and sound.

The chiefs who had come with the ships from Hilo continued to live aboard and gradually became exasperating to Vancouver. The last straw came when he discovered that five of his table knives were missing (not because the Hawaiians wanted the iron—they wanted the heavy ivory handles from which to make *palaoas*). This gave the captain an excuse to order all the chiefs off the ship except

Kamehameha; the distressed king was able to discover only three of the knives. Eventually he brought back one more, but the fifth had been given to a tabu chief and even the king could not ask for it.

While off Hilo an Englishman named James Boyd had come aboard with Kamehameha. He had been mate of the American sloop *Washington* (not the *Lady Washington*) and had left her to throw in his lot with Kamehameha—the king, aggressive, humorous, vigorous, frequently had this effect on sailors used to quarterdeck discipline and unimaginative leadership. Boyd had described himself as a shipwright; but he had been a little carried away—actually when he gathered the timbers for a ship requisitioned by the king, he had no idea how to lay the keel and set up the frame, nor could Young and Davis help him. Captain Vancouver judged the man to be honest and industrious, and he saw in this the opportunity of giving Kamehameha a present which the king would value above all others he might give. He sent for Boyd to have the timbers brought from Hilo to Kealakekua and set his ships' carpenters to building the framework. Kamehameha was speechless with delight, and when the work was under way, spent most of his days observing it.

Vancouver, as a gentleman, could not very well stay at Kealakekua without seeing the dishonored queen of whom he was so admiring, and eventually the matter cropped up again between himself and the king. Kamehameha's reticence broke down this time, and the truth of the matter came out. There were faults on both sides. Kaahumanu's infidelity with Kaiana could not actually be proved, and the king "acknowledged with great candor that his own conduct had not been exactly such as warranted his having insisted upon a separation," though "he alleged that his high rank and supreme authority was a sort of license for such indulgences." Having persuaded Kamehameha to admit this much, it was not difficult for Vancouver to make him admit that he wanted Kaahumanu back, and to persuade him to accept his kind offices. Kamehameha was anxious that no suggestion that he was a party to the matter be mooted abroad; his dignity would not allow it. The captain agreed with him and offered several alternative plans, but in the end the king himself proposed the best scheme. Taking two pieces of paper he drew with a pencil designs which he would recognize—one meaning that Kaahumanu was willing, the other that she was adamant. Vancouver was to invite her aboard ship, sound her out, and then send one of these slips of paper to the king under the guise of a joke.

When Kaahumanu answered Vancouver's invitation—he said that he wished to present her with a few tokens of his esteem—he quickly discovered that she was as eager for a reconciliation as was Kamehameha. Having given her a few gifts, he then proposed that he should send one to the king, and made a show of wrapping up the piece of paper in tapa and sending it ashore with a message to the effect that, as he was presenting favors to his Hawaiian friends, he had not been "unmindful of his majesty." As it was intended, this provoked no end of delight among the ladies. While they were still in the cabin, Kamehameha came aboard saying in loud tones before he entered that he had come to thank the captain personally for the great generosity he had shown and for his thoughtfulness on this occasion. The women were convulsed with laughter —all but Kaahumanu, who, at the sound of the king's voice, appeared "agitated." When he stepped into the cabin, he, too, lost his vivacious manner and at the sight of her attempted to withdraw. Vancouver, however, was stationed near the door and intercepting him led him forward and quickly joined his hand with the queen's. They said not a word for a moment and then at once fell into each other's arms, murmuring endearments, with tears rolling down their brown cheeks. The whole company showed such sympathy and pleasure at this reunion that Vancouver could not but feel well satisfied with himself. His pleased composure suffered a shock, however, when Kaahumanu insisted that he see her ashore and make sure she was well treated; indeed, she made him elicit a promise from the king that he would not beat her.

Traders in recent years had been taking advantage of the innocent Hawaiians—the phrase was then being born that they "hung their consciences on the Horn." The most serious offense was in giving defective firearms in trade. Not only were the guns worthless, but sea coal and charcoal were mixed with the powder to "water" it. While Vancouver was at Kealakekua a young chief, firing a defective gun, had lost several fingers of his left hand and the whole of his right arm up to the elbow; but for the work of the ships' surgeons, the Hawaiian might have died from the many wounds. This state of affairs gave Vancouver a good point in example of the advantages to the Hawaiians in being under the protection of the British crown. The men in Kamehameha's government understood by now that there were many nations in the world greater than their own—many maritime powers who might be expected to take advantage of Hawaii's position in the Pacific trade routes and of her natural wealth. Of these nations the Hawaiians preferred the British who had not only been their first contact with the outer world but reasonably consistent friends. The matter had undoubtedly come to a head, and it was understood that a conclave of chiefs would meet before Vancouver's departure to give him their decision as to whether they would accept Britain's protection or continue on as independent. Many of the chiefs were already at Kealake-kua.

The final assembly was delayed by the absence of two of the kingdom's foremost chiefs, the twins Kamanawa and Kameeiamoku. The former, as governor of Hilo, was unable to leave that province as its government was in a somewhat troubled state. As for Kameeiamoku, Vancouver had long considered him a scoundrel for his piracy of the *Fair American*, and had refused, in the past, to deal with him at all. Kameeiamoku being a ranking and influential chief, this disfavor had been injurious to him and he had been more or less exiled to Kohala, the province of which he was governor. On Vancouver's arrival he had withdrawn his court into one of the secluded valleys in the Hamakua cliff region. The Englishman well knew the effect of this special quarantine, and now he was in a difficult spot for it was imperative that Kameeiamoku be at the congress of chiefs. But with his usual ingenuity he bethought himself of a loophole; he had long preached to the Hawaiians the maxim of forgiving one's enemies; and now he would set the example by pardoning Kameeia-moku and inviting him to visit the ships at Kealakekua.

The recalcitrant chief was slow in coming. Not that he was uneager for a return to grace, but Vancouver's gesture struck him as so extraordinary that he could scarcely believe it and insisted on consulting the omens at each temple he passed on his way from Hamakua. The omens were progressively favorable, and at last he arrived—at the head of a fleet of canoes bearing some thousand retainers (Kamehameha told Vancouver that Kameeiamoku always traveled in such style).

The captain was at heart a little self-righteous and, despite his public magnanimity, he privately decided from the very first that he disliked Kameeiamoku's looks. The fellow was a scoundrel and, damn his eyes, he looked like one! After the introduction, Kameeiamoku made profuse apology for the offense which had been held against him, and that he had some provocation in it was testified by others of the chiefs; but, of course, no provocation justifies the murdering of strangers. Still, Vancouver was true to his word and reiterated the public pardon. Greatly relieved, the chiefs joined in with unusually high spirits at the party which the ships' officers threw that evening in the encampment. Kameeiamoku was made the butt of many a jest, for his period of exile had denied him the advantage of fraternizing with foreigners and his table manners were fierce. Put out of countenance by the ribbing he received, he decided to make up for his shortcomings by proving to the other chiefs that he could take drink for drink with them. Unfortunately it was a pathetic boast. Vancouver pointed out to him that the other chiefs were used to spirits and could take a good deal to drink without ill effect, but the admonitions fell on deaf ears. Kameeiamoku had a bottle of rum set before him and worked on it assiduously. All of a sudden he fell forward across the table. Retainers rushed forward to carry him out, and members of his own guard entered the tent, menacingly fingering their daggers. With his tongue lolling about in his mouth, Kameeiamoku was borne away making ferocious faces at Vancouver and muttering that he had been poisoned. The other chiefs grew uneasy; he looked convincingly poisoned. But the occasion was saved by Kamehameha who laughed uproariously, slapping his leg and rocking back and forth with enjoyment. Though a temperate man himself, he knew well enough the cause of Kameeiamoku's distress. Seeing the chief's bodyguard hesitating at the entrance and scowling at the company, he reached for Kameeiamoku's bottle and with great relish took a pull at it to demonstrate to everyone that there was no poison in it. Then he laughed again and explained that Kameeiamoku's indisposition was nothing that a little hot water could not fix. The treatment was applied, the evil spirits exorcised, and soon the chief was able to return to the party, apparently none the worse for his experience. But these had been touchy moments and the incident one out of which disaster might have rolled tumultuously; Vancouver thanked Lady Luck and fervently blessed Kamehameha.

The chiefs' congress had brought crowds of people to Kealakekua. Both villages were hives of humanity. There was a festival spirit in the air and smiling faces everywhere. As a special dispensation, Kamehameha arranged for a traditional hula to be presented at the near-by village of Keei. The *makahiki* season had ended and hence such entertainment was a breach of custom, but the occasion seemed to warrant it.

Vancouver arrived with the king and queen at about four in the afternoon and the chiefs who were in charge of the arrangements greeted the captain hilariously, with much joking over his having arrived at so unfashionable an hour—the performance would not start for some time yet. However, the Englishman had no cause to regret his early arrival for he was invited into the ladies' dressing room and allowed to observe the elaborate preparations. Kamehameha, "who was considered a profound critic," was frequently appealed to by the performers to make suggestions for the improvement of the costumes. They wore the *pa-u* (skirt) of tapa, many layers bound tightly around the waist and so plaited as to resemble, according to Vancouver, a "hoop petticoat"; in the arranging of the folds, the king took an active interest. In this instance, very little jewelry was worn; around one ankle, each lady wore a wreath of fragrant *maile*, and over her neck and shoulders a mantle of ti-leaves. The king and queen could not stay for the performance as it was against the religious custom. Kaahumanu was very reluctant to withdraw as she was herself an accomplished dancer and loved these entertainments. As soon as the royal pair had retired, the audience began to arrive. Crowds lined the village square fifteen and twenty deep, but whenever a ranking chiefess arrived a passage was quickly made for her to proceed to her place near the stage where mats were laid out; the chiefs, however, received no such courtesy and had to make their ways through the crowd as best they could.

There was some delay in the starting of the perform-ance. The audience began to call out, "*Hula! . . . hula! . . . po-elieli!*" ("Dance . . . dance . . . before it is too dark!"). After a few minutes the stage manager, who was one of the courtiers, came forward and apologized with a witty speech that caused laughter and a return of good spirits. The musicians then appeared—five men, each of whom stood holding a polished spear in his left hand and a short piece of wood in the other with which he drummed on the spear while chanting; each spear was "tuned" and the rhythms of the drumming were spirited and complex. Then the dancers, all ladies of the court, came out on the stage. The performance was dedicated to the sacred queen, Keopuolani, and, though she was not present, at the mention of her name everyone in the audi-ence, as a sign of respect, removed all ornaments above the waist. The dance lasted for an hour and was divided into four different tempos, combining serious pantomime to poems of praise with gay and abandoned songs of love and high spirits. Just as the heavens were awash with the brilliant colors of the sunset, the hula ended, and the audience, breaking up in good order, set out to walk the pebbled road back to Kealakekua.

In the evening Vancouver arranged a fireworks display. Kamehameha set off the first two rockets himself, but the other chiefs were not so eager in the matter. The display ended with the sending up of Bengal lights which hung lazily in the sky, lighting up the whole countryside; Vancouver announced that these were to light the villagers to their homes.

The squadron had already stayed on longer than anticipated and the captain was anxious to sail, but he had still received no satisfactory answer to his proposal for the island's cession to Great Britain. The chiefs appeared to be undecided. Mr. Menzies, the naturalist, had taken an expedition to climb Mauna Loa and as he had not yet returned, it gave Vancouver time to press his suit. On Sunday, February 23, 1794, there commenced a two-day tabu, and during this time the captain was invited to the *heiau* where, in the company of the priests, the matter was discussed in great detail. All of the chiefs had questions to ask relative to their exact status under the British crown, and the captain was able to answer these questions satisfactorily. The matter was finally decided then, and on Tuesday a formal conclave was held aboard the *Discovery*. The chiefs present were Keliimaikai, Kalaimamahu, Keeaumoku, Keaweaheula, Kaiana (by special permission), Kameeiamoku, and Kalaiuwohi. Kamehameha opened the meeting with a quiet, well-considered speech about the advantages of being under British protection, of being *kanaka no Beretani* (men of Britain); several of the chiefs proposed that once the matter was settled they should do a little empire-building for King George themselves . . . by taking Maui. The cession was then announced to the assembled people on shore and was received with good spirit.

Lieutenant Peter Puget, commander of the *Chatham*, went ashore, displayed the colors and took possession in the name of King George. A salute was fired by the ships. In Kamehameha's residence a copper plate was placed prominently; its inscription read:

On the 25th of February, 1794, Tamaahmaah, king of Owhyhee, in council with the principal chiefs of the island assembled on board His Britannic Majesty's sloop *Discovery* in Karakakooa Bay, and in the presence of George Vancouver, commander of said sloop; Lieutenant Peter Puget, commander of his said Majesty's armed tender the *Chatham;* and other officers of the *Dis-*

covery; after due consideration, unanimously ceded the said island of Owhyhee to His Britannic Majesty, and acknowledged themselves to be subjects of Great Britain.

Vancouver's comment on this incident—". . . whether this addition to the empire will ever be of any importance to Great Britain and whether the surrender of the islands will ever be attended with any additional happiness to its people, time alone must determine." But the affair had lost luster by the time the squadron reached England; Hawaii seemed far away and not very significant. So far as is known, the British government never officially recognized this new colony until many years later when the legality of the cession no longer had force.

Vancouver sailed up the coast to Kawaihae, with the king and queen and several of the chiefs aboard. At a farewell dinner, the Hawaiians were served with beef and mutton, that they might know the value of the gifts of cattle and sheep which Vancouver had presented them. Mutton was the favorite, Kamehameha casting the deciding vote.

On midnight, March 7, the king and queen, and Young and Davis, who had stayed aboard until the last possible moment, bade Vancouver a tearful farewell.

KAMEHAMEHA I

THE CONQUEROR

WAS KAMEHAMEHA THE NATURAL SON OF HIS greatest enemy, Kahekili? Such was the rumor, and it was never laid. Kamehameha's mother had visited at Kahekili's court before the prince was born; she was not an unattractive woman and Kahekili was an impulsive man. Furthermore, two of Kamehameha's chancellors were half brothers of this warrior king of the central islands: the twins Kameeiamoku and Kamanawa. It was said that Kahekili had sent them to the young prince of Hawaii with orders that they should watch over and be loyal to him. This loyalty was never questioned.

In the month of July, 1794, Kahekili lay dead in the stillness of a grove of *kou* trees near the sunny, ivory sands of Waikiki. His had been a full lifetime. His adventuring shadow had fallen across nearly every island event of importance in the last fifty years. Word of his death reached Kamehameha and he released the twin chiefs to allow them to perform last services for Kahekili. Sailing to Oahu, they sought his body and returned with it to Hawaii to entomb it in the recesses of a sea-hidden cave not far from Kailua. And so Hawaii gave eternal refuge to a man who had been her implacable enemy in his lifetime.

In his last years Kahekili had allowed his brother Kaeo, of Kauai, to govern most of the kingdom for him; he had seen too many battles—a man wanted peace in his old age. His son, Kalanikupule—who had been driven from Kauai by Kamehameha—governed Oahu. With his father dead Kupule felt that the rule of Maui, Oahu and the other smaller islands should fall to him;—his uncle Kaeo had served his term and now should return to Kauai. Kaeo planned to do just that—not because he intended to relinquish the kingdom to Kupule, but because he was homesick for his native island. Uncle and nephew, with their distinct opinions, met on Oahu. After a preliminary skirmish, matters seemed to be settled amicably—in favor of Kaeo. However, just as he was about to sail for Kauai, he discovered traces of defection among his troops, and, acting on the theory that warfare is the sovereign remedy for domestic ills, he suddenly attacked his vigorous young nephew.

Kupule, however, did not care to lend himself to such

a solution of his uncle's personal difficulties. Securing arms and ammunition—as well as a small group of volunteer fighters—from two English ships which then lay in Honolulu harbor, he flung himself against his uncle's army, and Kaeo fell before the onslaught.

Victory inspired Kupule to a prodigal sense of his own glory.[1] With the aid of the British ships he had, in the simplest of maneuvers, acquired nominal mastery over every island in the group with the exception of Hawaii. Why should he not strike at Kamehameha now while the gods were with him, and bring the whole archipelago under his control? But the action called for support. His first move was a carefully worked out plot to capture the two English ships. And he was successful.[2] On New Year's Day, 1795, King Kalanikupule found himself in command of the strongest fleet in the islands.

By the 12th of January he was ready to sail for Hawaii. But all the Englishmen aboard the two vessels had not been killed; two of the officers who had been spared effected a surprise mutiny, and with the aid of some of their sailors, recaptured the ships with the king and his

---

[1] The Englishmen had enjoyed their part in the battle so much that they celebrated the victory by firing off the great guns of their two ships. Through an oversight, one of the guns was loaded with shot and aimed squarely at a near-by American vessel, the *Lady Washington;* the charge passed cleanly through this vessel, mortally removing the captain and several of his officers who had been dining with him.

[2] The *Lady Washington* had left for Canton.

queen aboard. Quickly they set sail, taking the chagrined royalty with them. But they were sportsmen, these Englishmen, after a day or two, when they felt that Kupule had learned his lesson, they returned and, standing several miles off Waikiki, tumbled the unhappy monarch and his queen into a canoe, leaving them to paddle home. Then they sailed for Hawaii and sent letters to Young and Davis informing them of the recent turn of events.

It was undoubtedly Kamehameha's great opportunity. The men and arms which he had been assembling for so long were ready at a moment's notice. Immediately, his fleet put to sea on its most momentous adventure. Maui and Lanai, left at this crucial moment without governors, fell easily, and even supplied further addition to Kamehameha's troops. When he landed at Waikiki, his army, encamped along the shore, extended for nearly seven miles—from Waikiki to Waialae.

Kalanikupule's strategy was to retreat into the natural fortress of Nuuanu valley. There, surprisingly, he was joined by Kaiana, against whom feeling had arisen among the Hawaii warriors to such a point that he knew his only hope of repairing his fortunes lay in going over to the other side on the chance that his knowledge of European methods of warfare and his little company of well-trained followers might turn the tide of battle in favor of Oahu. But Kamehameha's men were not the Hawaiian warriors of a decade ago. They too had arms and Europeans to handle their cannon. They had learned to drill from Vancouver's marines, and Kamehameha himself was a master tactician.

The valley of Nuuanu, a carpet of green walled in by sheer and towering cliffs, slopes gently upward, ever narrowing, to a small deep cleft in the ridge of a long range of mountains; through this cleft, trade winds funnel with such violence that on some days a man can scarce stand against them. So long have these winds hammered against the mountain barriers that, with the aid of rains, they have cut away the buttressing spurs and ridges and made of the windward mountains a sheer precipice, striated and forbidding.

In sunlight and green shadow, Kamehameha's mighty army marched slowly up the valley of Nuuanu, driving all resistance before it. The men of Oahu, leaving their defenses to retreat to others farther up, knew that they could only go so far; at the bottleneck the earth dropped away, and the narrow trail down the cliff was not made for a retreating army. Relentlessly Kamehameha pushed on. His cannon, manned by Young and Davis, took dreadful toll in the scrambling masses of brown warriors. On and on. Panic ran through the Oahu ranks, and men were seen scrambling up the steep red walls of the narrowing ridges. Just before the fatal cleft was reached, Kaiana mustered enough brave men together to make a last stand. If his character was devious, lack of courage was not one of his weak points; tall and firm he stood, firing his musket with telling effect until a well-aimed shot by John Young brought him down. And now the first drops of a terrible cataract began pouring over the precipice, quickly increasing into a torrent of twisting and screaming bodies plunging to the rocks below. Kamehameha drove on to the very edge, the wind whipping his splendid cloak out behind him as he bent his body into it to steady himself while observing the chaos; his heavy round face was melancholy, his downward-slanting eyes squinted to mere slits against the glare of sunlight from the milky-green sea beyond.

Kalanikupule escaped. But his was a starving, hunted life among the dripping vines and muddy recesses of the mountain tops. Eventually he was captured and sacrificed to Kukailimoku that his lands might thus be symbolically absorbed by Kamehameha.

Now only Kauai remained to be conquered. And yet Kamehameha, with all the resources now at his command, with a creditable fleet a-building, with more and more arms pouring into his strongholds, with more and more white men to aid and advise him, never did succeed in actually conquering Kauai. Always something intervened. His first attempt, the year after the battle of Nuuanu, was thwarted by heavy seas in the channel; his fleet had to turn back. Then there was a revolt on Hawaii, led by Kaiana's brother; after putting this down, he remained on Hawaii until 1802, occupied with progressively complicated affairs of government. In 1803—having sent the king of Kauai a message demanding his submission and receiving no answer—he prepared for another attack, but this time a plague brought by a foreign ship struck the island of Oahu taking a dreadful toll of common people and warriors alike. Not until 1810 was the Kauai problem finally solved—and then only through the mediation of an American sea captain who contrived a meeting between the Kauai king and Kamehameha at which Kauai was made a suzerain state.[3]

In the absence of Kamehameha between 1802 and 1812, John Young governed the island of Hawaii. He had married the daughter of Keliimaikai, Kamehameha's brother, and was considered a ranking chief of the realm. By 1802 he was sixty years old.

Kamehameha had fulfilled his destiny. Attention turns now from internecine warfare to the increasingly complicated relations with the outer world. In these relations Hawaii was not like other kingdoms; her diplomacy was largely personal, deriving much of its character from the

[3] A plot to kill the king of Kauai at this meeting was exposed by Isaac Davis. The thwarted plotters poisoned Davis.

extraordinary king and relying, for the rest, on the scanty wisdom—and inspired intuition—of the counselors he gathered round him.

On the surface, Kamehameha was a musical comedy king, but none will gainsay him the tribute of being one of the greatest natural leaders that ever lived. And why should he not have been a musical comedy king on the surface? He lived in a time and in a place that were made for such frivolity, and he was thoroughly Hawaiian in that he delighted in the pleasant side of human relationships, delighted in show, delighted in the sheer exuberance of living in a world of continuous wonder and entertainment. When a foreign captain invited the king and queen to spend the night aboard his vessel, the two of them would keep him awake till dawn with their whispering and giggling; a ship's cabin, a Westerner's uncomfortable way of living, struck them as amusing. The king was forever changing his costume; after appearing in the uniform of a captain in the British navy, he might change to a simple *malo*. Why not? He had been formal, now he would be comfortable. His actions and attitudes were the result of the simplest logic, unhampered by foreign conventions.

Most of the foreigners who visited Hawaii during Kamehameha's reign were honestly impressed with him; only an unimaginative few found him absurd. Comparably, most of the foreigners with whom the king had any dealing were fairly honest; only a few—and they could not be called unimaginative—were outright scoundrels. Often the riffraff who jumped ship in Hawaii turned out to be decent citizens; here they were given a chance at domestic happiness and afforded equal opportunity.

Early in the year 1818 a mysterious ship put in at Kealakekua. She bore an unfamiliar flag, but had the name *Victory* painted on her stern. The crew was a blackguardly lot, speaking Spanish for the most part, except for the captain who was an Englishman named Turner. No mention was made of the purpose of the voyage. According to the king's custom they were liberally provided with foodstuffs, and for these they paid lavishly both in rum and in gold and silver ornaments which were recognized by some of the Europeans as being accouterments of a Roman Catholic church. The sailors, who spent most of their time in drunken revelry, hinted that they were pirates. When Turner became uneasy at their actions, he could not persuade them to leave. Providentally a Chilean warship arrived on the scene and took the *Victory* into her custody, but the crew managed to escape. The captain of the warship told Kamehameha that these men had pillaged a coastal town and stripped its churches during the revolution in Chile and Peru. The king at once ordered soldiers to bring in the pirates and all but Turner and the first mate were captured; likewise most of the stolen ornaments were recovered. Turner managed to make good his escape, but the mate was captured on the island of Kauai and promptly hanged.

Liquor was, of course, a source of frequent trouble in the early days. Kamehameha himself was temperate, but not all the Hawaiians were as wise. The heir apparent, Prince Liholiho, was particularly fond of the bottle. But for some reason it was usually the ladies who drank the most; none of the chiefs minded this, as they thought the attendant antics amusing to watch. (The ladies also were the foremost devotees of the weed, and made quite a ceremony of pipe smoking.) Most of the liquor was obtained in trade from visiting ships, but in time a small amount of distilling was done in the islands. The first in the business were some convicts who had escaped to Hawaii from the penal colony at Botany Bay in Australia; they were quick to perceive the advantage of the sugar cane which flourished in the islands.

The first article of trade the Hawaiians had to offer was food, but after a time the commercially minded captains discovered that sandalwood grew in abundance in Hawaii's forests, a commodity which commanded high prices in China. A local sandalwood industry sprang up with such vitality that in half a century it had exhausted itself. But for a time, the Hawaiian kings could call themselves truly wealthy. Kamehameha, however, discovered that he could not dispense with the middleman. In 1817 he purchased a brig which he named the *Kaahumanu;* he had it fitted out, loaded with sandalwood, and sent it to China under a hired captain. The vessel returned with East Indian rum, and bales of silk, but it was estimated that the king had lost some three thousand dollars by the transaction. On going over the accounts with his captain, Kamehameha was puzzled by a charge of one dollar a foot for pilotage in and out of the Chinese harbors; when the captain explained this matter to him, the king, always quick to learn, instructed his own pilots to charge the same price.

As his old counselors died, Kamehameha replaced them with young chiefs, most of them sons of his loyal old friends. The most important of these was Kalanimoku whose name came in after years to be synonymous with the title of prime minister. The Europeans gave him the affectionate nickname of Billy Pitt, or Mr. Pitt, after the great English prime minister. Another prominent figure of Kamehameha's later years was his brother-in-law, Kuakini, a brother of Kaahumanu; he started his official career as captain of the ordnance on Oahu, and later became governor of Kona—his name among the foreigners was John Adams, after the American president.

That Kamehameha considered himself a subject of

Great Britain is seen in a letter which he addressed to George III in the year 1810. But Britain did not take the Hawaiian king very seriously and gradually all mention of this suzerainty died out in the islands. During the War of 1812 some Americans jokingly pointed out the British flag which was floating over Kamehameha's palace and remarked that they ought to consider Hawaii as enemy territory and act accordingly. The king, when this matter was explained to him, said that he had any number of flags in his possession, and only flew this one because he liked its color; but he immediately had it taken down, and, shortly thereafter, had a Hawaiian flag designed.

Among the western powers interested in the development of the Pacific areas Russia was one of the most enterprising. The fur resources and fisheries of the North Pacific had first been discovered as far back as 1741 by the Russian navigator Bering. Imperial charter had been given to a company known as the Russian American Company whose base was at New Archangel (Sitka) in Norfolk Sound. In this severe climate the necessities of living were scarce and as a consequence the Russians drifted further south, as far, even, as California where they built a fort [4] just north of San Francisco. It was inevitable that they should sooner or later realize the advantages of Hawaii. After preliminary intercourse, Kamehameha in 1805

[4] Fort Ross.

made known to Alexander Baranov, the governor of the Russian company, that he would "gladly send a ship every year with swine, salt, batatas, and other articles of food, if (the Russians) would in exchange let him have sea-otter skins at a fair price"; however, his offer was not taken up, although the Russians continued to pay occasional visits to the islands.

In 1815 a cargo ship of the Russian company was wrecked on Kauai, and Baranov sent a German doctor named Georg Anton Scheffer to recover the goods and possibly establish some sort of trading post in the islands. On first arriving Scheffer presented himself to Kamehameha at Kailua as a naturalist wishing to do research in the islands, but after a time he made known his real errand and obtained an order from Kamehameha requiring Kaumualii, king of Kauai, to deliver up the goods as requested.

The German was a crafty operator. In 1816, after a year of exploring through the islands, he was reinforced by Russian ships belonging to the Alaska company and made his appearance on Kauai. Obviously the lost cargo was of no great moment. He succeeded in worming his way into the confidence of the king and, playing on Kaumualii's secret desire to be independent of Kamehameha, set himself up as virtual master of the island; the guileless king was even persuaded to sign agreements with the Russian American company and put his island, as well as half the island of Oahu, under the sovereignty of the Imperial Russian government. Scheffer went to Honolulu and built a blockhouse, raised the Russian flag, and laid out the ground plan of a fort. But the natives of Honolulu disliked him and were offended by his careless blasphemy of the places they held sacred. Kamehameha, receiving word of this, sent word to the Russians ordering them to leave the island. Scheffer was wise enough to abandon Oahu (shortly after his departure the fort he designed was completed under the direction of John Young). The German doctor returned to Kauai, where he was firmly entrenched, and built a fort overlooking Hanalei Bay on the windward shore, and later one overlooking Waimea Bay on the leeward. Eventually, under pressure of Americans who were interested in the sandalwood trade and annoyed at the high-handed doings of Scheffer, Kaumalii was persuaded, spurred by the orders of Kamehameha, to oust the doctor from Kauai, and in 1819 the islands saw the last of him.

Meanwhile, in 1816, a Russian naval expedition under the command of Lieutenant Otto von Kotzebue arrived in Hawaii from California. By courtesy he had with him a passenger, a colorful adventurer named Elliot de Castro. Kotzebue gives Elliot's biography thus: "Impelled by a desire to become suddenly rich, he had tried his fortune

in all parts of the world; but as soon as he had acquired
a little fortune, he lost it again by ill-judged speculations,
and was even once imprisoned in Buenos Aires and afterward in California. I was very much pleased on hearing
that Mr. Elliot had, two years before, resided some time
in the Sandwich Islands, as physician and chief favorite
of the king Kamehameha. The king had made him a present of much land (which he still considered his property)
and he succeeded very well; but still striving at wealth,
the hope of gain induced him to go to Sitka to Mr. Baranov where he expected to grow suddenly rich; and in
consequence of which he got acquainted with the prison
of California. . . . Mr. Elliot possesses a real knowledge
of medicine, and was for several years surgeon of the
hospital at Rio de Janeiro."

When the vessel arrived at Kawaihae, the knowing Mr.
Elliot recommended the Hawaiian Kualelo ("Jack Ingraham") as a pilot. Learning that it was a Russian ship he
was to pilot, Kualelo became uneasy but Elliot allayed his
fears and he guided the ship to Kailua. However, the
word had been passed and Kamehameha, believing the
ship to be hostile, had ordered soldiers stationed all along
the coast.

Elliot (who indeed seemed to have influence with the
king) finally persuaded him that the expedition was a
friendly one and Kamehameha ordered the vigil relaxed

and sent a chief to stay aboard while the vessel was at Kailua. He himself was not there for the arrival, being off fishing for *aku*,[5] but Kotzebue was bade welcome by the governor Kuakini and other men of rank. He was impressed both by the chiefs' "Herculean figures" and their costume which he described as consisting merely "of a black frock (coat) and a white hat." Kamehameha arrived soon after and greeted the Russians as they landed on shore.

Kotzebue wrote, "I now stood at the side of the celebrated Kamehameha who had attracted the attention of all Europe and who inspired me with the greatest confidence by his unreserved and friendly behavior." At the grass palace, European chairs were brought forth and the Russians made comfortable. The commander was impressed by the fact that though the king had European houses, he preferred his native one. "He imitates everything he knows to be useful and tries to introduce it among his people; palaces built of stone appeared to him superfluous, as the straw houses are convenient, and as he only wishes to increase the *happiness* and not the *wants* of his subjects."

The clothes worn by the Hawaiians usually called forth comment from the European visitors. Many of the villagers would wear only one article of a costume, suppos-

[5] *Aku:* bonito.

ing the hot European clothes to be merely decoration and contenting themselves with a mild show at no sacrifice to comfort. On state occasions, however, the chiefs would dress up. The garb which Kotzebue described as being worn by Kuakini seemed to be "the thing" among the *alii* at that time. One chief was so large that the waist of his frock coat was far up his back, the buttons would not button in front, and he suffered hotly and acutely, but fashion, seemingly, would not allow its removal.

Through an interpreter, Kamehameha addressed Kotzebue thus: "I learn that you are the commander of a ship of war and are engaged in a voyage similar to those of Cook and Vancouver, and consequently do not engage in trade. It is therefore my intention not to carry on trade with you, but to provide you without obligation with everything my islands produce. This affair is now settled and no further mention may be made of it."

The Russian attempted to voice his thanks, but the king silenced him and went on, "I shall now beg of you to inform me whether it is with the consent of your emperor that his subjects begin to disturb me in my old age? Since Kamehameha has been king of these islands, no European has had cause to complain of having suffered injustice here. I have made my islands an asylum for all nations, and honestly supplied with provisions every ship that desired them. Some time ago there came from the American settlement of Sitka some Russians, a nation with whom I never had any intercourse before. They were kindly received and supplied with everything necessary, but they have ill rewarded me for they behaved in a hostile manner to my subjects on the island of Oahu, and threatened us with ships of war which were to conquer these islands. But this shall not happen so long as Kamehameha lives! A Russian physician of the name of Scheffer who came here some months ago pretended that he had been sent by the Emperor Alexander to botanize my islands. As I had heard much good of the Emperor Alexander and was particularly pleased with his bravery, I not only permitted Scheffer to botanize, but also promised him every assistance, made him a present of a piece of land and servants, so that he might never want for provisions. In short, I tried to make his stay as agreeable as possible, and to refuse none of his demands. But what was the consequence of my hospitality? Even before he left this island he repaid my kindness with ingratitude which I bore patiently. Upon this, according to his own desire he traveled from one island to another and at last settled on the fruitful island of Oahu where he proved himself to be my most inveterate enemy, destroying our sanctuary—the *heiau*—and exciting against me on the island of Kauai, King Kaumualii, who had submitted to my power years before. Scheffer is there at this very moment and threatens my islands."

Kotzebue: "I assure your Majesty that the bad conduct of the Russians here must not be ascribed to the will of the Emperor who has never commanded his subjects to do an unjust act. But the extent of the empire is such that he is prevented from being immediately informed of bad actions, which, however, never remain unpunished when they come to his knowledge."

This explanation seemed to satisfy the king whose mood now changed from one of seriousness to one of light-hearted gaiety. He conversed with Kotzebue for some time regarding the state of the world and asked penetrating questions regarding conditions in Russia. He spoke so quickly that the interpreter was not always able to catch the shades of meaning, and evidently he spoke wittily for the courtiers were continually laughing at his remarks, delivered with arch good humor.

The Russian paid a visit to Kaahumanu whom he found in company with several other queens, all exceedingly stout, smoking a pipe which they passed around among themselves. Kotzebue declined it when it was offered him, but accepted a slice of watermelon. He found the ladies cheerful, but could not believe that they had ever been beautiful. One of Kamehameha's daughters was present at the interview. She was rather plain, but pleasant-looking, and was attended by three little boys, one of whom held a silk umbrella over her head while the other two drove away the flies by means of red feather *kahilis*.

The king entertained the officers at dinner that night in a house near the *heiau*. The table was set in European fashion, and each guest had a servant standing behind him with a *kahili* to wave away the flies; these attendants were quick to observe when a wine glass was empty and to fill it from a bottle of very good vintage. The Hawaiians did not join in the dinner as the food was not properly consecrated; the king and a few ranking chiefs did, however, sit at the table and ply their guests and themselves with wine. After healths were drunk to all of the guests, Kamehameha asked that a health be drunk to Emperor Alexander in a bumper. This done, one of the chiefs presented Kotzebue with a lei of feathers which Kamehameha himself had worn on ceremonial occasions. Then the affable monarch made a little speech.

"I have heard that your emperor is a great hero," he said, "and I love him for it, for I am one myself! And I send him this lei as a testimony of my regard."

After the dinner was over, Kamehameha would have it that the sailors who had rowed the Russian officers ashore sit down in their places and enjoy a feast of the same kind. The simple Russian tars were overawed by the splendor.

In the soft dusk then, the king led his guests to the *heiau* and pointed out the feathered, basket-work figures which were hung round with leis and before which offerings were heaped. One of the figures he embraced, and, turning to Kotzebue, said, "These are our gods whom I worship. Whether I do right or wrong I do not know, but I follow my faith, which cannot be wicked as it commands me never to do ill." After this he went alone into the *Hale Mana* where he remained a few minutes in silent devotion. As soon as he emerged he led the way to his own eating house, remarking, "I have seen how the Russians eat—now you may satisfy your curiosity and see how Kamehameha eats!" He sat down to a hearty meal while the Russians made themselves comfortable on the luxurious piles of *lauhala* mats. Dipping a finger into a calabash brimming with *poi* the king turned to Kotzebue and remarked, smiling, "This is the custom of my country and I will not depart from it."

Well might the Russian have been impressed for he caught Kamehameha in one of his best moods and saw the true man, the Hawaiian, who had survived the impact of more than thirty years of foreigners bringing new customs and new ideas. As a token of gratitude, Kotzebue gave the king two eight-pound brass mortars engraved with the name of his ship, the *Rurick*. In addition he presented him with a quarter of a pipe of wine [6] and some apples which had been brought from California; the apples were quite new to the Hawaiians and the *alii* tasted them eagerly being careful to preserve the pips that they might be planted.

According to the custom, Kotzebue had with him on his expedition an excellent painter, a man named Choris. His work was much admired by the Hawaiians, by the king himself, but though Kotzebue entreated, the latter would not for a long time allow Choris to limn him. It was nothing but modesty—surprisingly enough—on Kamehameha's part, and when finally he was persuaded to sit for a picture (because, said Kotzebue, the Emperor Alexander would surely want one), he squirmed and twisted and made faces at the painter in an agony of embarrassment. Nonetheless, Choris managed to catch a fine likeness, one so good, indeed, that he later made copies of it.

On leaving the islands, Kotzebue made no move toward his compatriots on the island of Kauai. Had he done so he might better have shown his gratitude for Kamehameha's hospitality.

Another Russian naval vessel, under Captain Golovnin, visited Hawaii the next year. Golovnin found Elliot de Castro, who had evidently given up hope of becoming "suddenly rich," acting as Hawaii's Minister for Foreign

[6] A pipe is approximately 105 gallons.

Affairs; but for his somewhat quixotic foibles, Elliot was an agreeable and intelligent man, and careful to obey all the Hawaiian tabus. Kamehameha was then (1818) living in Kailua. He greeted the Russian by shaking hands with him and saying in English, "How do you do," followed by "Aloha!" He was dressed, says Golovnin, "simply, in green velvet trousers, a white shirt, a silk handkerchief around his neck, a coffee brown vest, white stockings and shoes and a round felt hat." As with Kotzebue, the old king showed himself a courteous host.

While in the islands, Golovnin was told of an incident, illustrative of Kamehameha's integrity. A British ship had run aground off the island of Oahu. In her cargo were ninety ingots of copper, each weighing nearly 150 pounds, and these had been cast over to lighten her. The ship's crew was unable to salvage them. When, on the advice of his counselors, Kamehameha sent divers for the copper, he inquired as to the European custom in such matters. On learning that it was usual for the salvagers to take one-eighth of what they recovered, he would take no more than that, even though he might easily have claimed the lot. The rest of the ingots were returned to the captain of the vessel.

Another incident, this on board Golovnin's ship, illustrates the childish side of the king's nature. Noticing an attractive silk handkerchief worn by one of the Russians, a Baron Wrangel, Kamehameha removed it and was about to ask for it when Elliot de Castro stepped in and told the king he was being rude. Piqued at this, the old Hawaiian rolled the handkerchief up into a little ball, flung it at the baron, and remained sullen for some time thereafter.

Golovnin wrote of Kamehameha: "He is still strong, active, temperate and sober. We can see in him a combination of childishness and ripe judgment. Some of his acts would do credit to a more enlightened ruler. His honesty and love of justice have been shown in numerous cases.

"The petty faults which we may find in the old king will not obscure his great merits. He will always be considered an enlightener and reformer of his people. One fact which shows his good sense is this: None of the foreigners visiting his country enjoy any exclusive privileges, but all can trade with his subjects with equal freedom. Europeans are not allowed to own land. They receive it on condition that after death it shall be returned to the king, and during their lifetime it is not transferable from one to another."

LIHOLIHO

KAMEHAMEHA II

THE SUN WAS DOWN BEYOND THE HORIZON. ITS GO-
ing had flushed to a passionate brightness the
vaporous clouds floating in the distance against a
pale green sky. Kailua was enveloped in twilight. But
where the torches usually flared to guide home late fishermen, there were no torches, and along the shore where
the people were wont to gather and discuss with gaiety
and laughter the affairs of the day, there were no people.
But sound there was—a sound that struck a chill in the
heart—the melancholy wailing of priests and women.

Kamehameha was dying.

The Spaniard, Marin, who had a knowledge of European medicine, had been summoned from Honolulu. And
from all parts of the realm came *kahuna* chiefs, learned in
Hawaii's ancient medical lore. But man was powerless to
help Kamehameha.

Hewahewa, his high priest, ordered the *heiau* of Keiki-

puipui ('Fat child') done over to reaffirm the mana of its
gods. But when the time came, the king was too weak to
be moved. He sent, instead, his son Liholiho to make his
prayers. The priests wanted human sacrifices, but the old
king said no—the men of the kingdom were now sacred
to Liholiho, their mana could no longer be absorbed by
Kamehameha.

When he had conquered the islands, Kamehameha had
assumed custody of the powerful gods of each kingdom
and province; one such god was the poison god of Molokai, who, among other things, was responsible for causing
swelling of the abdomen. A titular priest of this god might
be able to exorcise it and transmute its poison to elixir.
Such a priest had formerly healed the king of an illness.
Now he was sent for again, and when he arrived, he had
two houses built to the god on the terrace of Ahuena,
close by the king's dwelling. Kamehameha was carried
into each one of these houses in turn, that he might "get
life before the gods." But he grew weaker and weaker.
And now, after three days, he had been returned to his
own bed.

It was May 7, 1819. At ten o'clock he was carried to
the eating house, but was unable to take anything more
than a little *poi* and some water. The chiefs took him back
to his sleeping quarters. They knew there was no hope.
In the shadowy thatched chamber, faintly lit by a gutter-

ing lamp set on the pebbled floor, men of his family and the *alii* whom he had loved stood at the foot of his couch of mats. One of his brothers spoke softly:

"*O ka lani*, we are all here with you, your brothers, your prince and Olohana.[1] Lay upon us your last command."

The king murmured faintly, "*I mea aha?*" ("What is this?")

"*I hua na mokou*" ("That we may have the fruit of your experience").

Kamehameha smiled. Strength seemed to return to him for a few moments while he spoke.

"*E na wale no oukou i kuu pono!*" ("Enjoy peacefully the honest principles for which I have stood!") He looked toward Liholiho, and went on haltingly, "My son, I leave you lord of a nation which ought, if you are wise, to satisfy your ambition, but which you will lose if you attempt to aggrandize yourself. You may judge from the sacrifices I have made of my comfort what this inheritance which I bequeath to you has cost me. The *alii* who are standing here now have shared my trials and I am indebted to them for the greater part of the glory I have acquired. They will be faithful if you are just—their love for me is the assurance. But your inexperience may lead you astray and you must guide your actions by their coun-

---

[1] Olohana—John Young.

298

sel. Never be hasty in punishing a fault committed by foreigners in the islands—put up even with a second offense; only on the third should you endeavor to repel them. If you act according to the advice I give you, I shall receive with pride the sacrifices with which you may honor me and the offerings your love may bring. Aloha! Bear my aloha to my wives. Aloha, my friends!''

He sank back on the couch. John Young, the faithful Englishman, came forward and, with tears in his eyes, bent to kiss the wrinkled brown cheek. Then Hoapili [2] knelt beside him and whispered that his body would be well hidden.

Not knowing what they could do to ease him, the chiefs tried once more to give him food and carried him again to the eating house (it was supposed he would be defiled by eating in a room where he had lived with women), but he had fallen into a coma and they had to bring him back to his bed. Shortly after midnight Kamehameha's great spirit departed his body, *lawe aku la Hikapoloa* (taken by Hika-of-the-long-night), to join the heavenly company in the lost islands of the gods; these islands may sometimes be seen, glowing faintly red on the horizon, at sunrise or sunset.

[2] Hoapili—this chief, son of Kameeiamoku, had been given his name ("Comrade") by Kamehameha, and charged with the task of secreting the royal body after death.

According to the custom, Liholiho and his wives immediately left the vicinity of Kailua for the duration of the
public mourning, lest his royal person be contaminated by
the atmosphere of death. As soon as he had gone, the riot-
ing began. John Young, long familiar with the orgies
Hawaiians indulged in at the death of a beloved *alii*,
boarded up the doors and windows of his house, remarking, "If my children attend they will never again cross my
threshold." The villagers went stark mad: they tore off
their clothes, knocked out teeth, mutilated their flesh,
indulged in every sort of licentiousness, drank themselves
to insensibility. There was no conversation, no laughter,
no serenity anywhere;—only a macabre, physical grief.

During this period the priests performed ceremonies
over the body. Many of the *alii* offered themselves as
sacrifices, but the priests reminded them of the dying
king's words that the men were tabu to Liholiho. Once
the body was interred within the *heiau* for the process of
disintegration, Hoapili effected an entrance and, accompanied only by his man, Hoolulu, removed Kamehameha's
remains. It has been said that the burial place he chose
was the same cave wherein reposed the bones of Kameeiamoku, Kehekili, and other famous *alii*, a cave whose entrance was beneath the sea near Kailua; it was a likely
hiding place, as Hoapili was Kameeiamoku's son and might
have known the secret. However, Kamehameha's sons

never did. Kamehameha III at one time persuaded Hoo-lulu to show him the cave; they had started off together, but such a crowd followed that Hoolulu refused to go on, nor would he again yield to the king's urging. And so it is said, "Only the stars know the final resting place of Kamehameha."

Some time before his death Kamehameha had made formal appointment of Liholiho as his successor; he had also —despite the precedent—appointed a separate custodian of the god Kukailimoku, Liholiho's cousin Ke-'kua-o-ka-lani ('The spirit of heaven'). It appeared indeed that Kamehameha had cautiously ringed Liholiho around with potentially alternative leaders.

When the young king returned to Kailua, after perhaps a week, a conclave was held at the famous Kailua beach, stage of Umi's battle with the gods and Lono's single-handed conquest of the kingdom. It was the sunset hour. Along the shore and in the water, the common people stood; the chiefs were seated facing them, with Kaahumanu in a position of honor. When the heralds proclaimed the approach of the king, the crowds bowed down. Liholiho walked proudly into the company, very splendid in a red-and-gold English uniform with a yellow feather cape flung over one shoulder. He stopped before Kaahumanu.

The queen spoke, "*O ka lani*, I disclose the will of your

father. Look upon these *alii* and these fertile islands. They are yours. But we shall possess them together." Still another check to his power! Kamehameha had trusted the good judgment—and strong will—of his intelligent queen to keep his son from error. He had appointed her *kuhina nui*, which was, in effect, chief executive of the kingdom, although Liholiho was technically and ceremonially the highest power. That the young king accepted his father's judgment, unfair as it might have seemed, was indicative of his temperament in which there was a surprising amount of humility.

He was, at this time, twenty-two years old. Until but a few years before, he had lived in seclusion from the sociable and active court life that had been part of the education of former kings, neither had he ever had any civil or diplomatic duty to perform. His education had been at the hands of his mother, the sacred queen Keopuolani; through her he had inherited a tabu so exalted that Kamehameha, his father, had not been allowed to enter his house and had to address him through the doorway. Thus, it was as though the heir to the throne of England had studied solely for the Church and knew no other customs than those prescribed by the most formal of church etiquette. In recent years, however, he had partially made up for his sequestration by a somewhat violent indulgence in a wholly different way of life. He had turned the merry prince with a vengeance.

In appearance Liholiho was tall and heavy; because he was neither athlete nor fisherman, he was not frequently exposed to the burning sun and as a consequence his skin was somewhat lighter than his father's, being of a golden, rather than a copper, hue. He had thick, lustrous black hair which he wore longer than the old fashion which dictated that a man's hair should be shaved off in a line above his ears. His eyes were a dark, luminous brown, wide-set beneath a "noble brow." His lips were full and shaped, but not thick; sensitive rather than sensual. The only ugly feature was his nose which was quite long and flat. Although heavy, he was not corpulent, though the softness of his indolent flesh sometimes gave that impression; but he had the proud stance of a Hawaiian *alii*, straight back and lifted head with steady gaze, and when clad in one of his splendid uniforms was very prepossessing.

Liholiho assumed the throne at a time when the whole foundation of his centuries-old society was crumbling, at a time when confusion under the impact of a new civilization had distracted most of the chiefs in his kingdom. The government was in a precarious position. On the one hand there were those chiefs whose defeat by Kamehameha still rankled and who were anxious for a return

to power; on the other, there were chiefs, led by Kekua
—custodian of the war-god, who believed in overthrowing
Liholiho and killing, or driving out, all the Europeans in
the islands. Furthermore there was coming to a head a
tremendous undercurrent of dissatisfaction with the ancient tabu system; it had done very well in the olden
times, but now it was in continual conflict with "the more
abundant living." Leaders of this movement included the
sacred queen Keopuolani, Liholiho's mother, and Queen
Kaahumanu, for under the tabus the women had always
suffered privation; they were forbidden to eat pork, certain kinds of fish, bananas, and many other staples of the
island produce—hence the eating tabu came to be a symbol
of all the traditional constraints. Word from Tahiti that
King Pomare had abolished the tabus there gave the Hawaiian agitators a precedent, if they had needed any.

How did Liholiho stand?—if he was uncertain, at least
he was unafraid. When his mother made a defiant gesture
by eating with little Kaui-keaouli ('Suspended in the blue
sky'), his brother (and heir), and when Kaahumanu followed suit by eating of forbidden foods, Liholiho remarked thoughtfully, "It is well to renounce the tabus
and particularly for husbands and wives to eat together;
—there will be less unfaithfulness and deception." His
chancellor Kalanimoku was in favor of abolishing the
tabus, and even old Hewahewa—Kamehameha's high

priest—confessed to thinking it a wise course, though in this he was not generally supported by the other priests of the kingdom.

Liholiho wavered. It was not easy for him to destroy with one fell gesture the traditions with which his whole education had been solely occupied. Meanwhile, he did not forswear his gods himself; indeed, he consecrated a *heiau* at a village a few miles up the coast, and made the subsequent celebration something of a scandal by his drunkenness. But, on the other hand, he willingly witnessed the baptism of his prime minister, Kalanimoku, which took place before the Catholic altar of a visiting French warship. This was in August, 1819.

Three months later he gave a large banquet at the palace in Kailua, to which he invited all the prominent *alii* and several Europeans. The tables were set according to the foreign style, but one was designated for the women and one for the men. When his guests were seated, the king, who appeared quite restless, suddenly rose and asked John Young to preside at his table. Then he wandered hesitantly toward the women's table; apparently, he had hoped that he would not be noticed. But there was a hush and all eyes were upon him and he saw a vacant seat near Kaahumanu; all at once he made up his mind, quietly sat down and began to eat with evident enjoyment. He ate alone. His guests were stunned when actually faced with the blasphemy for which they had so long been agitating. But no bolt of lightning struck down from the heavens. The king did not grow faint and fall to the floor:—on the contrary, he seemed more than usually cheerful and at ease. Suddenly the pent-up emotions burst forth in the cry, "*Ai noa . . . ai noa!*" ("The eating tabu is broken!") It was taken up by the serving men and the cooks and spread like fire through Kailua. Through Kona. Throughout the island. The whole archipelago. The king gave his order that all *heiaus* were to be destroyed and the images with them. Hewahewa himself with flaming torch lit the first pyre.

The breaking of the tabus was a signal for Kekua to declare himself. Gathering a sympathetic group of *alii* about him he went into open revolt at Kaawaloa. Likewise, in the province of Hamakua, dissenting chiefs organized an uprising. But Kalanimoku said: "It is not good policy to carry war into that quarter [Hamakua], for Kekua—the source of the trouble—is at Kaawaloa. Thither let us direct our forces. The rebellion at Hamakua is the leaf of the tree. I would lay ax to the root—that being destroyed, the leaves will soon wither." Kekua was Kalanimoku's nephew; Liholiho's cousin. Keopuolani, the sacred queen, pleaded to be allowed to go and reason with him. However, the mission failed. Kekua was adamant, determined to be king, sure that the gods were on his side as they had been on the side of Umi and Kamehameha when they had challenged the hereditary king.

The royal troops marching to Kaawaloa met their first resistance just beyond Keauhou, but were able to drive the rebels before them for some distance until a series of stone walls offered temporary entrenchment. From this shelter they were driven by Kalanimoku, who was an able warrior as well as politician. At Kuamoo ('Lizard Back') the battle-to-death began in earnest. Kekua's men fought bravely, their wives at their sides, helping to load the muskets and often firing them as well. But Kekua had been wounded, and after losing a great deal of blood, fainted. His people rallied round him and revived him, propping him up against a stump of lava from which position he continued to fire. At last a bullet pierced his heart, and he fell to the side, his soft feather cape covering his face. Seeing him fall, his wife, who had fought loyally at his side, called for quarter from the advancing Kalanimoku, but someone shot just as she cried out and she fell across the body of her husband. After this disaster, there was ragged action and sniping from the rebels until nearly sunset, when most of the troops were finally surrounded or dispersed and the king's army returned victorious to Kailua.

And so the tabu system was ended. Hawaii found herself in the position—unusual for that era—of being a kingdom without a religion, for the king and his counselors had no substitute to offer. Strangely enough, however, two months before these events, a party of young New Englanders, unaware of Kamehameha's death, had sailed from Boston to bring the gospel to the heathen in Hawaii.

Behold, then, the brig *Thaddeus* off the eastern coast of South America in this eventful December of the year 1819! Aboard were the strangest, bravest, most uncompromising group of youngsters that ever sailed toward the southern seas. Fresh from college, burning with faith, they had set out under the auspices of the American Board of Commissioners for Foreign Missions to bring the Word to the benighted savages of Hawaii. Several of the young men were on their honeymoon, a queer honeymoon; they had married their wives but a few weeks before sailing and had taken them as partners in Christian enterprise rather than as loved ones. Those were the days when young men took up the Church with the same zeal as modern college students take up radicalism.

There was the Reverend Asa Thurston and his wife, Lucy. The reverend Asa was a hefty, handsome bear of a man, a Yale athlete; in his college days he had been the Bully of the Bully Club—later Skull and Bones—but sorrow in his family had turned him to the Church. He was the most virile member of the group, though not the least zealous in his faith. His wife, Lucy, whom he had only known for a month prior to sailing, was—by surely the kindest of heavenly dispensations—an indomitable, charming woman, as idealistic as he and a perfect partner.

Then there were the Reverend Hiram Bingham and his wife; a physician, Dr. Holman and wife; two teachers and their wives, Mr. Whitney and Mr. Ruggles—Whitney had been a sophomore at Yale but "was impelled to go to the heathen at once!"; and Mr. Chamberlain, a farmer who had had a pleasant home in central Massachusetts, had brought his wife and five children, "rather than withhold their personal labors from the heathen." With them was Mr. Loomis, a printer, and his wife; and four Hawaiian boys who had been in America for ten years studying for the Church—one of these was George P. Kaumualii, son of the King of Kauai (an *illegitimate* son,[3] as the missionaries discovered to their distress during the voyage). It was the religious enthusiasm shown by these Hawaiian youths that had largely prompted the Board of Missions to send this company to the barbarous islands.

Mrs. Thurston wrote of the young missionaries' prospects: "We cut loose from our native land for *life*, to find a dwelling place, far, far away from civilized man, among barbarians, there to cope with a cruel priesthood of blood-loving deities; and to place ourselves under the

---

[3] It would be hard to say what constituted legitimacy in Hawaii.

iron law of tabus requiring men and women to eat separately. To break the law was death." But in Mrs. Thurston's case, at least, the prospect was not a gloomy one
for "to be connected with such a husband, and engaged
in such an object, in the present state of the world, is, of
all situations in life, what I choose."

After nearly half a year at sea, the *Thaddeus* reached
Kawaihae in March, 1820. The first man aboard was one
James Hunnewell, who breathlessly gave the news: "Kamehameha is dead! His son Liholiho is king. The tabus
have been abolished, the images burned, the temples destroyed. There has been war, but now there is peace!"
And what news this was to these young New Englanders;
it was as though God had answered their prayers.

And then the natives arrived, curious as usual to see
what ship was this and what it had to offer in trade.
Little did they know! Imagine the confusion of these
well-brought-up New England youngsters at viewing
their flock for the first time! Handsome, very physical,
men and women came aboard wearing no clothes at all,
only a casual cloth about their loins. Embarrassment readily obscured the missionaries' more spiritual emotions.
They welcomed with relief and admiration the kingdom's
prime minister, Kalanimoku, who had had the tact to
appear in civilized clothes (he wore "a white dimity
roundabout, a black silk vest, yellow Nankeen pants,

shoes, and white cotton hose, plaid cravat and fur hat").
Mr. Bingham went ashore at Kawaihae and was shown the
heiau of Puukohala; he wrote, "This monument of idolatry I surveyed with mingled emotions of grief, horror,
pity, regret, gratitude and hope." Such a medley of emotion was experienced by most of the company after their
first glimpse of the islands they had come to conquer with
their morality.

As the king was at Kailua, the *Thaddeus* did not linger
in Kawaihae. When she sailed for Kailua, however, she
had aboard most of the prominent people of Kawaihae,
including the fat, irrepressible dowager queens of Kamehameha. The missionary ladies quickly went to work
making civilized clothes for their new charges. The most
successful dress was one they made for Kalakua, a younger
sister of Kaahumanu (also a widow of Kamehameha, and
later wife of Hoapili). This was a dress of white cambric,
the length of the skirt being adjusted to Brigham Young's
famous dictum—"Have it come to the tops of their shoes"—
but the ladies found that in Kalakua's case, her bare feet
"cropped out rather prominently" and somewhat spoiled
the effect. Nonetheless, the royal lady was received with
admiration and enthusiasm by the populace of Kailua.

Mr. Thurston and Mr. Bingham went ashore at Kailua
to call on the king. They were introduced to his Majesty
by one of the converted youths, Thomas Hopu, who

called them "Priests of the Most High God who made heaven and earth." Liholiho greeted them courteously and listened while letters were read explaining the purpose of the mission. Then the two Americans retired leaving the matter to his consideration.

Again Liholiho was faced with an important and difficult decision. He was not, of course, unfamiliar with the Christian God, although he was unaware of the attendant code of morality. Subsequently he was prevailed upon to call a meeting of his counselors in which the matter was fully discussed, but Young explained to the missionaries that such a conclave offered no real hope of a decision for at least a year, and recommended that the Americans ask to be allowed to remain on probation. The missionaries acted on this advice, and it was good, for the king was relieved of immediate decision and had a chance to satisfy his curiosity as to just what these stiff and earnest people wanted to make of his kingdom.

Among those who urged Liholiho to accept the missionaries outright was his favorite wife Kamamalu (his half-sister). But the king answered her argument by saying sadly, "If I do, they will allow me but one wife, and that will not be you."

A meeting was held aboard the *Thaddeus* to determine who should stay in Hawaii and who should go on to Honolulu. When Liholiho heard that the missionaries were planning to set up a station at Honolulu, he commented: "White men all prefer Oahu. I think the Americans would like to have that island." In the end it was decided that the Thurstons and Dr. and Mrs. Holman should stay in Kailua, as well as two of the Hawaiian converts.

In Mrs. Thurston's writings there is scarcely a mention of what she must have felt, a twenty-five-year-old girl who had never been outside New England, set down to live in a thatched house among brown-skinned people who had never seen a white woman before, much less heard of the strict code of living which she considered the only code. But because of her consuming faith, she had believed the Hawaiians to be so barbarous and so unenlightened that perhaps the actual conditions made her feel somewhat easier. And she was fortunate in having a strong-minded, strong-bodied husband at her side. Still, Lucy Thurston could have done it alone, for she was an amazingly courageous woman. In later life she had to undergo an operation for the removal of one of her breasts; without anesthetic, she stayed conscious and unprotesting through an hour of the cruelest agony, perhaps, a woman could ever undergo. But she was a woman:— she did mind the mustiness and discomfort of the thatched house which was allotted to her and her husband, and minded the fleas (which had been brought first by a

Western ship, and had accommodated themselves to thatched dwellings more readily than had the white people who brought them).

The two Hawaiian converts, in their best Boston clothes, lived leisurely lives in Kona, much admired by their countrymen; they had homes to go to and servants to attend their needs. But their teachers were not so fortunate: the missionaries had to build their homes out of their faith. A missionary's salary was four hundred dollars a year, with a fifty-dollar allowance for each dependent, and in these early times, when goods took half a year to come from New England to Hawaii, dollars were as pennies. Had it not been for the king who gave houses, furniture and guards, and for the kindness of those at home who sent out clothes and domestic necessities, the missionaries could never have had these things; four hundred dollars could scarcely purchase a bedstead. The demands on their comfort and their faith were so great that after a year, the Holman family gave up the struggle and returned to New England. The Thurstons were left alone to convert the island of Hawaii.

The worst the missionaries suffered was seldom from the Hawaiians, but from the white sailors who lost no opportunity to pour out their scorn of the godly and to preach counter-doctrines and immorality to the confused Hawaiians. The Hawaiians knew by now that white people were not gods, but they still considered them as superior beings, and they knew not which way to go when these superior beings pulled at their either arm offering, on the one hand, immortality, and on the other —more fun—immorality. Mrs. Thurston faced the situation bravely and even fairly; when she saw Hawaiian girls making a show of the trinkets they had received from the sailors who had had their favor, she heaped her scorn rightly, not on the girls, but on the sailors. It is a difficult thing to be right when those in your image defy you.

The Hawaiian nation was well prepared for the services supplementary to religion which the missionaries had to offer. Years of association with foreigners had taught the Hawaiians the value of being able to read and write;—and, in some cases, they had even learned respect for the Christian God. A school was established in Kailua which was attended by Liholiho and his little brother (and heir) Kauikeaouli; two of the queens, Kamamalu and Kinau; Governor Kuakini; one of John Young's sons; two young men of the court, John Ii and James Kahuhu; and other people of rank. Within three months the king was reading a little of the New Testament, and others were attacking the reading lessons in Webster's spelling book. Unhappily, this ideal state of affairs did not last for long. Liholiho was more of an experimentalist than an enthusiast. He found that his studies interfered with his drinking. From the first he had been dubious of learning; he had asked a missionary to write his name and, on seeing it, remarked, "It looks neither like me nor any other man." Still, he would not condemn the system as a whole. He commanded the five-year-old heir apparent to learn his lessons for both the king and queen; he told the boy that application to the arts would make him a fit ruler and a wise and good king. His imagination captured by the idea of learning by proxy, he ordered his favorites, Ii and Kahuhu, to study hard under the guidance of Mr. Thurston, and he always insisted that the two should wear civilized clothes, even though other members of the court dressed after the traditional fashion.

Other chiefs, however, were not so light-hearted about their education. Kalanimoku humbly took his instructions in letters from little Dan Chamberlain, age five, and the missionaries delightedly fell upon the phrase "—and a little child shall lead them." Another diligent student was the Kona governor, Kuakini. He and Keeaumoku already knew how to speak English, but their remarks were interlarded with the heartiest of fo'c'sle expressions and they had to unlearn much of this accomplishment. In later years Kuakini used to read the English Bible through regularly. He built, of his own accord, the first Christian Church in the islands, on the site of the ancient *heiau,*

Keiki-puipui ('Fat child'). And he was an earnest deacon of the church; he made it a law that no women without bonnets and no dogs were to be allowed in the church—sleepers were rapped over the head with a long cane by policemen who stood by for the purpose; he became so particular, indeed, that any woman entering his premises without a bonnet was liable to have all her hair shaved off in punishment.

The foremost members of the Kailua congregation in later years were Naihe—son of Keaweaheulu—and his wife, Kapiolani, who lived some sixteen miles distance at Kaawaloa. Kapiolani made one of the most courageous gestures of the times by going into the crater of Kilauea, an act which most Hawaiians, even though they had forsworn their ancient gods, were still afraid to chance. Naihe was the chief orator of the realm, and well beloved by all who knew him; so well beloved indeed that Kapiolani took the precaution of having an attractive maidservant wear her hair over the face, trimmed at the nose, lest Naihe succumb to her honest admiration and her somewhat obvious charms.

The missionary ladies excited much interest among the Hawaiians. White men they were used to, but the women were strange. For one thing, they did the cooking; this put them into the servant class, and as servants they might have been dismissed but for the astonishing learning they had. "They are white and have hats with a spout, their faces are round and far in. Their necks are long. They look well." From this Hawaiian description the missionary ladies received the nickname "Long Necks." Children, too, came in for their share of curious admiration; never before had children been seen with clothes on—they were like dolls, and as entertaining. The Thurstons soon became accustomed to having a large audience outside their house day and night.

In the year 1821 the royal court removed to Honolulu. It was Kalanimoku's opinion that the government should be established in one place and not moved about according to the king's fancy; and the most promising village in the islands was certainly Honolulu. The king made his progress by easy stages aboard the newly purchased yacht, *Haaheo o Hawaii*. This yacht had known an interesting history. It had been built by Retire Becket, a famous Salem shipbuilder, for the wealthy merchant-captain, George Crowninshield, the first American yachtsman. The vessel, known as *Cleopatra's Barge*, was so elaborately designed that wherever it called, in America and in the waters of the Mediterranean, it occasioned wide interest. Its appointments were sumptuous; the paneling of the cabin was of mahogany, inlaid with bird's-eye maple, the mahogany chairs were covered with red velvet and gold lace, and it boasted elaborate silver and china services. The original cost to Captain Crowninshield had been fifty thousand dollars, a fabulous price for these times; Liholiho had purchased it for ninety thousand. On the night he arrived in Honolulu the village had never known such an uproar. The cannon of the yacht, and cannon on Punchbowl and in the fort, thundered out in salutes, making the night livid with their flashes; and criers ran through the streets demanding hogs, dogs, *poi*, and other tribute for the king. On the following day when Mr. Bingham went to call on him, Liholiho was so hung-over that he could not speak; his queen, Kamamalu, courteously lifted his inert hand in salute to the missionary.

Although the court was now officially established at Honolulu the king was of a restless disposition and continually toured the islands, traveling in elaborate style. One of his trips was of particular consequence. While on a horseback ride to Waialua on Oahu to oversee the progress of the sandalwood cutting, he had the impulse to visit Kauai. It was an island his father had never actually conquered. Accordingly, he appropriated a sailing canoe, and in the company of Boki, governor of Oahu (Kalanimoku's brother), Naihe and Kapiolani and some thirty retainers set sail across the stormy channel. The boat was not very seaworthy, the weather unseasonable, and in a short time all the *alii* pressed him to return to Oahu. But Liholiho had brought along some bottles of cheer and would hear nothing of their pleas. He remarked that if the others wanted to return, he would swim to Kauai. "Fear nothing," he said in his lordly manner, "Caesar is with you."

And so, it seems, were the gods with them. They arrived at Kauai safely. King Kaumualii was no little surprised at this unexpected visit. He wondered whether Liholiho had come to demand his absolute subjection. But he did not allow this question to prevent him from giving his suzerain lord a friendly welcome. In the presence of his chiefs and several foreigners, he addressed the king thus: "King Liholiho, hear!—when your father was alive, I acknowledged him as my superior. Since his death, I have considered you as his rightful successor, and, according to his appointment, as king of the Islands. I have plenty of muskets and powder, and plenty of men at my command—these with the vessels I have purchased, the fort, the guns, and the island, all are yours. Do with them as you please. Send me where you please. Place what chief you please as governor here." The young king was silent for a long moment. He was impressed by Kaumualii's courtesy, and he liked the man's looks. He replied slowly: "I do not come to take away your island. . . . I do not wish to place anyone over it. . . . Keep your island and care for it just as you have done, and do what you please with your vessels."

The king's abrupt departure, unarmed, had caused consternation among the members of his court in Honolulu. Immediately, the yacht was made ready and many of his counselors and wives set out to join him. But the first to arrive at Kauai was Boki's wife, Liliha; she had been so anxious to be with her husband that she had set sail in a single canoe with only four rowers. When the small white sail was seen in Waimea Bay and the king learned who it was, he cried out in admiration, "*Aloha ino!*" (a phrase which defies translation—"much love," being a poor expression of its meaning). When the rest of the retinue arrived, Kaumualii invited the royal party on a tour of the island, a lavish progress which consumed forty-two days. At the end of this time, Liholiho returned to Oahu with Kaumualii aboard his yacht. Whether this was forcible kidnapping or a return of courtesy—as Kaumualii was always careful to say—is hard to judge. Whatever it was, the king of Kauai never again returned to his kingdom. One reason for this was that Kaahumanu, the co-ruler of the kingdom, fell in love with him and married him, and she was a possessive woman. (Later, she fell in love with his son, too, and married him, making a happy family group. One of the missionaries relates how she arrived at church in a newly acquired carriage. There were no horses to pull the carriage, so ten or twelve husky retainers served instead. Uncertain as to how her family should be seated, the portly queen had finally hit on the scheme of sitting in the driver's seat herself, while Kaumualii—husband number one—sat in the carriage proper, and his son—husband number two—sat in the rear in place of a footman.)

Meanwhile, the missionaries had made some progress with their cause. The Hawaiians found the Christian religion to their taste—though for various reasons. Some women, accustomed from earliest youth to memorizing the names of their ancestors, took particular interest in those parts of the Bible that concerned themselves with a long list of "begats"; these the Hawaiians learned by heart and felt pleased with their progress toward the ultimate redemption. Others enjoyed the hymn-singing (and it is from these early hymns that the harmony of Hawaiian music stems). And again, there were those who honestly found spiritual uplift in their new faith; among these was the king's mother, Keopuolani. The king, himself, however, was a difficult pupil. At one time when he was invited to attend church service, he sent word to Mr. Bingham: "I am tipsy, and it is not right to go to church drunk. When I have got through, I will come." And Kalanimoku, the admired of the ladies, when approached while gambling, answered, "I have business and cannot go. My heart will be with you, though my body is here."

Still, Liholiho was not wholly recalcitrant. He honestly believed in the principles of Christianity, but found that they hampered his enjoyment of life. Attending a family worship at the Bingham house, he said seriously, "Jehovah, he's good. I like him. The devil, I no like." Mr. Bingham approached him once when the barriers were down, and the king told him, "I cannot repent at once. *He nui loa kuu hewa* (my wickedness is great); but in five years I will forsake sin."

In the year 1822 Liholiho received the present which had been promised to his father by Vancouver—a small schooner with six guns; it had been built in Sydney by the direction of the British government and was called the *Prince Regent*.

Liholiho wrote King George IV:

"May it please your Majesty,

"In answer to your Majesty's letter . . . I beg to return to your Majesty my most grateful thanks for your handsome present of the schooner, *Prince Regent*, which I have received. . . .

". . . The whole of these islands having been conquered by my father, I have succeeded to the government of them, and beg leave to place them all under the protection of your most excellent Majesty; wishing to observe peace with all nations, and to be thought worthy of the confidence I place in your Majesty's wisdom and judgment.

"The former idolatrous system has been abolished in these islands, as we wish the Protestant religion of your Majesty's dominions to be practiced here. . . ."

For a long time, the young Hawaiian king had considered making a voyage to England and America. Not only was this because of his restlessness and desire to see new places, but he was also anxious to confer with the governments of these nations concerning the international status of Hawaii. In October, 1823, a conference of the chiefs was held at Lahaina, Maui, and as a consequence of their discussion, it was decided that Liholiho and a small party of courtiers should sail for England aboard the English ship *L'Aigle*, Captain Starbuck. The proposal that the king should go on his own yacht was abandoned as impractical. To go with him, the king selected his favorite wife, Kamamalu, Governor Boki and his wife Liliha, and several other chiefs, including a son of John Young. One of the missionaries, Mr. Ellis, was invited to come along as interpreter, but at this Captain Starbuck balked. It later turned out that the crafty captain wanted to have full control of the expense money the king took aboard.

The royal company sailed from Honolulu on November 27, 1823. Before the ship's boat left the dock, Kamamalu with great emotion apostrophized before the multitude assembled to bid farewell.

"Ye skies, ye plains, ye mountains and wreathing green sea,
 Ye nobles and people of the land, know now my love for you.
 Aloha, aloha my native land,
 Land for whose sake my father strove:—alas! farewell!"

The only pause in the voyage was at Rio de Janeiro where the British consul-general gave the Hawaiian royalty an elaborate ball and the Emperor Dom Pedro gave them a courteous reception. On May 22, 1824, the ship arrived at Portsmouth. On being given notice of the Hawaiian's arrival, the British government appointed the Hon. H. F. Byng to be aide to the royal party. Quarters were arranged for them in the Osborne Hotel in London.

When Captain Starbuck forwarded Liholiho's money chest to the Bank of England, it was discovered that ten thousand dollars were missing from the original twenty-five thousand with which the king had left Hawaii. There was no explanation other than a bill for three thousand dollars which covered the expenses in Rio. Liholiho did not like to make a fuss, and consequently the matter was never pursued.

At first, the Hawaiians created an odd impression among the people of London. The queen and Liliha wore, as formal attire, loose trousers and bedgowns of colored velveteen. But the Hon. H. F. Byng soon secured tailors and dressmakers and the royal company was dressed to the latest fashion. The Hawaiian king and his cortege were elaborately entertained, and became in a short time the rage of London. Ladies clamored to learn the secret of the handsome turbans which Kamamalu wore, and the gentlemen found Liholiho a nobleman and a sport.

An audience was arranged with King George IV, but before it could take place, several members of the Hawaiian party came down with measles. Among the sufferers were the king and queen. King George sent his own physician to attend them, but his ministrations were of little avail. Kamamalu was dying. Liholiho, weak himself, was distraught with grief, and spent all of his time with his sweet-natured wife whose vivacious spirit was lost in suffering. They caressed each other and murmured endearments in their native tongue. But finally she died. Liholiho, for whom was held some hope of recovery, was so distracted by her death that he himself no longer cared to live and died six days later, the 14th of July, 1824.

EPILOGUE

ND NOW THIS NARRATIVE IS CONCLUDED. THE BODIES of the Hawaiian king and queen were carried back to the islands by a British warship. Kauikeaouli inherited the throne, as Kamehameha III, and during his early years Kaahumanu acted as regent.

A new sort of adventure was beginning in Hawaii, less flamboyant perhaps, but in its way exciting. But the focus of history shifts to the newcomers, those white strangers who, in the very beginning, had been absorbed into the Hawaiian race, yet who now have absorbed the Hawaiian race into theirs.

The next years were the youthful years of the western pioneers, the senescence of old-time Polynesia. Still, the old spirit lived on deep in the hearts of the Hawaiian people, and lives today, though it is, perhaps, not easy to find. Yet I believe it will continue to live, that rare humor and kindliness and love of living, so long as there are palms to nod along the peaceful, silver shores, so long as the mountains are draped in their lustrous cloaks of blue and green, so long as there is a Hawaii Nei.

KAUAI
Kumukahi Channel
IIHAU
Kauai Channel
OAHU
HONOLULU
Kaiw
NORTH
PACIFIC
OCEA